The Reference Shelf

The 21st Century

Edited by Hilary D. Claggett

The Reference Shelf
Volume 71 • Number 5

The H.W. Wilson Company
New York • Dublin
1999

The Reference Shelf

The books in this series contain reprints of articles, excerpts from books, addresses on current issues, and studies of social trends in the United States and other countries. There are six separately bound numbers in each volume, all of which are usually published in the same calendar year. Numbers one through five are each devoted to a single subject, providing background information and discussion from various points of view and concluding with a subject index and comprehensive bibliography that lists books, pamphlets, and abstracts of additional articles on the subject. The final number of each volume is a collection of recent speeches, and it contains a cumulative speaker index. Books in the series may be purchased individually or on subscription.

Visit H.W. Wilson's Web site: www.hwwilson.com

Cataloging-in-Publication data is available from the Library of Congress: www.loc.gov

Production Editor: Beth Levy

Printed in the United States of America

Contents

V. The Society of the Future

Preface

What will life be like in the 21st century? The answers to that question depend upon several factors, including whom you ask, when you pose the question, your definition of "life," when you believe the 21st century begins (2000 or 2001; see below), and, finally but not incidentally, who you are. For invariably when we ponder the answers to these questions, we are really asking, what will life be like for "us" in the 21st century? If you are a well-paid young executive in a cosmopolitan American or European city, the answer is likely to be quite different from that which might greet a middle-aged displaced worker whose once-valuable skills are no longer needed in today's economy, an inhabitant of an impoverished remote village in the developing world, a creative artist or writer trying to work within the constraints imposed by an authoritarian government, or a witness to genocide in Rwanda, Bosnia, Kosovo, East Timor, or Chechnya.

This question of what the future holds for whom is closely related to whom you ask, because people tend draw on their own personal experiences when answering. That is not to say that a middle-aged white American male has nothing valuable to contribute to the discussion about others' experiences of age, race, gender, nationality, or what have you. On the contrary, it most often means that, in the case of the writers whose thoughts are encapsulated in these pages, their professions dictate their answers (with the obvious exception of journalists reporting on other industries, in which case the subjects shape their answers). For example, a demographer will evaluate the dual forces of population growth in some areas of the world and population stability in other areas, the aging of America, the replacement of African Americans by Hispanics as the most populous minority in the country, and the gradually dwindling numbers of the white majority. A scientist may discuss anything from global warming to global cooling to advanced robotics, while a marketer will focus on shopping habits and consumption patterns and a geopolitical strategist will emphasize the futures of nations, war, and peace. Then you have the nonspecialist: call her a futurist, call him a science-fiction writer, or call her a social commentator. All of them have in common the ability to conceive of the future and express those conceptions clearly. They base their answers not on the expertise gained from years of honing one's craft but on a generalist's simultaneous apprehension of a wide range of considerations, and they draw from a variety of disciplines. When it comes down to it, no one can claim to be an expert on the future, but some folks have stronger ideas than others about what may happen, and some people (not always the same ones) have spent a great deal of time and effort trying to figure it out for the rest of us. Gathered here are several of the more intriguing postulations that turned up in a survey of recently published books and periodical literature.

As with every title in the *Reference Shelf* series, the goal is to present the reader with a broad variety of viewpoints in order to aid her or him in coming to an informed conclusion. A secondary purpose of *The 21st Century* and its five companion numbers in the 1999 volume is to stand as a historical record of the current thinking on one topic (albeit an extremely large and unwieldy one in the present case). In an era in which many people have unprecedented access to full-text sources, the *Reference Shelf* volumes are more relevant than ever because they organize and contextualize the bounty of otherwise unfiltered data with which we are blessed, or, as it were, cursed, in the Information Age.

One of the outstanding characteristics of the Information Age is the primacy of the computer and its effect on nearly every aspect of our lives, from work to play. Because most predictions of life in the next century are merely clever extrapolations of current trends, it is no surprise that many of the writers whose articles are collected here mention the computer in some role—as a toy, an entertainment vehicle, a replacement for a stock broker or bank teller, a powerful tool, or a weapon—but Ray Kurzweil, whose book *The Age of Spiritual Machines* is reviewed in Part Five, goes farther than most. We have long become accustomed to the idea of artificial intelligence, regardless of whether we know how it works or what its limits may be. But what about artificial spirituality? The term sounds like an oxymoron, and it is unless you revise your definitions of "artificial," "spirituality," and even the notion of life itself. "Regardless of the nature and derivation of a mental experience, spiritual or otherwise, once we have access to the computational processes that give rise to it, we have the opportunity to understand its neurological correlates," Kurzweil argues in his book. "With the understanding of our mental processes will come the opportunity to capture our intellectual, emotional, and spiritual experiences." Others have contended that we may someday be able to preserve for posterity the essence, so to speak, of our very selves—that is, our minds and the way we think—in a virtual reality limbo to be called into action or animation (neither word fits; our vocabulary is not evolving at the same rate as our technology). That's one way to think about definitions of life. Another is to think about quality of life; that question is addressed in a wide range of articles devoted separately to the fate of the planet and its denizens in the event of a new Ice Age, an aging global population, increased individual longevity, and a return to hand-to-hand urban guerrilla warfare.

Among the factors that influence the various responses to our enquiry about life in the 21st century is when the question is asked. In 1967, Herman Kahn and Anthony J. Wiener of the Hudson Institute predicted in their book *The Year 2000* that we would be working much fewer hours while producing more than ever. As Geoffrey Colvin points out in an article included in Part Two, the "leisure revolution" did not pan out. Neither, he notes, did the dire predictions of the *Global 2000* report commissioned by President Jimmy Carter in 1980. "With utter confidence it predicted a colder, hungrier, poorer world of poisoned seas and food wars," Colvin writes, adding that both views were informed by the conditions prevalent in their respective times. But one need not reach back that far into the past to find pessimistic predictions of what the next century will bring. In 1991, in the wake of the crumbling of the Berlin Wall and the lifting of the Iron Curtain, rapid changes were sweeping the former Soviet Union and its former satellites. Communism had failed, the United States was experiencing a mild recession, and Japan's and South Korea's economies were booming. In this context, the veteran journalist David Halberstam, writing in *The Next Century*, quoted the Japanologist Chalmers Johnson: "The Cold War is over; the Japanese won." Halberstam suggests that as we "were already entering the next century . . . it was our not very secret secret that the American Century was over as well." But what has happened since then? After recovering from a mild recession in the early 1990s, the U.S. economy rebounded, the Dow Jones soared into the quintuple digits, interest rates, inflation, and unemployment all remained relatively low, and we became, for better or worse, the world's policeman. Meanwhile, the global markets reeled from an Asian financial crisis, the Balkans were plunged into a genocidal maelstrom, and Muscovites were being asked to guard their apartments because terrorists had stepped into the vacuum left by the KGB. Perhaps the American Century *is* over—but if so, it sure seemed to have had one heck of a last hurrah.

Therefore, in the context of today's prosperity—however relative or selective it may be, and regardless of whether it is largely perceived rather than actual—one might expect a rosier picture to be propounded by contemporary pundits. Yet one must not make too much of the literal effect of context upon analysis, because today Panglossian pronouncements coexist quite happily with doom-and-gloom forecasts. In *The Future and Its Enemies: The Growing Conflict Over Creativity, Enterprise, and Progress*, Virginia Postrel posits a dynamic future evolving from today's uncertainties. She identifies the enemies of progress as those who would wish for, or plan for, a static, controlled future. Jettisoning the old divisions of left wing and right wing, she suggests that a new dichotomy has formed outside of traditional definitions. "Do we value stability and control," she asks, "or evolution and learning? . . . Do we crave predictablity, or relish surprise? These two poles, stasis and dynamism, increasingly define our political, intellectual, and cultural landscape. The central question of our time is what to do about the future. And that question creates a deep divide." On the other side of that divide is Eugene Linden, the author of *The Future in Plain Sight: Nine Clues to the Coming Instability*. Crediting the stability of recent decades with our success and prosperity as a species, Linden warns us that a less stable future—one characterized by volatility in everything from the weather to the financial markets—would likely be a dangerous future. He argues that nine trends of the present point toward a chaotic future, and he explores eight scenarios of life in 2050. How can the same environment support such seemingly contradictory visions of the future? It can because global systems are so complex, the multiple effects of their interactions so unpredictable, that things could go either way, and evidence can be found that supports both sides. And even though Halberstam's predictions may appear in 1999 to have been colored by the times in which he was writing, his ideas may yet be borne out in the longer run.

This brings us to the scope of *The 21st Century*. Unlike Linden, most people whose articles are collected here confine their predictions to the next decade or so. Which brings is to the question of when the decade, the century, and the millennium actually begins. Because there is no year zero, there being only one year between 1 B.C. and A.D. 1, purists believe that the 21st century and the third millennium will not begin until January 1, 2001. But the appeal of the triple zero in 2000 is not to be denied, and the fact is that most New Year's celebrations around the world are being planned for December 31, 1999 into January 1, 2000. In *Questioning the Millennium: A Rationalist's Guide to a Precisely Arbitrary Countdown*, Stephen Jay Gould explains why the issue will never be resolved to everyone's satisfaction. (Even after the fact, arguments can be expected to continue about when the turn of the century should be said to have occurred.) According to Gould, this is the third consecutive century to see this unresolvable debate, the first such arguments having debuted in 1699 and continued through 1701. In the modern era, the debate, which is really a battle between high culture (2001 advocates) and low, or pop, culture (year 2000 celebrants), fought out in the media. At the inception of the 20th century, Gould reports, high culture won by imposing January 1, 1901 as the beginning of the century in magazine covers, headlines, book titles, and the like. But over the course of the century, pop culture, perhaps driven by its superior ability to penetrate the global marketplace and earn untold amounts of wealth for a lot more people, has clearly become the dominant culture, and if it decrees that 2000 shall mark the new century and the new millennium, then so be it. Gould concludes, "The old guard of [the Royal Greenwich Observatory in Cambridge, England] may pout to their heart's content, but the world will rock and party on January 1, 2000."

In another section of *Questioning the Millennium*, Gould attempts to document the "subtle shift in our primary definition of the millennium—from the duration of a blissful age following a forthcoming apocalypse, to the measured passage of a thousand years, perhaps preceding the same apocalypse." The concept of the millennium is addressed in the first two sections of *The 21st Century*. The first part examines awareness of and attitudes toward the advent of the second millennium in A.D. 1000. The second part is concerned with various aspects of today's millennial fever: definitions, celebrations, past predictions, and, inevitably, the Y2K bug, which is the source of some of the more fearsome apocalyptic visions being promulgated today.

I. The Year 1000 and the Second Millennium

Editor's Introduction

We will begin our examination of what life may have to offer in the 21st century with a look at the turn of the century and the dawning of the new millennium, namely, January 1, 2000. (The debate about when the century actually turns, on January 1, 2000 or January 1, 2001, is touched upon in the Preface.) Discussions of the advent of the third millennium, and its attendant elicitation of fears and hopes (whether apocalyptic or confined to Y2K anxiety or both—they're not mutually exclusive), seem often to give rise to intense curiosity about how our forebears handled millennial anxiety—if it existed—1,000 years ago. For this reason, we begin with a section devoted to the year A.D. 1000.

Was it a time of terror or a time much like any other? Again we return to the prior assumption of for whom was it or wasn't it a time of trepidation? For Christian Europeans. As the writers whose articles are included here point out, other important cultures of the 10th century, including Islam, the Song dynasty in China, and the recently decimated Mayan civilization in the Americas, were marking time by altogether different calendars. But did Christian Europeans, who of course did not yet identify themselves as Europeans, feel a sense of something afoot circa A.D. 1000? The debate is a live one among medieval scholars.

Patricia Bernstein, the author of the first selection here ("Terror in A.D. 1000?" *Smithsonian*), delivers a fine summary of the various positions taken by the two all-or-nothing opposing camps as well as the recent controversy stirred by Richard Landes, a founding historian of the Center for Millennial Studies at Boston University, who argues for a third position, that something (not necessarily widespread panic and divulgence of all worldly possessions) may have happened among ordinary folk that was not recorded by the clerics. The fourth and last article in this section, by Jeffrey L. Sheler ("End-Times Visions," *U.S. News & World Report*), provides a brief recap of the debate.

Landes himself is the author of the second selection, "The Apocalyptic Year 1000: Then and Now," originally published in *The Year 2000: Essays on the End*, edited by Charles Strozier and Michael Flynn. The original version, complete with footnotes, can be found on Landes's web site, www.mille.org. Aside from the omission of footnotes, the version reprinted here is identical to that posted on the author's site. In this essay, he argues that the truth about what happened can be found neither in earlier centuries' Romantics' claim of universal terror nor in the later Positivists' certainty that the year 1000, and its anticipation and passing, had no effect upon the majority of Europeans. Landes expounds the thesis that events taken by the populace to be apocalyptic may have had a transformative effect on the believers' subsequent behavior. "The collective penance [that the peasants, fearing an apocalypse, had allegedly engaged in after famines, earthquakes, comets, and other portentous events]," he writes, "can produce a massive change of 'atmosphere' in which people embrace their enemies in tears of mutual forgiveness." For people felt not only fear but hope, if they felt anything at all about the new millennium—hope for an age of peace. When the end did not come and the peace, which they did try for a time to uphold, did not last, the believers were disappointed, but their faith was not shattered. "Disappointment triggers not discouragement," Landes argues, "but renewed efforts to reignite the apocalyptic flames that had made the movement possible." A period of reform followed and a sense of identity was forged, according to Landes, who concludes his essay by explaining why it is important for us today to understand whatever our own society's reactions to the year 2000 will prove to have been in light of our ancestors' experiences. "The belief that the end is at hand is one of the most powerful and radical motivators in the human psyche," Landes writes, "combining the most urgent passions with the most deep-seated megalomanic tendencies. It is the adrenalin rush of religious beliefs. People in the grip of such beliefs are capable of extraordinary deeds, and immune to the kind of skeptical logic with which we insulate ourselves from the appeal of apocalyptic time. We ignore such sentiments at our own risk, and even, I might add, at the risk of our own impoverishment."

The third selection, Jay Tolson's "Of Kings and Commoners" (*U.S. News & World Report*), puts Landes's theories in historical context by describing not the millennial beliefs and activities of 10th-century Europeans but the overall direction in which their political system was headed. He argues that although the reality of nascent feudalism fell far short of its ideal—security—it nonetheless paved the way for the more stable political system of the nation-state, in which the nation, rather than a nobleman (or later, king, in an absolute monarchy), is supposed to be the guarantor of rights and liberties for those who obey its laws and live within its boundaries. Just as we sometimes attribute to the feudal system the instability and savagery that seems to have characterized the Middle Ages, so too may we be tempted to lay the blame for our 20th-century world wars, genocides, and terrorist regimes on the current global arrangement, which is still dominated by the nation-state, albeit less and less so. Despite its faults, the system has also arguably made possible an extended era of stability and prosperity for a great number of people. "How citizenship will fare in an age of weakening nation-states—so far the strongest protectors of the rights and liberties of citizens—is one of the great questions of our time," Tolson concludes.

Terror in A.D. 1000?
(What Really Happened 1,000
Years Ago)[1]

While we look to the new millennium with both trepidation and amusement, medieval scholars argue about what really happened at this time 1,000 years ago.

Popular accounts of the turn of the last millennium paint a world gone mad. Commentators tell us that medieval Europeans believed that the new year would bring the Last Judgment and the end of the world in a horrifying blaze of hellfire and damnation.

"Almost a thousand years ago," reported Liane Hansen on National Public Radio's *Weekend Edition* in 1996, "Europe was going slightly crazy. People had the terrors, and churches were crammed with penitents looking for last-minute redemption. The pious were awaiting the coming of either the Redeemer or the Devil. The reason? The millennium was ending, and apocalypse seemed right around the corner."

The conviction that the world was going to end, so the story goes, brought a continent-wide panic so intense that farmers abandoned their fields, soldiers left the battlefield, people of property gave all they owned to the church and everyone waited at the altars, to see what their fate would be.

A 1997 *U.S. News & World Report* article explained that during the year 1000, "many feared the end of the world, and huge numbers of the faithful stopped taking care of their houses, families, crops, and trades." In a recently reissued 1988 book entitled *A.D. 1000: A World on the Brink of Apocalypse*, Richard Erdoes imagines the scene at St. Peter's Basilica on the last day of the year 999: "Many did not dare to look, lying face down upon the multicolored marble floor, their arms spread out in the shape of a cross. A few were seized by holy ecstasy, waiting to be united with Christ. As the minutes passed and the fateful hour was about to strike, a deathly silence filled the venerable basilica."

As the year 2000 approaches, it has become commonplace for the media and the public to regard the late tenth century as a time of paralyzing fear, widespread panic and universal confusion. While easy to embrace, this vision of the long-distant past is more fantasy than fact. There was no general panic, no universal abandonment of life while all awaited

Popular accounts of the turn of the last millennium paint a world gone mad.

---

1. Article by Patricia Bernstein from *Smithsonian*, July 1999 v30 i4 p114. Copyright © 1999 Patricia Bernstein. Reprinted with permission.

death and judgment. Documents, royal speeches, papal bulls and chronicles of the time offer little evidence of mass hysteria. For the past 100 years, medieval historians have groaned over the public's penchant for believing that the turn of the last millennium was a time of great horror and upheaval. In fact, they've even dubbed it the myth of the "Terrors of the year 1000."

One medieval historian, however, recently has challenged the old guard with his belief that lots of millennium-related activity did occur and that the Terrors myth may, in fact, contain elements of truth. The resulting academic debate has become lively and contentious: the hypercharged word "conspiracy" has even entered the fray. At the root of this often arcane but fascinating debate is the issue of how we think about the past, the upcoming millennium and our role in shaping history.

It is true that the centuries leading up to A.D. 1000 were dark times. Waves of foreign invaders, including Magyars, Saracens and Vikings, as well as outbreaks of epidemics and famines, had carved great swaths of destruction across Europe. Europe's most glittering jewel—Rome—lay in ruins. Once a thriving city of about a million, Rome now claimed only 50,000 people, "a pale shadow of its luminous former self," writes James Reston, Jr., in *The Last Apocalypse: Europe at the Year 1000 A.D.* Laundry hung from the windows of the once-magnificent Colosseum, now an apartment building. On the coasts of England and northern Europe, villagers lived in constant dread of the appearance of Viking long ships and their fierce occupants, who took either their gold or their lives. The horsemen of the Hungarian Magyars devastated central Europe, and the ruthless armies of Al Mansor ruled Spain with fear.

In A.D. 991, at the battle of Maldon, the Christian Anglo-Saxons of England took up arms against the heathen Danish invaders. While the Christians lost that battle, similar battles pitting Christian against pagan played out across Europe for the 40 years leading up to A.D. 999. "Something great and mighty was under way throughout the continent," Reston writes. "Europe Christianized, almost all at once." With these massive changes shaking Europe, and a long history of brutal invasions, it's not hard to imagine that ordinary folks may well have lent an ear to self-appointed prophets who roamed the countryside preaching that the end was near. No doubt some doomsayers declared that the Last Judgment would arrive 1,000 years after the birth of Jesus Christ.

After all, Saint John darkly warned of the coming of the apocalypse in Revelation: "And I saw an angel come down from heaven, having the key of the bottomless pit and a great chain in his hand. And he laid hold the dragon, that old serpent, which is the Devil, and Satan, and bound him a

For the past 100 years, medieval historians have groaned over the public's penchant for believing that the turn of the last millennium was a time of great horror and upheaval.

thousand years, And cast him into the bottomless pit, and shut him up, and set a seal upon him, that he should deceive the nations no more, till the thousand years should be fulfilled and after that he must be loosed a little season." After all the fearful and the unbelieving and the corrupt were cast into a fiery lake, there would be "no more death, neither sorrow, nor crying, neither shall there be any pain: for the former things are passed away."

A handful of prophets, especially those whose appearance coincided with a heavenly or earthly "portent"—famine or epidemic, comet or earthquake—may have stimulated local reactions. But primary documents of the time are few. Noted medieval historian Bernard McGinn, of the University of Chicago Divinity School, points out that "medieval folk lived in a more or less constant state of apocalyptic expectation difficult to understand for most of us today." McGinn, whose views represented the gospel of all American medieval historians of this century until recently, argues that "apocalyptic traditions" occurred throughout the Middle Ages but that "it is by no means clear that fears of the end were more general ca. 1000 than at other periods in the Middle Ages." One historian declares with exasperation that he would like to "wring the neck" of the legend of the "Terrors of the year 1000."

How, then, did the tale get its start? And why has it been believed for so long? The short answer is that historians from the 16th century on found the notion of millennial activity surrounding the year 1000 territory too rich to resist. As with all historians, their interpretations reflect the shifting streams of events in their own day. Over time, these interpretations flowered into the Terrors myth.

Much of the dramatic detail of the myth comes from a brilliant French historian of the 19th century, Jules Michelet, who lived in the shadow of the French Revolution and whose work reflected the changing relationship between church and state. But the roots of the myth date back more than two centuries before Michelet to a church history prepared by Caesar Cardinal Baronius in 1605.

The 1500s witnessed waves of religious upheaval, known collectively as the Reformation. The reform of the Roman Catholic church, the birth of Protestantism and the freeing of religious thought also spawned millennial interest, not only coloring the interpretation of current events but the past as well. Cardinal Baronius wrote: "Now begins the first year after the year 1000. It was falsely said that this year would mark the end of the world or its imminent ruin. The man of sin, the son of perdition, the Antichrist, in a word, would soon appear. These rumors resounded from Gaul throughout the world. Almost everyone believed them: the simple were afraid of them, but the wise scarcely accepted them."

One historian declares with exasperation that he would like to "wring the neck" of the legend of the "Terrors of the year 1000."

Baronius' account of millennial activity in the year 1000 passed into many standard references and sources of knowledge. In 1769, a historian and clergyman in the Church of Scotland, William Robertson, breathed more life into the legend of the Terrors in the popular *The History of the Reign of the Emperor Charles the Fifth*. For Robertson, a product of the Age of Reason, the medieval church was a cesspool of "illiberal superstition," and Europe floundered in a state of dark ignorance. It made sense to Robertson that in the decades preceding and following the turn of the first millennium, a "general consternation seized mankind; many relinquished their possessions, and, abandoning their friends and families, hurried with precipitation to the Holy Land, where they imagined that Christ would quickly appear to judge the world." Robertson's book influenced an entire generation of Europeans, most notably Jules Michelet. With passion, Michelet seized upon the idea of excessive millennial activity and gave it such reality and narrative power that it became part of literature.

The famous historian grew up in a turbulent time in French history as Emperor Napoleon took on Europe with legions of well-trained French troops. Michelet's childhood was sad and somber. Growing up in Paris in the first decade of the 1800s, he was from a family so poor that his father spent nearly a year in debtor's prison, and they had trouble staying warm in winter. "For nourishment," he wrote, "I was accustomed to such frugality that often it was sensuous for me to eat some green beans." In those early days he acquired a lifelong distaste for autocratic authority, spurred by his hatred of Napoleon, who had destroyed the fortunes of the Michelets by closing down the family printing shop. Eventually, Michelet would transfer some of his hatred of authority to the church which, he believed, had let down the French people. The notion that religion inspired terror and panic seems to mirror Michelet's disappointment with the Catholic Church itself.

When he became the head of the historical section of the National Archives at 32, Michelet immersed himself in original documents. As he navigated the galleries of the archives, he claimed, the "distant sufferings of so many souls, smothered in past epochs, moaned in a soft voice." By then his fanatical French nationalism, which he described as his only religion, had begun to blossom. More than anything else, this would color his interpretation of events leading up to the turn of the first millennium.

By the time he had begun research for his monumental *The History of France*, Michelet had already determined that the church and Christianity were dead. He wrote in his journal that France must take the place of God "whom we miss" and that his beloved country must fill the "incommensurable abyss left by an extinguished Christianity."

As part of this centuries-long story of the relationship between the people and the church, Michelet told his version with such unforgettable and dramatic language that it made an indelible impression not only on historians who came after him but on the popular imagination as well. "It was an universal belief in the middle ages, that the world was to end with the year 1000," he reported. "Woe on woe, ruin on ruin! . . . The captive expected [the end of the world] in the black dungeon, . . . the serf expected on the lea, . . . the monk expected in the abstinences of the cloister, in the solitary tumults of his heart, amidst temptations and lapses, remorses and strange visions, a miserable sport of the devil who gamboled cruelly round him and who, plucking aside his bed-clothes at night, whispered merrily in his ear, 'Thou art damned.'"

For Michelet, however, the story involved more than just panic and fear but also hope and peace. For the people, at least their oppressors, the damned, would receive a deserved comeuppance at the hands of Divine Justice. "It must, too, have had its charm for the imagination," he writes, "that moment when the shrill and piercing trumpet of the archangel was to ring upon the ears of tyrants. At that moment from dungeon, from cloister, and from the field filled by the villein, a fearful burst of laughter would have risen amidst the weeping." When the world did not end in 1000, Michelet wrote that "humanity took courage." People rose up from their collective "death-struggle," full of a newfound energy that would eventually lead to the Crusades and form the roots of French nationalism.

The story of the Terrors took on an even stronger anti-church rhetoric after Michelet, reports Peter Stearns in his book *Millennium III, Century XXI*. Later French writers suggested that greedy churchmen had encouraged millennial fears deliberately so that people would give their material possessions to the church in hopes of salvation. During the 19th century, writers vied with each other in describing this period of history—each attempting to heighten the drama of the story and add more macabre details to the tales told by their predecessors. The myth of the Terrors reached full flower as it found colorful expression in poem, play and book.

By the late 19th and early 20th centuries, however, a new generation of historians loudly decried the Terrors as an apocryphal story concocted from the inflamed minds and fantasies of Michelet and his fellow Romantics. "Alas for human fallibility!" comments American historian George Lincoln Burr in 1901, smugly dispensing with the Terrors as a bad practical joke that would not fool modern historians, schooled in rigorous critical thinking and the scientific method. For nearly all of the 20th century, no one seriously challenged Burr's definitive and biting analysis. No one, that

By the late 19th and early 20th centuries, however, a new generation of historians loudly decried the Terrors as an apocryphal story concocted from the inflamed minds and fantasies of Michelet and his fellow Romantics.

is, until Richard Landes, a medievalist in the history department and director of the Center for Millennial Studies at Boston University, who is interpreting year 1000 history with a new twist.

Landes is creating controversy by insisting that a lot of apocalyptic activity did occur around the turn of the last millennium. He is reexamining the year 1000 documents with a fresh eye. He says that if more emphasis is placed on the accounts of rumors and reports of troubling signs and natural wonders—such as famine and the appearance of comets—then one can find evidence that the people across Europe were expecting a Last Judgment scenario. He also draws attention to historical references to pilgrimages, penitential processions and peace assemblies, which he argues might have come about as a result of apocalyptic concerns among the people. At the outset Landes establishes that he is "not arguing that we should reintroduce the Romantic notion of the 'Terrors of the year 1000.'" He acknowledges that a universal panic may have never materialized. Landes aims rather to introduce the idea that apocalypticism—involving both fear and hope—did occur on a greater scale in the period surrounding the year 1000 than at other times.

Many historians, while intrigued by some of the bits of evidence that Landes has turned up, fail to swallow the argument that there was more millennial activity than meets the eye. The academic battle lines are drawn. Bernard McGinn, who has analyzed medieval apocalyptic thought for many years and is editor of the *Encyclopedia of Apocalypticism*, has commented that he thinks "a hidden millennarianism is a figment of his [Landes'] imagination."

Landes responds that "the 'anti-Terrors' school has an aggressive naivete in its approach to the texts, indignantly dismissing the possibility that the clerics who compose our sources might be under discretionary pressure." It's a point as convincing as it is difficult to prove: holding most of the power to control what was written down, the church could effectively quiet those who wrote about millennial activity. Landes proposes that instances of millennial fever often went unrecorded because the chroniclers who wrote the history afterward knew that the world had not, after all, ended. In addition, he points out that the very idea of setting a date for the end of the world was forbidden by church policy, so chroniclers may have exercised great caution in writing about this matter. Landes argues that "silence is the Church party line."

Of the half-dozen first-person accounts of millennial activity, none are more controversial than that of one Burgundian French monk named Rodulfus Glaber, who penned a five-volume history that speaks directly to life at the turn of the millennium. The monk with the chatty writing style has become like the witness in a controversial murder trial: it's

> *Landes is creating controversy by insisting that a lot of apocalyptic activity did occur around the turn of the last millennium.*

hard to tell where the truth lies once one has discounted his obvious excitability, his instinct for the dramatic and his inclination toward fantasy and superstition. His veracity will remain in question because his testimony is ten centuries old and one of few sources that survives. The fact that Glaber wrote of his experience meeting the Devil—a man with goat's beard, pinched nostrils and blubbery lips, who appeared in a vision at the foot of his bed—has given pause to many medieval historians. Bernard McGinn makes only brief mention of him in his *Visions of the End*, a collection of medieval apocalyptic texts.

To make matters worse, the monk earned a rich reputation as a troublemaker. At age 12, in the year 992, Glaber entered his first monastery. Throughout the next 50 years, as many as six monasteries, including those in Auxerre, Dijon and Beze, and the Abbey of Cluny, would find ample reason to rid themselves of his troublesome presence. Yet his experiences traveling the French countryside between monasteries—even going as far as Italy—would give him a view of the world not available to his more cooperative, sedentary brethren. In the early eleventh century he witnessed the construction of many new stone church buildings across France. These churches appeared to him as the world making a new start, "cladding itself everywhere in a white mantle of churches." Was this a reaction to the recent turn of the millennium or simply the result of the Christianization of Europe?

Glaber recorded that millennial fever built up in the year 1033 because it marked the year of Christ's death and resurrection, the time when many felt that judgment was at hand. Glaber told of heresy, or devil worship, among the Lombards. When famines were said to have turned men into cannibals, he wrote, "it could portend nothing other than the advent of the accursed Anti-Christ who, according to divine testimony, is expected to appear at the end of the world." And when pilgrims flocked to Jerusalem in large numbers, Glaber wrote, "it was believed that the order of the seasons and the elements . . . had fallen into perpetual chaos, and with it had come the end of mankind."

A critical point in the debate is the calendar issue (*Smithsonian*, February 1999). When exactly did the millennium change over? (Complicating the question is confusion over the date of Christ's birth.) The idea that people across Europe followed many different calendars is a strong argument against a widespread response to the millennium. In the age of ubiquitous digital watches, Greenwich mean time and the televised drop of the New Year's ball in Times Square, it's easy to forget that regions varied dramatically as to when they celebrated the end of one year and the beginning of the next. Some ushered in the new year on January

The idea that people across Europe followed many different calendars is a strong argument against a widespread response to the millennium.

1, others at Christmas, on Good Friday or the day after, or on Easter. The year was different from place to place.

It's conceivable that many unlettered people didn't know that a new year was at hand, nor that one century was changing to another. Life was measured by the progress from one season to the next, from seedtime to harvest, from one holy day or festival to the next—a cycle that repeated again and again and was likely to go on doing so.

Richard Landes insists that it is insulting and condescending to imagine that people of the tenth century would not know or care what year it was. If the prevailing religious tradition hinted about the time and shape of a person's ultimate destiny, then the year and date would have been of consuming interest to many. Landes cites the English monk Saint Bede the Venerable, who complained in the year 700 that the "rustics" kept bothering him, wanting to know when the foretold end of the world would take place. They were the ones, Landes says, who eagerly anticipated the end of the world, because they believed that it would bring release from this vale of tears.

Indeed, the notion of the apocalypse lies deep in the fabric of Christianity, borrowed and adapted from Jewish traditions. The Christian reading of the Jewish bible, or the Old Testament, led them to regard themselves as the new Chosen People.

For a persecuted and downtrodden minority, the idea of an apocalypse at the millennium where they would inherit a new and better world had recognizable and deep appeal.

For a persecuted and downtrodden minority, the idea of an apocalypse at the millennium where they would inherit a new and better world had recognizable and deep appeal. By the fifth century, however, Christianity had shed its beleaguered minority status and emerged as a powerful and dominant force throughout most of Europe in the form of the Catholic church. As Norman Cohn argues in *The Pursuit of the Millennium*, the now staid and tradition-laden church elite "had no wish to see Christians clinging to out-dated and inappropriate dreams of a new earthly Paradise."

Church doctrine forbade the assigning of a specific date to the end of the world. "It is not yours to know the times that the Father has put in his power," wrote Saint Augustine of Hippo. The church took pains to refute anyone who claimed to know exactly when the end would arrive. A person should always live, the church instructed, as if the end of Days and the Last Judgment could arrive tomorrow. Whether church doctrine could banish the appeal of the deeply rooted apocalyptic tradition among common people is difficult to say. The effect of the doctrine on written documents, however, may have been large. Landes points out that "virtually no text survived to our day that was not copied and preserved by monastic institutions whose decisions were made long after any apocalyptic moment had passed." Landes argues that mention of apocalyptic activity would have been censored, most evidence destroyed.

In the final analysis, of course, the argument that there is an absence of critical documents and important witnesses to the events surrounding the first millennium can never be proof that fevered response did occur. The absence of this evidence makes for a negative argument, which is not enough to convict either in a court of law or in academe.

No amount of argument among medieval scholars will answer definitively the question of what happened. It is clear that Europe was undergoing momentous changes as it Christianized. It's probably safe to assume that a massive seizure of panic did not take Europe in its grasp. It remains open to debate, however, whether the turn of the last millennium caused significant activity or not. The mystery remains, the debate continues.

Curiously, the only undisputed cases of extreme millennium-related activity, such as mass suicide, come not from the first millennium but from our own times. On March 26, 1997, in a wealthy community of San Diego, California, 39 members of the Heaven's Gate cult committed suicide so that their souls could be transported to the "Next Level" by a starship hiding behind the Hale-Bopp comet.

No amount of argument among medieval scholars will answer definitively the question of what happened.

Perhaps it's best, then, to look at the behavior of people today for clues to how people may have reacted back then. Despite generations of scientific advance and universal public education, millions of people in our own day believe in alien abductions, listen to channelers who claim to speak with the voices of the dead, and fear the impending approach of black helicopters representing the New World Order. Far more Americans feel vaguely unsettled, concerned that normal life will grind to a halt as computers fail to switch over to the new millennium. Some people have contemplated that the Y2K bug could drop airplanes from the sky, shut down power grids across the world, or activate nuclear missiles. Even today, the line between fantasy and fact, myth and reality, is not always clear.

Meanwhile, the legend of the Terrors, detached from the current academic debate, continues to thrive because of our willingness to believe that the early Middle Ages was a time when the sun scarcely rose by day and the people languished in a benighted twilight, so different from our own enlightened time.

For posterity, Landes and his colleagues at the Center for Millennial Studies are recording the modern response to the new millennium by tracking "apocalyptic discourse" in books, chatrooms on the Internet, television and radio news programs, newsletters and newspapers. Perhaps this information will prove useful for historians at the turn of the third millennium. We can only wonder what tales the people of 2999 will tell about how we reacted to the change of the second millennium.

The Apocalyptic Year 1000: Then and Now[2]

The year 1000. What a host of images it calls forth. Signs and wonders in the heavens; ghastly plagues and famines on earth; the populace—from the highest to the lowest—on their knees in dread, in churches, in fields, terrified at the coming Judgment when this Day of Wrath turned into a Day of Doom, and man confronted his eternal destiny. With such brushstrokes did the Romantic historians of the mid-19th century paint their lurid pictures of a world febrile with expectation in the tenth century and energized with relief in the eleventh. To this day, the guides who take us through the churches of France tell us that the *potentes* of those years, fearing for their souls, gave large portions of land to the clergy, especially to the monks, thus triggering the great explosion of church-building that Radulfus Glaber, the historian of the millennium, describes in such poetic terms: "It was as if the whole world had shaken off the dust of the ages and covered itself in a white mantle of churches."

No! said the new professional school of historians at the end of the 19th century: nothing of the sort. First of all, there is no scriptural basis for the year 1000: it represents not a date, but a period (Revelation 20:7). Second, we have almost no evidence for such a picture: half the lurid texts about 1000 are either outright fakes from the sixteenth century, or describing events at a different date: 909, 950, 1010, 1033. Indeed, given how rarely documents even use Anno Domini, it seems that contemporaries neither knew nor cared about the date. And if, perchance, some few did evince an interest, they could not be certain when it came due. There are no serious documents indicating that people were "paralyzed by the terror" of the Coming Day of the Lord in the year 1000. When all is said and done, the careful historian is left with a small handful of texts of doubtful significance, which pale in comparison with the overwhelming majority of the documents from the period showing no interest whatsoever in eschatology. The big picture of contemporary documentation suggests that the famous "terrors" spring not from the documents of 1000, but from the fevered brain of the Romantic historians who have contaminated our understanding of our past with their unrestrained imaginations, leaving us not real history, but legends. Contrary to this novelist's reconstruction, Positivists depict a year 1000 that passed amidst wide-

2. Article by Richard Landes from *The Year 2000: Essays on the End*, ed. Charles Strozier and Michael Flynn. Reprinted with permission. To save space, the original end notes of this article have been deleted. To read this article with end notes, visit the Center for Millennial Studies Web site at www.mille.org.

spread indifference, in many places unnoticed... a year like any other. If you do a survey of media pieces on 2000, say since the *Le Monde* article [from the 1970s] entitled "2000 semaines jusqu'à a l'an 2000": some (I suspect a minority) refer to the Romantic notion of the terrors before rapidly moving on to our own times. Some, bowing to the experts, dismiss it. In both cases it plays little part in the narrative or analysis of 2000: most often it serves as a kind of contrast. Then, they were superstitious and thought God would put an end to the world; now we no longer believe in a God who intervenes in history... on the contrary, it is not God but humans with the immaturity and massive technological abilities who threaten the planet. In the final years running up to the year 2000, with the flood of books hitting the market on the subject, such "glances" become more lengthy if not necessarily more penetrating. And what are the causes and consequences of these two, radically different views of the last turn of the millennium in European (also Christian, also Western) history?

Why, whether one follows the Romantics or the Positivists, is there so little connection between 1000 and 2000? Partly, I would argue, because since the late nineteenth century, when the Positivist position first dismissed the year 1000 as a myth, little work had been done on the eschatological thinking of the period; as a result major debates, like the one about the so-called *mutation de l'an mil*, or the one about the origins of popular heresy, are carried on without a mention of apocalypticism as a potential actor in the course of events and developments. And if this is true of the key issues at the turn of the millennium, it is all the more so about subsequent events, in that century, in later ones. This in turn is partly due to the Augustinian fallacy of the historically correct: because every apocalyptic believer in an eschatological year 1000 proved wrong, it does not really matter whether many or few so believed; they were not particularly significant. Not then, and surely not now, at the distance of almost a millennium. Such a conclusion is the result of what I call capstone historiography—i.e., a widespread tendency among medievalists to succumb not only to the quantitative impression of the sources (as Ferdinand Lot put it: few texts, few beliefs), but also to accept the texts at their face value: to believe, for example, what a writer says about the way he (far more rarely she) and fellow contemporar[ies] interpreted events. What escapes us when we take this approach is that in most cases, our texts are written retrospectively, with the same knowledge that we have (i.e., the expectations proved false). This neglect of the temporal perspective in considering our sources—no belief is more subject to dramatically different interpretation than one about the immediate future (what we call 20/20 hindsight and what I call the fallacy of the historically correct)—leads us to neglect the

Why, whether one follows the Romantics or the Positivists, is there so little connection between 1000 and 2000?

fact that the retrospective narrative is not only historically accurate, but also (in terms of our exclusively clerical composers), politically correct. Those scribes who preserve, copy, compose, erase, and edit the wealth of manuscripts they inherit, are not scientists dedicated to preserving the record; they are committed believers, trained in the Augustinian tradition which says that one cannot know the end, must not interpret current events in terms of an apocalyptic scenario, and must interpret 1000 as an allegorical number symbolizing perfection, not as a fixed number of years before the parousia. With their knowledge of what should have been, they could and did "correct the record," sparing their heroes—the founders and benefactors of the institutions they lived in—the embarrassment of so grievous a slip in the Augustinian norm. These men were no more likely to preserve evidence that the great figures of the day—King Robert, Emperor Otto, Pope Gerbert, Abbot Odilo of Cluny, William of Dijon, Abbo of Fleury—were subject of apocalyptic concerns than historians of modern science are eager to dwell on Isaac Newton's fascination with apocalyptic calculations based on the Book of Revelation. Their work as composers and archivists is not to be taken at face value. If there were a brief moment when some of the leaders of Christendom openly embraced an apocalyptic year 1000, sponsoring the kinds of extraordinary and often dangerous or (retrospectively) ridiculous behavior that such beliefs entail, it would be too much to expect them to tell the story faithfully. It would be like arriving the day after the emperor had paraded naked before the entire town and asking the courtiers what happened. You might get the real story in the street; but historians, unfortunately, are stuck with primarily the "official record" of the courtiers. Starting from this revised record, Henri Focillon (one of the few historians of the period to grant significance to the approach of 1000), made a key distinction between the enlightened elites and the superstitious commoners. These latter may have been swayed by such foolish fears, but certainly not the great figures who built Europe. They were almost like two different races of men.

This approach has a number of characteristic analytic tendencies which, in the case of apocalyptic beliefs, tends to (dis)miss the significance of the documentation. Thus, they interpret the relatively few documents from this period that are actually dated Anno Domini as a sign of indifference among contemporaries, and consider the learned discord over the date as a sign of that age's limited scientific abilities and general confusion. But one can read this data in precisely the opposite fashion and draw a picture of a generation acutely aware of the date, whose (relative) silence in certain documents indicates anxiety rather than indifference. First, consider the Easter Tables then in use: every single religious establishment which owned even half a dozen codices would have tables first drawn up by Bede (724) and spread in the following generation by the Carolingians. These tables all used AD dating in their first column, followed by all the information necessary to determine when to celebrate Easter that year. In other words the assumed knowledge, the point of entry into the Easter material, was the date. No one could make the most vital liturgical determination in Christendom without knowing the year. Indifferent to the meaning of 1000 or not, there is no possibility of arguing ignorance of the date.

But, we are told, the year 1000 had no eschatological meaning. It appears in the famous (and explosive) passage of Revelation in reference to a future period of time, a millennium to begin at some point, rather than a period to end. This is true, and would hold as an argument were we dealing with the millennial expectations of the early Christian centuries. But starting in the third century, the coming millennium was linked to a scheme of seven millennia from creation: the sabbatical millennium of peace and justice and plenty would come at the end of this sixth and last millennium of travail and darkness. The year 6000 was variously dated to 500 and 801 AD by successive generations of Christian chronographers; and at the approach of each date, some chronographers engage in a "countdown" of years from their day "to the completion of this millennium." Moreover, with the passage of this second millennial date, evidence suggests that the new focus of the end of the millennium was retargeted to 1000. Finally, and perhaps most ironically, this millennial calculation, which Augustine had done so much to drive out of the Church, and whose "marginal" appearance in the documentation led the specialists of Christian chronology to miss its significance, was reinforced by Augustine's own insistence that the current millennium, since the time of Christ, marked the period of the (invisible) millennial reign of the saints, thus giving either 1000 or 1033 a different, but no less eschatological significance: rather than awaiting the beginning of the millennium of Revelation 20:1-6, mankind awaited its end (20:7-14) in a cosmic battle between good and evil. The widespread knowledge of AD among clerics, and the eight-centuries-old tradition of counting down to an eschatologically significant "fin-du-millénaire," sheds a different light on the scholarly "confusion" concerning the precise date of 1000. On the contrary, all of the dates offered by the "anti-terreur" historians as "alternative" dates for 1000—968, 979 or 1033—reflect not a variety of equally plausible dates in circulation, but a series of efforts either to speed up the millennium's arrival, to postdate it, or to salvage a coming millennium after its passage. The disagreement, then, which crops up only in the final generation before the year 1000, is not a sign of confusion, but of either anxiety or enthusiasm about an approaching eschatological deadline.

Starting in the third century, the coming millennium was linked to a scheme of seven millennia from creation.

Nor did it have any serious impact on the widespread acceptance of the common date AD, still in use.

As for whether the lay populace also knew the date, that is
obviously a matter of sheer conjecture. We have precious little on what they knew, and that is so spotty that it would be
hard to confidently generalize from it. But conjecture we
must, and it is better to do so in an informed manner than
merely by asserting conclusions based on the principle that
peasants are illiterate, stupid, and insignificant (what our
clerical sources call "dumb" or "hornless" oxen). The first
issue, then, is to ask whether they wanted to or not. If the
date were meaningful to them (a question to which we shall
return), then there were certainly channels to find out—the
sources are full of stories about wandering holy men, monks
who jump the monastery walls (like Glaber), religious leaders who reject any kind of ecclesiastical discipline. Like children with watches, the rustics may have wanted to know
just how much longer to wait. If Bede could complain of rustics who importune[d] him over how many years remain in
the millennium (i.e., at the approach of 6000 AM II), one can
easily imagine that the crowd in Paris who, in 970, heard
that Antichrist would come in the year 1000, might be
equally insistent on knowing when that date might come.
Having questioned the basis of an "insignificant year 1000,"
one needs to go further. What are the historiographical consequences of the kind of capstone historiography that has
given us this "year like any other" and effectively atrophied
our ability to think about an apocalyptic year 1000. Above
all, such a view disconnects the year 1000 from any discussion of the great issues—millennial or social—of the past
thousand years of Western Civilization, indeed it has even
disconnected it from developments in the very century it
inaugurated, those revolutions of agriculture, of commerce,
of urban and rural freedoms, of church reform, of law, of
knightly piety, those mutant forms of behavior which produced, by the end of the eleventh century, the communes,
the Investiture Conflict, the Crusades. However he or she
cuts it, the medieval historian describing the large sweep of
the story, must somehow start the tale of the High Middle
Ages sometime around 1000 (950-1050). Those who start
their tale in 950 invoke slow, imperceptible changes and
begin discussing the visible changes in the mid-eleventh century; many simply start ca. 1050, or a year before, when the
reform Pope Leo IX had lifted the relics of Saint Remi, and
demanded that all simoniac bishops (i.e., all of those assembled), come and resign their office for having polluted it with
their lucre. None of this, generally, is associated with the
year 1000.

To the contrary. Looking at the documentation of 1000 in
the context of the longer tradition of apocalyptic thought and
preaching within the church—from its origins in the Gal-

lilean and Judean hills, through the conversion of the Roman emperor himself, to the conversion and ascendance of these barbaric tribes to the true faith and, under the name Charlemagne, to the imperial title—in this longer trajectory, I would argue, the year 1000 stands out as a year of outstanding eschatological importance to high and low alike. And its passage, far from exposing some foolish fantasy that soon dissipated, had immense consequences for the shape and direction of European culture. As the end of the second Christian millennium approaches, we are in a position to understand what happened at the approach and passage of the first.

Background to 1000: On the Nature of Christian Apocalyptic Thought

Christianity begins with the announcing of the good news, that is "The kingdom of heaven is at hand." Whether that kingdom was meant as the chiliastic reign of the saints in this world, or some eschatological Last Judgment, it promised an imminent and public release from all the pain and suffering that the righteous suffer in this world where power is wielded by the brutal and immoral. It is important to keep in mind that for the believer, the promise of this final deliverance from evil lay at the core of much Christian thought: the Day of the Lord was, for the true believer, not one of fear but hope, not one of terror but of vindication. One has only to read the Book of Revelation to get a sense of how powerful—indeed violent—the dreams of final deliverance might become. However often Christians might cite the principle that "the Kingdom of Heaven is within," they continued to look for the Parousia. Bishop Hesychius, convinced that the End had come, and criticizing Augustine for his insistence that we cannot know the time, argued that the hope of the imminent Parousia was the food with which he nourished his flock. Especially for the meek, who awaited to inherit the earth, the moment was eagerly awaited. But it never came. (Or has not yet... for the historian this is the key.) And in the meantime, each generation had to deal with both its hopes and disappointments. In time there emerged two different positions: the Augustinian and the Hesychian, or what I would call the owls and the roosters. The roosters crow about the imminent dawn of redemption, of a public settling of accounts, exciting their flocks to extraordinary efforts of self-sacrifice, to the white hot fervor of a full-blown Sermon on the Mount; the owls try [to] hush the roosters, arguing that only mischief, disappointment, and loss of credibility can come from such hastiness, emphasizing that in this perduringly fallen world the Kingdom of Heaven can only [lie] within, and that precious few are capable of a full embrace of ethics so glorious as those Jesus enjoined upon the faithful. At times of great uncertainty and unrest—when the sky

The year 1000 stands out as a year of outstanding eschatological importance to high and low alike.

filled with signs and wonders, when famines, plagues and wars devastated the countryside, when rumors of prodigies and marvels spread, when long-awaited eschatological dates reached their term—the roosters crowed loudly and the owls were helpless to resist. When, as they always did, things quieted down, the owls gained the upper hand. And it is they who control our documentary record. Thus the capstone historians who dismissed 1000 as a "year like any other" overlooked a key variable: the end is not merely paralyzing terrors, it is also extravagant hope; hope to see an end to the injustice of suffering in this world, hope for a life of ease and delight, hope for the victory of truth and peace. In this perspective, some of the very things that in one argument appear as "life as usual" appear in this perspective rather differently. The massive effort and success of imperial missionaries from Germany and Byzantium to convert the pagan peoples—Scandinavian, Slav, Hungarian—is not "proof" that people did not just freeze in terror, it is, on the contrary, an illustration of millennial enthusiasm: at once massive in scope and successful in endeavor. Similarly (a point to which I shall return), when the high aristocracy began to gather the commoners into large open-field assemblies to establish a social peace, this was not [a sign] of a confidently determined church keeping the social machine finely tuned, but of a fundamental social crisis and a (shocking) appeal to the most profoundly chiliastic hopes of the masses to resolve it.

Let us approach the year 1000. In 750 the Carolingians adopted Bede's Anno Domini in historiography, computus, and some diplomatics, thus enabling them (as Bede had intended) to avoid mentioning the approaching of the year 6000 Anno Mundi. Thus on the first day of AD 801 (= 6000 AM), Charlemagne received the imperial crown in Rome. Everyone knew; no one wrote about it. Did anyone speak openly about 6000? Were references to this date in the ceremony? Did anyone pass from the coronation as a *continuatio imperii Romani*—Rome stands, the Antichrist cannot come—to something about a messianic emperor, a new and final Christian millennium? We are forced to conjecture, because for the second time, Christian scribes have proved capable of maintaining a strict and disciplined silence about an apocalyptic year. Using AD permitted not only to leave-off discussion of the ever-more apocalyptic year 6000, it permitted focus on one still comfortably off in the future: 1000. When Thiota the pseudo-prophetess (note, her very title is retrospective) came to Mainz in 847 announcing the end of the world for the following year and gathering a large and devoted following of commoners and even clerics, the official rejoinder to her apocalyptic calculation was (as it had been for the last 600-700 years), that still 152 years remained until the year AD 1000.

The Approach of 1000: The First Millennial Generation (960–1000)

About 950, Adso of Montier-en-Der wrote a politically conservative treatise on the Antichrist addressed to the West Frankish queen, Gerberga, in which he made three key points about the contemporary scene: First, although [a] great Antichrist would be born in the East of the tribe of Dan, he would be preceded by many antichrists, who would rebel against their place in the social order. Second, the Antichrist could not come until the Roman Empire had fallen, and as long as there were Frankish kings who "ought to be emperor" that empire was still "standing." And third, one variant current among our "learned ones" (*doctores*) foresaw a mighty emperor who would unite the entire world in his Christian peace for a century or more and then go on pilgrimage to Jerusalem where, in laying down his crown, he would voluntarily put an end to the Roman empire and inaugurate the final, eschatological scenario.

Adso's text became immensely popular, read, copied, sent as a present to Heribert when he first rose to the episcopal see of Cologne in 999 with a new preface, advising him to read it carefully as a guide to the times. It was attached to a treatise on the Vices and the Virtues which urged a deep and abiding penitence, and a struggle with one's old ways. Although capstone historians are likely to read the manuscript history of the text as evidence of a purely literary phenomenon, the likelihood is greater that behind every written text lay ever-widening gyres of readers, auditors, reciters and embellishers. If so erudite an apocalyptic calculation as the years in which the Annunciation and Crucifixion coincide could spread "throughout almost the entire world," then the mythical narrative that Adso gave voice to could easily move from the world of written to that of oral discourse. If Brian Stock can speak of "textual communities" in the early eleventh century who take the apostolic verses as their source of bonding, then one can certainly imagine that such communities, drawing on Revelation and Adso's *Vita Antichristi*, could have formed in the generation before the year 1000. The immense impact of Adso's work on the subsequent eschatological imagination of the West for two centuries attests precisely to such oral popularity. Let us, then, read the treatise as *roman à clef*. To Adso in 950, the line which "ought to" produce a Frankish emperor was Gerberga's husband Louis IV of the western Franks, the last direct descendent of Charlemagne's royal (millennial) line. He was not thinking of her brother, king Otto of the East Franks, a Saxon from [a] dynasty whose royal pretensions had only arisen in the course of the tenth century. Within a generation all would change: by 962, Otto had become emperor, and by 987–91, Louis family had lost the throne to a new and local aristocratic dynasty. As we approach the year 1000, there-

Signs and wonders, disasters and omens gave rich body to this apocalyptic political and social picture.

fore, Germany and France go in exactly opposite directions in playing out the eschatological scenario Adso had laid out. In the East, the Ottomans pursued a grand and triumphal strategy in which all the symbols of Apocalypse and imperium were combined: converting the pagans (far more successful than Charlemagne), renewing the Roman empire in Rome, reforming the papacy (Gerbert the peasant scientist), opening the tomb of Charlemagne (emperor of 6000) on Pentecost of 1000. Although he was not of the imperial blood, Otto III was nonetheless emperor; and a close look at his "overheated mysticism" suggests that he conceived of himself as that messianic emperor spoken of by those *doctores* Adso mentioned. In the West, everything fell apart. The constant pressure of local strongmen to assert their dominion over the population (*potentes* vs. *pauperes*), already strong under the last Carolingians, broke its bounds. In every place where the ruler did not assert constant vigilance, new castles went up... not to protect against invaders, but to dominate the countryside. Castellans and their bully-boys, the milites, asserted a new kind of peace, one in which the difference between an armed *bellator* and an unarmed *laborator* was clear; and the advantage went to [the one] with arms and control over the local courts. Not only was the church helpless to reign in these newly-powerful, these *nouveau puissants*, not yet socialized to the exercise of that which they so ruthlessly laid claim to, [it] was often enough their victim. To the victims of this revolution in social relations, the new men could not help but seem like so many antichrists, rebelling against their place, intensifying warfare and pillage, embittering the life of the peasants whose produce they lived off. Especially in the south, the fall of the Carolingians meant the end of the monarchy—many dated their charters by Anno Domini with Christ reigning; and the new dynasty got off to a difficult start. In the year 1000, accused of incest by the church, excommunicated by his own teacher, Gerbert the pope, King Robert stood as the symbol of royal impotence. Whereas the Ottonians rode the top of the wave of apocalyptic hopes and fears of 1000, the Capetians wiped out early. Signs and wonders, disasters and omens gave rich body to this apocalyptic political and social picture: famines, plagues, invasions by the Danes, beached whales, monstrous births, a bright Halley's comet in 989, widespread outbreaks of *sacer ignis*, earthquakes, eclipses of the sun and moon. The roosters were crowing continuously. As early as the 960s, Lotharingian computists were predicting the end for the year 970, when the Annunciation and the Crucifixion coincided: Friday, March 25, when Adam was created, Isaac sacrificed, the Red Sea crossed, Christ incarnated, Christ crucified, and the Archangel Michael would defeat Satan. Against this rumor, a Paris preacher urged the classic Carolingian response: "not now, in the year 1000." Abbo, a very smart and energetic young man, who would have to live with that delayed promise some 30 years off, objected strenuously, emphasizing Augustine's radical agnosticism. "We cannot know," he would have argued, "these texts are not to be taken literally; we must look within and do penitence." The fact that Abbo was right did not put an end to the issue: the coincidence happened again in 981 and again in 992. However big or small we imagine them (Abbo spoke of a rumor spreading through almost the entire world), these waves of date- based apocalyptic expectation were only dress-rehearsals to the year 1000. Here the evidence seems quite powerful: we have a dozen chroniclers and annalists who specifically speak of the passage of 1000 (again retrospective), another dozen surviving examples of Easter Tables that either end in or begin in 1000 (in the middle of a 19-year cycle), another half-dozen texts which explicitly link the year 1000 to apocalyptic behavior. Perhaps the single most spectacular text, written in a contemporary hand, in the margins of a Bedan Easter Table, describes a tremendous earthquake, "sign of the sure completion of all the prophecies and the imminent fulfillment of all our hopes." We also know how Christians met these moments of crisis: public processions, often with relics, gathering the entire populace in acts of penitential contrition. Such moments may not last, but their memory does (they are, I would argue, depicted on the bottom stratum of the tympanum at Autun); and it is up to us to figure out how it influenced events. One can, therefore, with little difficulty, draw a text-based picture of an apocalyptic year 1000, one filled with both long-term eschatological projects (Otto III) but also specific and public apocalyptic moments when, as the Romantics claimed and the Positivists mockingly dismissed, people literally stood in fear and trembling. The important point for the historian is to go on. What happened after? After the catharsis of public penitence? After (even the most committed began to realize that) the end did not come? After normal time resumed?

Historians . . . tend to miss the full range of apocalyptic behavior because they look for only one kind of manifestation— generally extravagant and often destructive behavior.

Historians who like to categorize the phenomena they study tend to miss the full range of apocalyptic behavior because they look for only one kind of manifestation—generally extravagant and often destructive behavior. Thus when confronted with the case of public apocalyptic moments—vast assemblies of people convinced by some combination of signs, wonders, disasters, prophets, and times, that the end is upon them—the historian tends to believe that, with the passage of time, they realized that they were wrong in their fears, and, with a huge sigh of relief, they returned to their former lives. This approach misses the key transformation provided by apocalyptic beliefs. The approach of the Apocalypse calls for all sinners to, in this final moment, "Repent, for the Kingdom of Heaven is at hand." If large numbers collectively feel this imminence, if a plague or an earthquake or a sign in the heavens shakes the confidence of even the most determined and powerful members of a society, if people gather in vast assemblies and engage in penitential activity, reaching unimagined heights of confession and renunciation, then the fear can and will pass, not only because the end fails to come, but because the collective penance can produce a massive change of "atmosphere" in which people embrace their enemies in tears of mutual forgiveness. Thus the delay of the end might be viewed not merely as a reprieve, but as the salvation of God, bestowed on his chastened people; not the continuation of the world as we know it, but the inauguration of a new age in which the peace of men, the peace of iron, gives way to the Pax Dei.

The Aftermath of 1000, the Approach of 1033: The Second Millennial Generation.

It is in the transformation of penitence to joy that new social bonds are made, that vendettas are abandoned, that feuding enemies embrace, that weapons are laid aside.

Things did not, I would argue, return to "normal." Capstone historians, with their unidimensional caricature of terror-filled apocalyptic beliefs, tend to look for relief, a sentiment one might well expect from clerics like Abbo who had been saddled with this volatile eschatological promise by his Carolingian predecessors. And indeed we find it: Adam of Bremen, writing a chronicle on the northeastern frontier of Christendom, gratuitously noted that the year 1000 from the incarnation had been completed *feliciter.* But I think the more significant sentiment to follow is hope, and its post-apocalyptic sister, disappointment. Here one finds some of the most pregnant activity—the first and vigorous stirrings of a popular Christian culture of vast movements, of radical dissent and reform, of widespread pilgrimage, of collective actions. The key to these developments is to be found in the apocalyptic dynamic itself, which goes through some fairly predictable stages. Let us begin with the penitential movements, which most closely fit the stereotype of apocalyptic fears. These public outpourings of confession and remorse have an electrifying effect on people, unleashing the full force of the apocalyptic ethics of the sermon on the mount, leading them to beg forgiveness for crimes from neighbors and enemies, to swear off a life of evil and turn with an open heart to God. Again, granted, the texts describing such moments often go on to give us the retrospective perspective, in which promises are broken and evil ways return. But it is in the transformation of penitence to joy that new social bonds are made, that vendettas are abandoned, that feuding enemies embrace, that weapons are laid aside. It is in this atmosphere that a Christian peace first emerged, most notably in the south of France, where royal authority was non-existent. Here we have the mutation of Rogations-like penitential processions into a full-fledged chiliastic movement in which the elites and the populace met on the same terrain—one favorable to the populace—and attempted to inaugurate God's peace on earth.

The peace started in the south, where royal power and authority were close to non-existent. It constituted an effort by the highest aristocracy, lay and clerical (dukes, counts, abbots, bishops). It combined all of the most passionate and populist elements in the ecclesiastical repertory—major relics and the huge religiously enthusiastic crowds they drew, collective oaths, messianic rhetoric, and, of course, the self-abasement of the participating warriors who, swords sheathed, openly participated in the infectious deeds of contrition and mutual forgiveness, mutually swearing to renounce their ways and to leave the non-combatants alone. At the least, it was an oath renouncing terrorism (a standard form of warfare); at the most, it was an oath to live in a society where to shed the blood of a Christian was to shed the blood of Christ. Some of the early assemblies, like the one in Limoges in 994 were clearly undertaken in a dramatic, indeed apocalyptic atmosphere of crisis: the detailed and lurid descriptions of the plague of *sacer ignis*, of the penitential fast, of the vast crowds accompanying the saints—like the children of Israel crossing the Red Sea and following Moses to the Promised Land—the miraculous healing and joyous celebration, and the ensuing pact of peace and justice sworn by the warrior elite. This is the most striking expression of apocalyptic sentiment at the approach of the millennium: it contains both the fears and the hopes so characteristic of such beliefs; it spreads with great rapidity through most of the south during the final decade of the millennium; it mobilized an entire culture. It also probably stepped over the bounds of Augustinian eschatological discourse. It has clearly chiliastic elements—the very notion of the rule of God's peace on earth, brought about by voluntary rather than forced restraints, by mutual love and forgiveness rather than fear of retaliation, all this suggests a kingdom of the saints. Whether the clerics at these assemblies were openly roosters and explicitly invoked millenarian themes is difficult to gauge. Like Charlemagne's coronation, we cannot look to the written record for a clear sense of what went on. They surely invoked God's wrath and imminent Judgment as a reason for the evil-doers (here the warrior aristocracy) to repent: as Hesychius had said, that was part a fundamental part of preaching. Indeed, if we need an example of terrified paralysis at the advent of the year 1000, we might see it, as Michelet put it, in the sword hand of the warriors who attended these Peace assemblies. Nor need one be explicit to raise hopes; much of the symbolism—from the name of Pax Dei to the presence of the saints (relics), to timing—certainly allowed participants to believe that they were participating in the descent of the heavenly city to the earthly city. Of course they were participating in nothing of the sort. Within a relatively brief time (indistinguishable in the texts) the warriors were back at it, building their castles, coercing their own peasants, fighting their wars, pillaging churches and burning their enemies' villages and crops. Conventional historians tend to treat this outcome as decisive: the Pax Dei failed in its effort to instaur peace; it was eventually replaced by more pragmatic institutions, enforced by arms. It appears often as a footnote in a survey, an illustration of how bad feudal anarchy could get. Given the widespread assertion that the economic revival of the eleventh century was due to the return of peaceful conditions to Europe, this is, in a left-handed way, an admission of the messianic pretensions of the movement: only in terms of a messianic program of "complete peace" does the movement fail. But the dismissal does not take such pretensions seriously. We know that the extravagant hopes aroused by apocalyptic expectations rarely dissipate with their failure, especially when they spawn large and (at least momentarily) successful movements. Disappointment triggers not discouragement, but renewed efforts to reignite the apocalyptic flames that had made the movement possible. The annals of modern apocalyptic movements is filled with the efforts to overcome the cognitive dissonance of a belief so powerful it had moved mountains (in this case, the warrior lords to the peace assemblies) but had not delivered its full (absolute!) promise. In fact, the Peace movement is a genuinely radical anomaly: the normal means for dealing with the complaints of the peasantry in this period was either slaughter (as in Francia in 859) or a more purposeful cutting off of hands and feet (as in Normandy in the late 990s). The very calling of assemblies represented a major concession to the populace. It gave them a voice.

If this represents the kinds of "concessions" that commoners could expect from an aristocracy frozen in terror at the thought of the Last Judgment, as Michelet would put it, their eagerness to see the approach of the year 1000 is perfectly understandable. Nor should [it] come as a surprise then, that in the case of the apocalyptic year 1000, they preferred to recalculate the end rather than shrug their shoulders and go back home. And we find precisely this recalculation: from the millennium of the Incarnation to that of the Passion (1033). As Glaber put it: after the passage of all the wonders and prodigies around 1000, there were no lack of sagacious men who predicted no less for the millennium of the Passion. And as that second millennium approached, we find the same revival of peace councils at which popular participation became increasingly prominent. It is to this millennial generation that we need to turn if we would understand the period and its significance. Here in this 33-year span we have a generation steeped in apocalyptic hopes—those disappointed mass movements of the previous generation, now openly discussing apocalyptic themes. This overheated atmosphere gives us many of the themes which will, over the next centuries, give us the profoundly creative and deeply conflicted culture we have labeled the High Middle Ages—communal movements, pilgrimages and church building, revolutionary church reform, colonial warfare, radical religious dissent, execution of heretics and pogroms against the Jews. Thus, in 1010, when Al Hakim destroyed the Holy Sepulcher in Jerusalem, partly as a reaction to the increased fervor and numbers of Christian pilgrims there, it was greeted in the West with apocalyptic dismay: chroniclers speak of him in tones reminiscent of the Antichrist; the pope called for crusade, the reforming monks blamed the Jews, and the frustrated and frightened populace gave them the choice of conversion or death. Perhaps the single most enduring effect of this millennial generation was the development of a process of apocalyptic reform, in which movements like the Peace, which were launched at times of intense apocalyptic expectations, become, upon "reentry" into normal time, institutionalized as "reform" movements. Thus, the entire eleventh century is known as a time of fervent reform, beginning the with monastic orders (especially Cluny), moving into the secular clergy with the reform of the canonical houses, finally becoming a full-fledged church reform in the second half of the century under the tutelage of the popes. Behind these clear and well documented movements lie a more charismatic impulse, that of the apostolic life, that of the effort to live the ethics of the Sermon on the Mount in a committed community.

One can detect all these elements clearly in the millennial generation—from the popular heresies which were apostolic movements too radical for the clergy, to the vast movement of church building and parish organization. Indeed, Radulfus Glaber's famous passage about Western Christendom "shaking off the dust of the ages and covering itself with a white mantle of churches" specifically in 1003 suggests that within the millennial generation, church reformers like his patron William of Volpiano viewed the remarkable renewal of Christian life a sign of a new age. Thietmar, bishop of the German town of Meerseburg in the north wrote about a new dawn spreading over Europe. Both these exceptional characterizations of an optimistic future-oriented Europe are written around 1020, and refer specifically to the year 1003/4, the period immediately after the Antichrist's reign. Reform is the post apocalyptic form of the spiritual renewal that the advent of the millennium brought. At the approach of 1033, the prognosticators proved correct. The Peace movement once again gained momentum, starting in the 1020s, this time in both north and south, and under the auspices of the king of France. Even the German emperor met with King Robert in 1023 to declare a universal peace. In 1028 a rain of

Perhaps the single most enduring effect of this millennial generation was the development of a process of apocalyptic reform, in which movements like the Peace . . . become . . . institutionalized as "reform" movements.

blood fell on the Aquitanian coast, prompting a worried exchange of letters between the duke, the king, and two of his most trusted ecclesiastical advisors about what it might portend. Soon thereafter, a devastating famine struck the entire land for three years and a exodus of pilgrims to Jerusalem began to swell. Glaber describes how in the year 1033, both of these gathering waves of popular religious activity—the pilgrimage to Jerusalem and the Pax Dei—reached their peak. Innumerable pilgrims made their way to Jerusalem and the Mount of Olives (traditional site of the parousia), prompting wonder among their neighbors and disapproval from the ecclesiastical hierarchy. Meanwhile those who stayed were not idle: the Peace swept France from the south to the farthest reaches of the north, gathering people in vast assemblies. Some bishops even claimed that they were instructed to proclaim a universal peace by a letter sent from Heaven.

Rather than a church filled with quaking and superstitious fools, we find the advent of the millennium energizing the entire culture.

Glaber's description of these councils will serve as a good basis to reflect on both the meaning of the millennial generation and on its subsequent impact on European culture right up to the present. At the height of the enthusiasm aroused by these peace assemblies, he describes how the entire people raised their palms skyward and shouted "Peace Peace Peace." They believed, he tells us, that they were making (Glaber uses *spondo* = to marry) a covenant (*pactum perpetuum*) with God. This is an extremely rare passage, one that tells us how commoners thought (they are so rare, most medievalists have given up on even guessing what they thought), how they perceived their actions, how they identified themselves; and it is no accident that it describes the peak moment of millennial expectations associated with the year 1000.

Rather than a church filled with quaking and superstitious fools, we find the advent of the millennium energizing the entire culture, leading them to a full-hearted acceptance of a Christian covenant with God. This marks the moment when the commoners became genuinely enthused about Christianity (it had previously been largely an imposition from above). It marks the point where Europeans first thought of themselves as God's New Chosen People. I would compare this moment with the previous case of a Chosen People, the covenant at Mount Sinai; the Peace, in its two millennial decades of the 990s and the 1020s/30s, constituted the defining moment in European cultural identity, the key moment when European Christians first developed a sense of mission and of religious unity. This "reading" poses several problems: first, I have imperceptibly shifted from France to Europe; second, the Peace plays a very small role in the history of Europe, far from the centrality of the Exodus in Jewish self-identity; and third, if, as Glaber himself admits, and the documentation of the following centuries repeatedly confirms, the aristocracy broke their promises and went back to their bellicose and oppressive ways, what can the significance of a moment, no matter how exalting it may have seemed, be in the long run? Let me answer these questions in reverse order. First: as Glaber says, it was the *potentes* who broke the oaths. The populace may well have been "returned to their plows," subjected to the "evil customs" of their lords, enserfed for centuries; but that does not mean they either liked it or accepted it. Just because our sources reflect the perspectives of the aristocracies (Glaber is quite daring here in blaming the elites), does not mean that the commoners ceased to think, to protest, to organize, to take action. When seen in this light, all of the most revolutionary activity of the eleventh and subsequent centuries—from the "Gregorian Reform" (really a papal revolution) and the Crusades to the urban and agricultural revolutions (the communes), to the heresies and pilgrimages—feature an unusually active popular participation. Indeed, I would argue that the dynamic of modernity, which we tend to identify with the period following the Renaissance, actually began in the eleventh century. We have missed it because we think of modernity purely in secular terms. But secular modernity is really the second phase; the first began and developed in a profoundly religious, biblical idiom. Religion as the opiate of the masses is only one side of the story. Second: the reason that the Peace plays so small a role in European history is the product of capstone historiography. Obviously, if the elites turned against the restrictions of the Peace movement (as Glaber tells us explicitly and our other sources confirm implicitly), then they were not interested in dwelling on what they had rejected. Just as the French revolutionary aristocracy, which had renounced their "feudal privileges" in an emotional oath on the night of August 4, 1789, proceeded to water down the concessions in subsequent (written) publications of the oath, and to pass the incident over in silence after the Restoration of the monarchy in 1815, so the clerical elite tended to invoke the Peace only on certain restricted occasions. Thus, after 1033 there are few councils until the end of the eleventh century, and no historian gives the movement the prominence that those of the millennial generation did.

I would argue that the dynamic of modernity, which we tend to identify with the period following the Renaissance, actually began in the eleventh century.

Capstone historians, accepting the documentation as a reasonable reflection of the age, have confirmed the spin that aristocratic sources have given the movement: even in cases where the elites invoke the Peace of God in sweeping terms (Pope Urban and the Crusade), there is little close analysis of what kind of popular appeal is involved in such an invocation. Rather than dismiss the analogy with the Israelites because of the contrast, I would pose the following question: why, and with what consequences for the shape of their respective cultures, did the Israelite religious elites remember their moment of covenant as central to their people's identity, whereas European Christians forgot it? Finally, what about France. Were you, in the year 999, to bet on France or Germany as the leader of Europe in the coming centuries, you would have been crazy to choose France. Germany was ruled by the most powerful and competent dynasty in Europe; it had solved the problem of invasions, exercised control over the papacy; had a court and culture to rival, indeed surpass that of the Carolingians. France was leaderless, in a state of anarchy, attacked from within and without; its most energetic people entering into a monastic movement that prized a continuous round of prayer as the height of piety. And yet, a century later, the situation is completely reversed despite the fact that the French king was, in 1100 as in 1000, excommunicated by the pope. By 1100 France is the undisputed cultural powerhouse of Europe and would remain so for at least another century. All the great religious movements—monastic and canonical reforms, popular "heresies," even the church reform—started in France and spread over Europe; so did the architectural and artistic styles known as Romanesque and Gothic; university culture was most varied and influential in France; and, of course the Crusades (which are only the most dramatic part of a larger phenomenon of invasion and colonization which continued well into the twentieth century) are so much a product of French culture that, to the Muslims, the term for European was Frank. Why is this? I would argue that all of these cultural and social developments are in some way the product of the peace movement, itself a chiliastic millennial movement: in a pattern that is typical of the paradoxes of apocalyptic movements, rather than in the regions in which the leadership kept control (Germany), it is precisely where they lost control and were forced to tap into popular elements that the most creative social developments emerge. These movements do not disappear, especially ones of the unprecedented scope and intensity of the Pax Dei. (I cannot think of a millennial movement to compare with it: over 40 years long, involving the entire society, spreading over a sizeable region.) However disappointing the results may have been (I am not sure they were as paltry as conventional historians would have us believe—these same historians then talk about the "peaceful conditions of the eleventh century" to explain the urban and commercial revolutions), they were not forgotten. And the trace of both the memory, and the effort to recreate the paradise lost, is to be found in the central role that various kinds of apocalyptic expectations played in subsequent European history.

In fact Michelet's invocations of the year 1000, replete with references to the serf standing in his ploughed furrow in the shadow of the odious tower, letting out a terrible laugh as Doomsday struck, can be understood as an effort to revive the revolutionary fervor of France in the midst of the reactionary consolidations of the nineteenth century. For Michelet, the Revolution came when the French people could no longer wait for a God who tarried interminably. Nor is it a coincidence that the violent reaction of the Positivist school to this reading comes immediately after the commune of 1871.

From the millennial generation onwards, one can trace a continuous, if periodic, presence of widespread apocalyptic expectations of an eschatological date: 1065, 1096–1100, 1147–50, 1166, 1179–86, 1200, 1212, 1233, 1260, 1290, 1300–1304, 1333, 1356–60, and so on. Indeed, preliminary investigation suggests that each century's end is marked by an apocalyptic generation which stretches from the final '90s to the '30s (this is especially true of 1200–1233, 1300–1333, 1500–1533). Once we have paid attention to these moments, all of which elicit vast outpourings of social and religious activity among the commonfolk, we will begin to restore to our own history this vital dimension. In the process, I think that we will find that much of what we call modern is actually a phenomenon which started out apocalyptic and, in mutating to adjust to the failure of expectations, took on its more stable and recognizable forms. As opposed to the capstone historiography which affirms—even finishes—the work of our distorting sources, I propose a genealogical approach, one which restores the mistaken but powerfully consequential apocalyptic origins of much that makes us what we are today. What does this mean for this coming millennium? Here I, as one who spends more time with eleventh-century colleagues than contemporary ones, cede to those who can discuss it more specifically. But before doing so, let me touch on three points:

First, I think that for the last millennium, European (and, in the last half a millennium, Western) culture has had a powerful, if textually "marginal," strain of millennial thought, which has been repeatedly triggered by apocalyptic expectations. Among these, dates have played a significant role in creating widespread and long-lasting apocalyptic moments. Thus, I think it is a safe bet to predict that while God (probably) will not bring History to an End and redeem/punish mankind in the year 2000, there will be no lack of people to predict and to believe that S/He will. And if one can predict prodigious and exceptional developments for the years surrounding 2000, one can expect no less for the bimillennium of the Passion. Indeed there is a curious irony at work which revitalizes apocalyptic thought just when, as a cultural elite, we imagine it has faded. As opposed to those who feel that the coming year 2000 will just be a party hyped by the media, I think we are in for another millennial generation.

As opposed to those who feel that the coming year 2000 will just be a party hyped by the media, I think we are in for another millennial generation.

Second, the difficulty that modern intellectuals have in dealing with apocalyptic beliefs (and here I speak specifically of historians, but suspect it applies to many others as well), is a function of the literary culture that we have inherited. Despite all the efforts of modernity to liberate itself from the confines of religious discourse, it has been least successful where apocalyptic discourse is concerned on two counts: First, apocalyptic rhetoric is one form of religious communication which has not been slowed by the advent of an atheist/agnostic intellectual culture; quite the contrary, one might argue it has increased. Second, we have yet to really appreciate its power. Partly because we, as an elite culture dedicated to dismissing superstition, have an inbred sympathy for the Augustinian position, partly because we are repeatedly reminded of the mischief that apocalyptic prophecies can bring on (the secular forms of the twentieth century—Marxism and Nazism have proved staggeringly destructive), we tend to fear and, whenever possible, ridicule the belief. In this, we are the direct inheritors of those elite and highly educated ecclesiastical figures like Augustine and Jerome, who heaped contempt on the superstitious folly of the masses. Thus, most academics and intellectuals are unaware that Hal Lindsay has become the best-selling living author for writing books that do precisely what Augustine forbade, reading contemporary events as the fulfillment of the prophecies in Revelation.

The problem may even go deeper than that. We are part of an intellectual culture peculiarly given to both retrospective disguise and prospective unmasking. Christianity is only the first, paradigmatic, example of such apocalyptic revision and revelation; and modernity and "post-modernity" are only the most recent examples of its protean ability to take secular as well as religious shapes. The fact that in our own days, volume upon volume denying the apocalyptic origins of Christianity can be written by the most sophisticated practitioners of all the latest intellectual techniques of deconstruction and sociological analysis, illustrates the point with special poignancy: our apocalyptic past and future remain dangerously threatening territory. As exegetes like Derrida have argued, much of our discourse denies through an eloquence that masks a silence; our most agile narratives and analyses impart a systematic spin, a brilliant cloth with which to cover our nakedness.

However these insights of deconstruction may or may not apply to other dimensions of our culture, one could not hope for a more penetrating approach to the textual silences about apocalyptic matters that lies at the heart of so spectacular and consequential an event as the coronation of Charlemagne in 6000 Anno Mundi, or the (rather less complete) textual silence concerning the advent and passage of the first Christian millennium. The real question, the real challenge to our current historical culture, is to stop assisting in this challenge, to stop interpreting it as an index of indifference and assuming that it corresponds, grosso modo, to the contents of oral discourse. Once we begin to retrieve the apocalyptic genealogy of our own past, we begin to understand how so many fundamental yet surprising elements of our own culture owe their past to an apocalyptic project that managed, despite the failure of its initial hopes, to become a functional element within "normal" time. Jesus, no matter how brilliant, charismatic, and great-hearted, was also wrong; so was Charlemagne, so was Francis of Assisi, so was Bacon and Newton, so was Marx, and so was Hitler. The error has been no impediment to their ability to shape our culture, only to our understanding of what motivated them and their followers. And once we understand this, we can begin to look at the approaching year 2000. As looney and discredited as "Apocalypse 2000" may seem to us at this point (many who believe in an eschatological year 2000 would not [now] openly avow such beliefs precisely for fear of ridicule by a public consensus which will not take such a discourse seriously), that does not make it less significant. The belief that the end is at hand is one of the most powerful and radical motivators in the human psyche, combining the most urgent passions with the most deep-seated megalomanic tendencies. It is the adrenalin rush of religious beliefs. People in the grip of such beliefs are capable of extraordinary deeds, and immune to the kind of skeptical logic with which we insulate ourselves from the appeal of apocalyptic time.

We ignore such sentiments at our own risk, and even, I might add, at the risk of our own impoverishment. For apocalyptic beliefs need not be purely violent, sectarian, dualistic, and self- destructive. Some of the most extraordinarily generous and noble expressions of the human heart are the product of an irenic belief that the kingdom of God will usher in an era of genuine mutual affection and joy, that the instruments of war will be beat into those of peaceful labor; that the predators will cease to prey on those who cannot fight back; that nation will not lift up sword against nation.... Indeed, the very foundation of Christianity, the preachings of one Jesus of Nazareth, seem to be just that: Peace on earth; goodwill towards men. As the Peace of God movement illustrates, millennial moments have the ability to mobilize large numbers of people, and to give their emotions a collective force. And over the long run (the eleventh century in this case) it can produce both the most exceptional cases of civil society (the communes) and the most violent cases of savagery (the knightly crusade).

At a time when one culture critic after another speaks of Western and global culture as having reached profound and urgent social, technological, natural, and political crises, we

The belief that the end is at hand is one of the most powerful and radical motivators in the human psyche, combining the most urgent passions with the most deep-seated megalomanic tendencies.

need not only the genius to find solutions, but also the social will to implement such solutions. Those who try to mobilize large numbers to accept new paradigms of social interaction (like the environmentalists) will inevitably, like the pope, use apocalyptic rhetoric, even when they might deny its origins. Not to do so, would be to neglect a major force of social transformation, and those owls who chastely restrain themselves will likely be drowned out by those roosters who do not hesitate to act. It can be argued that hope is one of the most sublime human emotions, one that sets us squarely in the time of past and future, that sublimates our passions by reorienting us from present gratification to future enjoyment. It has been shown that optimists are wrong more often than pessimists, but accomplish more. We are, I would argue, a particularly accomplished and vigorous culture precisely because of our roosters. We should not disown them. On the contrary, on the eve of the third Christian millennium, we should acknowledge such impulses as a fundamental part of our world, and seek ways to help those "ridden" by these passions to reenter "normal time" with irenic contributions to civil society, rather than with the savage violence of suicidal destruction.

Of Kings and Commoners[3]

In the year 999, somewhere off the western coast of France, an Arab dhow heads for the distant city of Paris, where two passengers, a North African Jewish merchant and his Muslim trading partner, have important business. "Even though there was no reason why the Christian millennium should trouble Jews or Muslims sailing alone upon the universal ocean," says the narrator of Abraham B. Yehoshua's recent novel, *A Journey to the End of the Millennium*, "the Moroccan ship, advancing at the pace of a fast horse, seemed to have absorbed something of the new religious fervor radiating from the nearby Christian coast."

It's an intriguing idea, but how credible is this notion of a spreading apocalyptic contagion, circa 999? Probably not very. To Muslims, the coming year was 391, and though there were divisions within the extended Islamic community, it was still a flourishing civilization. To the Chinese of the Song dynasty—more than a fourth of the world's 280 million population—the year called gengzi promised further stability and prosperity. In fact, to find a people who could lay certain claim to living in apocalyptic times, you would have to travel to the land of the Maya: During the 10th century, they had seen their civilization, the most advanced in the Americas, undergo a dramatic decline. Yet no evidence suggests that the Mayan calendar assigned special significance to the year 10.8.12.5.0.

Even within the Christian core of Western Europe, it is hard to say what most people made of the year "M," as it was then written. Did it mark the Second Coming of Christ or the beginning of Satan's reign? Not even the apocalyptic moment was clearly established, since it could be 1,000 years after the birth of Christ or 1,000 years after his crucifixion. Either way, there were terrible portents, such as a famine in Burgundy that gave rise to cannibalism, or the Muslims' destruction of the Holy Sepulcher in Jerusalem in 1009. But there was also the Peace of God movement, an effort by clergy, the higher nobility, and commoners to limit the devastation of warring feudal lords. In short, throughout what was just beginning to be called Europe, there was, as Princeton historian Natalie Zemon Davis observed in her White House Millennium Lecture last January, "no clear-cut apocalyptic movement led by a single prophet and focused on the single year 1000, but rather a millennial spirit spread over several decades." Richard Landes, a co-founder of the Center for Millennial Studies at Boston University, even argues that the very inconclusiveness of the millennial

---

3. Article by Jay Tolson with additional research by Nancy L. Bentrup from *U.S. News & World Report* p.34-40+ Aug 16-23 1999. Copyright © 1999 *U.S. News & World Report*.

moment, the general murk of disappointment and relief, had a paradoxically decisive effect on Europe's subsequent development. The year 1000, he says, "was the moment when a people defined itself and laid down a path for a millennium to come."

More surprising is the fact that the early medieval world, with its crazy quilt of contending empires, theocracies, principalities, baronies, and bishoprics, bears a startling—if reverse-image—resemblance to our own, in which the dominant political form, the nation-state, is losing some of its sway. Today's challengers to the sovereignty of nations include transnational institutions like the World Bank and the International Monetary Fund, a border-defying global economy, and scores of competing allegiances that range from the supranational (the European Union) to the subnational (Catalonia or Quebec). As the late Oxford scholar Hedley Bull first observed more than 20 years ago, our emerging political order might turn out to be the "secular equivalent of the kind of universal political organization that existed in Western Christendom in the Middle Ages."

Christendom Out of Chaos

The political-military order governing most of A.D. 1000 Europe was the system later dubbed feudalism. Based on oaths of allegiance, it arose after the breakup of Charlemagne's Holy Roman Empire in the early ninth century, as kings or great lords granted fiefdoms to lesser lords in return for their loyalty and services. The goal of feudalism was security, from both lawless lords and marauding barbarians, but it often meant the opposite, particularly when the upper nobles were weak and the lesser barons were free to roam about like junior Mafiosi, pillaging and plundering at will. A German prelate in 1016 sized up the situation bleakly: "The king of Burgundy has now nothing save his title and crown. . . . He is not capable of defending either his bishops or the rest of his subjects against the dangers that threaten them. Therefore we see all betaking themselves with joined hands to serve the great. In this way they secure peace."

Yet out of this semichaos, a more stable political order was taking shape. Although no kings or prelates would succeed in re-creating Charlemagne's empire, they would set Europe on the road to nation-states within the framework of an increasingly coherent civilization. That civilization—Christendom—consisted not only of a religion but of literacy and learning, art and architecture, rule of law, and the powerful idea and commercial practices of urbanity. To be sure, there were stark contrasts between the ideals of this civilization and the realities of everyday life in the year 1000: Most people were peasants, illiterate, ill fed, and leading wretched lives in actual or virtual slavery. Their fate was largely dependent upon their lords, to whom they owed around 100 days of labor a year as well as a portion of what they grew

The early medieval world, with its crazy quilt of contending empires, theocracies, principalities, baronies, and bishoprics, bears a startling—if reverse-image—resemblance to our own.

on their allotted few acres. And everything they worked for could easily be destroyed or taken by one of those lawless barons who took a shine to his neighbor's fiefdom.

For a truly civil society to emerge, Europe needed peace and order within as well as security on its periphery. And as James Reston Jr. shows in his book *The Last Apocalypse*, Europe began to find both around the year 1000. To the east, for example, a constant threat throughout the 10th century had been the Magyars, 10 tribes of nomadic warriors who had arrived from the vast, grassy steppes of Central Asia and settled in the Carpathian basin in 896. Launching sporadic, havoc-wreaking raids upon Central and Western Europe, these fierce horsemen seemed to relish terror for terror's sake, destroying churches and castles and, as Reston writes, even drinking the blood of their victims. "No man ever more ardently desired a drink of cold water than these cruel savages longed for the day of battle," a 10th-century German observed. By the end of the century, however, the marauding hordes were transformed into a bulwark of stability when their leader converted to Christianity and brought seven of the 10 tribes into the new kingdom of Hungary.

The Scandinavian Norsemen posed an even more constant menace to the core of Western Europe. Swooping down upon the Anglo-Saxons, the French, and the Germans in their famed wave-treading longboats, they plundered, pillaged, enslaved, and conquered. Yet during the 10th century, the Vikings, like the Magyars, succumbed to civilization envy. These most adventurous of sea explorers not only brought order and relative unity to their own realms in Denmark, Norway, and Sweden as each successively converted to Christianity, but they also established more permanent roots in other lands, including Normandy and Russia.

Perhaps the most dramatic instance of this civilizing transformation was the Viking conquest of England. As the year 1000 approached, Anglo-Saxon England was still absorbing Norse invaders of the previous century. But the victory of 3,000 Norsemen at the Battle of Maldon in 991 launched a new ratcheting up of Danish interference in the affairs of the island kingdom. In 1013, the Danish leader Sweyn of Forkbeard saw weakness in King Ethelred (the "Unready") and seized England outright. Sweyn and his successors would rule the kingdom until 1066, when it was conquered by William and his Normans—themselves descendants of Norsemen.

A pattern emerges. A succession of peripheral peoples threaten the core of Western Europe but eventually are drawn into its emerging order by the attractions of religion, literacy, lawfulness, a stable agricultural economy, and the first flickering of an urban life. In turn, these new Europeans play a role in stabilizing the political system, forging some of the early protonations—including Hungary, Russia, and England—and indirectly spurring the rise of others.

An Islamic Golden Age

But Christendom hardly represented the only, or even the most compelling, version of civilization in the year 1000. The Islamic community, or *umma*, although less unified than earlier in the millennium, still had impressive geographic reach. From its Arabian and Middle Eastern core, it extended west across North Africa into Spain and east into Central Asia and the Indus River basin. A powerful military, cultural, and commercial civilization, it not only remade those regions of the world that it conquered but challenged other civilizations wherever it came into contact with them.

Just three years before the millennium, Moorish Spain scored one of its many decisive victories over the Christian powers of northern Iberia: The Muslim general Almanzor razed the town of Santiago de Compostela and the holiest of all Christian shrines on the peninsula. Almanzor's martial superiority had its equivalent in the condescension of a Moorish vizier and historian, who penned this assessment of Christendom a few years after the millennium: "So great is the multitude of Christians that God alone can number them, and they can boast of sagacious princes and illustrious philosophers. Nevertheless they believe that one is three and three are one."

Muslims were at the top of this society, but as in other Islamic towns and cities, non-Muslims were tolerated as long as they paid a special tax.

Cordova, the caliph's capital (caliph means successor, or lieutenant, of the prophet Mohammed), was itself a powerful symbol of Islamic civility and order. With some 450,000 residents, it was Europe's largest city and possibly the largest in the world. More important, it ranked with Constantinople, Baghdad, and Kaifeng as a major center of commerce, art, architecture, and learning. "When a rich man dies in Seville," a saying went, "his library is sold to Cordova," which may explain why the city's library was reputed to be the largest in the world. Located on the Guadalquivir River in south-central Spain, Cordova boasted graceful bridges, paved and lamp-lit streets, a sewerage system, and aqueducts that provided its residents a steady supply of pure water. Its vast array of mosques, public baths and gardens, palaces, grand villas, and modest but well-built homes made the city a model of cultural refinement. Muslims were at the top of this society, but as in other Islamic towns and cities, non-Muslims were tolerated as long as they paid a special tax. Christians, Jews, and others were welcome to partake in the largest, most sophisticated commercial order the world had yet seen.

But important changes were taking place around the year 1000, moving the umma's center of geographic and cultural gravity from the Mediterranean world to the East. The shift had actually begun in the eighth century with the demise of the second, Damascus-based caliphate and the rise of a new one in Baghdad. The Baghdad regime expanded into Persia and beyond into Central Asia, spawning rival Muslim dynasties as it grew. By the year 1001, a new dynasty of Central Asian Muslims, the Ghaznavids, had extended its reach into the northwestern region of India.

Islamic conquests in South Asia, combined with earlier Muslim trade activity throughout the Indian Ocean basin, reinvigorated and deepened Islamic civilization, even as they gave rise to a new regional order. As Dutch historian Andre Wink writes in *Al-Hind: The Making of the Indo-Islamic World* (1990), by the year 1000, Muslims had effectively built a "world economy in and around the Indian Ocean—with India at its center and the Middle East and China as its two dynamic poles." The making of this "Arabic-speaking Mediterranean," as Wink calls it, had two immediate effects on the peoples of the South Asian subcontinent. First, it spurred the growth of their economies by creating trade outlets along the coast. And second, by the contrasting example of their hard-edged monotheism, Muslims compelled Indians to develop and assert their own distinctive Hindu civilization. When King Rajaraja of the powerful Chola empire built a huge stone temple dedicated to the god Shiva, he did so not only out of piety. "The size of the building reflected his political ambition," says Wink. The Chola empire, John Man explains in his forthcoming *Atlas of the Year 1000*, became "the linchpin of Asia's maritime economies, sitting astride Arab routes to southeast Asia, and reaching out to China."

A growing player in the Indian Ocean trade, China itself had taken off around the year 1000, again partly as a result of the Islamic challenge. Centuries earlier, in 751, Chinese forces of the Tang dynasty, attempting to extend the influence of the Middle Kingdom into Central Asia, were trounced by a Muslim army not far from Samarkand. Humiliation led to instability back in China, as powerful generals entered politics and fomented rebellion. During the first half of the 10th century, warlords continued to vie for mastery, but in 960 the commander of the palace guard, Zhao Kuangyin, prevailed. Founding the Song dynasty, he pensioned off the troublesome generals and replaced military provincial governors with civil functionaries.

The hallmark of Song rule, particularly that of the first, northern Song dynasty (960–1126), was its emphasis on orderly and virtuous governance, achieved largely through an efficient bureaucracy staffed by mandarins who passed rigorous state examinations. The 20,000 mandarin officials bore a heavy responsibility for governing this empire of some 80 million people. But they were also expected to embody the very traditional cultural values that were the essence of Chineseness. Never was this more the case than under the Song, when a revival of Confucian teaching gave a particularly strong moral flavor to the dynasty.

Milestones of 1000

Kings, Invasions, and Scholarship at the Turn of the Millennium

955 Otto the Great defeats the Magyars at the Battle of Lechfeld, ending 50 years of raids.

960 Zhao Kuangyin becomes first emperor of China's Song dynasty, which lasts until 1279.

970 Al-Azhar, the world's oldest university, is founded by the Ismaili Fatimids in Cairo.

985 With the help of Vikings, Vladimir establishes the first Russian dynasty in Kiev.

985 Maharaja Rajaraja (the Great) becomes ruler of the Chola kingdom in Southern India.

987 Hugh Capet establishes a royal dynasty in France, which rules until the Revolution.

987 The Toltecs move into the Yucatan Peninsula, formerly Mayan land, and found their empire.

Milestones of 1000

994 Viking chieftain Olaf Trygvesson is baptized at Andover, England, after surviving a mutiny

996 Otto III, a 16-year-old, is crowned as Holy Roman Emperor by his cousin, Pope Gregory V.

996 Al-Hakim, the infamous "Mad Caliph" of the Fatimids, begins his long, cruel reign.

999 Gerbert of Aurillac becomes Pope Sylvester II, the first Frenchman to hold that title.

1000 The Icelanders are converted to Christianity under orders from Olaf Tyrgvesson.

1000 Magyar leader Vajk is consecrated King Stephen I of the Christianized Hungary.

1002 Otto III dies, and with him the dream of a renewed Holy Roman Empire.

Not to be involved in the moral order of the Middle Kingdom was to be a barbarian. Hence the earlier consternation caused by defeat at the hands of the Muslim barbarians. But in addition to causing political discord, the setback led to a burst of unprecedented economic activity, including the rapid development of coal, steel, and armaments industries and an equally speedy evolution toward market-regulated commerce. For almost four centuries after 1000, China so decisively led the world in technology, industry, and commerce that one of the great historical mysteries is how it lost its lead.

But consider just a few of the accomplishments achieved by the Song: a level of iron production in 1078 that would be double that of England seven centuries later; the manufacture of the first printed books; the development of explosives, including gunpowder; the construction of six-mast, four-deck sailing junks capable of carrying up to a thousand men and employing pivoting sails, watertight compartments, and mariner's compasses. Consider, too, the rapid urbanization of Song China, symbolized most dramatically by the dynasty's new capital, Kaifeng—by 1020, its population approached 50,000—and the proliferation of business and stores, which remained open through the night. "People no longer found their way about the town by the names of districts," observes the French Sinologist Jacques Gernet, "but by the names of streets." Advances in industry, transportation, and city living all gave the domestic economy such a forceful shove that it expanded beyond the power of officialdom to regulate it, and soon adventurous merchants were moving into the even less manageable arena of international commerce. But a harbinger of China's later stagnation can be glimpsed, even at the height of the Song renaissance, in officialdom's reluctance to lose too much control. Fearing ungovernable merchants and industrialists as much as they feared unruly generals, the administrative class waged a steady regulatory war against the freewheeling ways of ambitious entrepreneurs—proof that the tension between central political control and the market economy long predates the China of Mao Zedong and his successors.

Another aspect of China's fate was bound up with the contempt of its long-nailed mandarins for hands-on experimentalism and tinkering, which are so essential to sustained progress in science and technology and perhaps even to a true "scientific revolution." China produced too few intellectuals of combined practical and theoretical brilliance, too few Leonardos or Francis Bacons who would bring visionary genius to bear on the fine workings of the material world—one reason, among many, that Europe would catch up with and surpass China's formidable lead.

Europe: A Bad Gamble

In the year 1000, of course, Europe would have looked like a very dubious long shot in any wager on the future of civilizations. Any gambler bold enough to bet on Christendom almost certainly would have placed his chips on the eastern Mediterranean empire of Byzantium. Then in an upswing, it had retaken lands earlier lost to Muslim armies and acquired new territory in the Balkans. The center of Byzantine greatness, Constantinople, dazzled visitors with its monumental imperial and religious architecture as well as its buzzing, cosmopolitan bazaars.

Western Europeans on the Crusades of the 11th, 12th, and 13th centuries came to consider Constantinople, its court awash in purple silk and hammered gold, a center of decadence, intrigue, and vice; they would even contribute to the dismantling of Byzantium, which the Ottoman Turks in 1453 would complete. But in 1000, Western Europeans could point to nothing in their realms that could equal the grandeur of the Eastern Roman Empire.

Indirectly, though, Byzantium would have a hand in Western Europe's rise. At the millennium, the Germanic portion was ruled by the naively idealistic Otto III, whose mother, Theophano, a Byzantine noblewoman, filled his mind with Greek culture and delusions of imperial grandeur. Hoping to restore the unity of the Holy Roman Empire, Otto squandered much of his short rule on intrigues in and around Rome and allowed his realms in Germany to grow rebellious. But for all his grandiosity, Otto deserves lasting credit for raising to the papal throne his former teacher and perhaps the greatest man of his time, the French cleric Gerbert of Aurillac, crowned Pope Sylvester II in 999.

Of the many explanations for Europe's ascent, one of the more interesting was first advanced by the French historian Henri Focillon in his book *The Year 1000*. Focillon attributed great significance to a shift in relative power and influence from the Gothic eastern Franks to the Romanesque western Franks—and with it the flowering of a social order grounded in contract, law, and the restraint of power through civil society.

A milestone in this transformation was the death of the last Carolingian ruler of France, Louis V, in 987. Partly as a result of many years' plotting by Gerbert against both Louis V and his father, a non-Carolingian nobleman, Hugh Capet, was elected king by the assembly of notables at Senlis. Hugh became the first monarch of the Capetian dynasty, which, with its two branches, the Valois and the Bourbons, would rule an increasingly unified France until the French Revolution.

A stable French dynasty only partly accounts for Europe's new social-political equilibrium. Just as important, Focillon believed, were the combined efforts of kings and clergy "to

Milestones of 1000

1002 Brian Boru becomes high king of Ireland, and Irish culture thrives again.

1003 Sylvester II dies, after spending his reign crusading against nepotism and simony.

1013 Denmark's King Sveyn becomes England's ruler by defeating Ethelred the Unready.

1054 The Patriarch of Constantinople is excommunicated, formalizing the Church's schism.

1066 William the Conqueror and his Normans defeat King Harold at the Battle of Hastings.

neutralize or restrain feudal warfare." More recently, Richard Landes has argued that peasants, too, had a hand in making the new order. In the peace councils of the Peace of God movement, where throngs gathered in fields outside great towns or castles on dozens of occasions preceding both 1000 and 1033, great lords, clergy, and peasants came together to form a compact against the excessive, unruly violence of the brigand armies of lesser lords. "In these large but still face-to-face gatherings," says Landes, "with the church taking the lead, men of war took oaths before the populace to respect the rights of churches and of unarmed peasants. It was a social contract by public oath and acclamation: The workers would feed society, the prayers would assure its salvation, and the fighters would provide for safety."

The peace councils extended the contractual practices of feudalism beyond the aristocracy and clergy to the peasantry. They established an early civil society, in which the rights and obligations of individuals and corporate bodies were clearly delineated. And they forged an alliance between great lords, or kings, and a new class of people, the commoners. This alliance would in turn be essential to the rise of absolute monarchies, the precursors of modern nation-states.

It is significant that the word enfranchise originally meant "to be made a Frank." For it was among the western Franks that peasants first acquired a kind of legal-political standing. From this starting point, commoners would slowly become the agents of their own destinies, owning their own land or moving into towns, working in crafts and trades and starting their own businesses, and eventually taking their full place as citizens. The enfranchisement of the common people would be as important as—and directly related to—the commercial, scientific, and political revolutions that would make Europe, and its offspring in the Americas, the most dynamic civilization in the world.

How citizenship will fare in an age of weakening nation-states—so far the strongest protectors of the rights and liberties of citizens—is one of the great questions of our time. It is certainly one for which future historians will seek answers when they look back at the second millennium as we now do at the first.

How citizenship will fare in an age of weakening nation-states—so far the strongest protectors of the rights and liberties of citizens— is one of the great questions of our time.

End-Times Visions[4]

During the final fretful moments of the year 999, according to one ancient chronicle, a throng of worshipers huddled in the flickering candlelight of St. Peter's Basilica in Rome, weeping and trembling as they awaited the turn of the millennium. Many were certain it would unleash the holy terror of Christ's Second Coming and the end of the world.

So convinced were some Christians that the apocalypse was upon them that they gave away all their possessions and fled to the magnificent Vatican sanctuary clothed in sackcloth and ashes. As Pope Sylvester II calmly intoned the familiar Latin phrases of the midnight mass on that dreaded millennium eve, fearful believers prostrated themselves on the polished marble floor, their eyes closed in anticipation of the trumpet blast that in a moment would herald the arrival of Judgment Day.

Nourished by signs. It mattered little to the anxious worshipers in Rome that the pope and other church leaders apparently did not share in such urgent apocalyptic expectations. There were plenty of other priests and abbots who had expounded for years on how the turbulent events of the late 10th century fit perfectly with the Bible's vivid descriptions of the Earth's final days.

As the pontiff concluded the sacred liturgy, "the crowd remained rooted, motionless, transfixed, barely daring to breathe, 'not a few dying from fright, giving up their ghosts then and there.'"

Re-creating this vivid scene in his 1988 book *A.D. 1000: A World on the Brink of Apocalypse*, Richard Erdoes concedes that the account is based largely on historical hearsay and that "things might not have happened just that way." Nonetheless, Erdoes argues, it accurately portrays the "all-pervading dread of the apocalypse that held humankind in its grip" at the turn of the last millennium. Among the peasant masses of Europe, wrote the eminent French historian Henri Focillon, "belief in the end of the world was reawakened by the approach of the fateful date, and nourished by signs and wonders; . . . the time which the apostles prophesied had come."

Just how widespread were the "terrors of the year 1000" remains a matter of debate among modern historians. On one extreme are the startling images, drawn mainly by 19th-century French historians, of a European continent engulfed by apocalyptic panic. On the other extreme is the contention of many modern scholars that there is no credible

---

4. Article by Jeffery L. Sheler from *U.S. News & World Report* 127, no. 7 p.40-41 Aug. 16-23 1999. Copyright © 1999 *U.S. News & World Report*. Reprinted with permission.

evidence of end-times anxiety attached to the turn of the millennium, and that most peasants had little awareness of calendrical time other than the agricultural seasons and the cycle of Christian feast days. Some, like Bernard McGinn of the University of Chicago, insist that while there was "a broad stream of apocalyptic expectation" throughout medieval Europe, "it is a mistake to single out the year 1000 as a special case."

In the middle are historians like Richard Landes, director of the Center for Millennial Studies at Boston University, who find indications of heightened apocalypticism surrounding the year 1000—a period, says Landes, [that is "one of the high-water marks of such beliefs in European—or any—civilization."

Attempts to pinpoint the time of the Second Coming date to Christianity's earliest days. In the Gospel of John, Jesus says, "I will come again and receive you unto myself." And in the Gospel of Matthew, Jesus lists an assortment of signs that he says would point to the end—"wars and rumors of wars . . . famines, and pestilences, and earthquakes in diverse places."

Most biblical scholars think the first disciples were convinced Jesus would return in their lifetime. When he did not, the church developed a more detailed theology on the matter based on sometimes controversial interpretations of the New Testament book of Revelation and on the Hebrew prophets Ezekiel and Daniel. And despite Jesus's warning that no one would know "the day nor the hour" of his coming, the church continued to watch for signs and to speculate on the timing of the end.

Don't panic. But by the fifth century, the influential theologian Augustine of Hippo argued forcefully against literal readings of biblical prophecy and detailed speculation about the timing of Christ's return. Augustine warned against making apocalyptic predictions so that "when we fall into a panic over present happenings as if they were the ultimate and extreme of all things, we may not be laughed at by those who have read of more and worse things in the history of the world." The church officially endorsed Augustine's view at its Council of Ephesus in 431. Yet it did not cool the apocalyptic fervor of many clerics and laymen, which grew more intense as the year 1000 drew nearer.

While not all end-of-the-world expectations were focused precisely on the year 1000, some scholars say the 50-year period on either side of the turn of the millennium was rife with apocalyptic belief.

While not all end-of-the-world expectations were focused precisely on the year 1000, some scholars say the 50-year period on either side of the turn of the millennium was rife with apocalyptic belief. The French medieval monk Radulfus Glaber, a chronicler of the 10th and early 11th centuries, reported an outbreak of heresies in France and Italy around the year 1000 that he interpreted as the unleashing of Satan as prophesied in Revelation. Glaber and others report portentous "signs and wonders"—earthquakes, comets, famines, and volcanic eruptions—that were widely interpreted at the time as heralds of the end.

Focillon, in his historical study *The Year 1000*, notes a marked decline in artistic and cultural activities in monasteries toward the end of the 10th century, a period he describes as "an evening of the world."

When the year passed and the world was not destroyed, writes Focillon, mankind breathed a sigh of relief and "gratefully set out on a new road." The disappointed apocalyptic hopes of the year 1000, adds Landes, "were the mother of a dynamic culture which, in both high medieval and modern incarnations, we call the West."

For Further Reading:

The Last Apocalypse: Europe at the Year 1000 A.D. by James Reston Jr.

The Year 1000: What Life Was Like at the Turn of the First Millennium by Robert Lacy and Danny Danziger

The Year 1000 by Henri Focillon

Atlas of the Year 1000 by John Man

A.D. 1000: A World on the Brink of Apocalypse by Richard Erdoes

II. The Year 2000 and the Third Millennium

Editor's Introduction

The question for 1,000 years ago may have been to pray or not to pray, but today it's to party or not to party, and if we're partying, are we doing it on December 31, 1999, or on December 31, 2000? As the articles in this section demonstrate, the world is readying itself for the biggest celebration of all time, in 1999 and throughout 2000. To those who are inclined to avoid the hype altogether for fear of acting like a lemming, this editor suggests that you might regret having no answer for your kids or your friends' kids who will inevitably ask you, around 2012 or so, what it was like to witness the dawn of a new millennium. Do you really want to sleep through it?

Perhaps marking the occasion in a somnolent (as opposed to somnambulant) state is the best option after all, for the event cannot possibly live up to expectations and is bound, therefore, to be anticlimactic. Indeed, Henry A. Grunwald asks that very question, "Can the Millennium Deliver?" (*Time*), in the third selection.

If you attend one of the events described in Dan Johnson's roundup of the global celebrations ("Millennium: The Biggest Party Ever—And You're Invited," *Futurist*), you probably have the best shot at not being disappointed. Here are a few of your options: Attend an Eiffel Tower egg-laying ceremony, in which the "egg" cracks open to reveal hundreds of television sets broadcasting events from around the world. Travel the Via Francigena, a medieval network of pilgrim routes, in Tuscany. Ride a new subway extension from London to the Millennium Dome in Greenwich. Attend Berlin's millennial festival, "Images and Signs of the 21st Century." Join half of million people to watch the ball drop in New York City's Times Square or listen to 100 rock bands on 4,500 acres in southern California. Cruise on the *QE II* from New York City to Cairo to dance at the Cheops monument. Or just stay home and brace yourself for the effects of Y2K, addressed in the fourth selection.

In the second article, "Making Sense of Past Visions of 2000: What Were They Thinking?" (*Fortune*), Geoffrey Colvin assesses recent predictions for what life would be like in the year 2000. One view took shape in the 1960s and predicted a leisure revolution brought about by technology. Technological innovations would make us so productive that the economy would continue to grow at the postwar rate, meaning that by 2000 we could all work much less and enjoy 13 weeks' vacation a year while maintaining a high standard of living. The truth seems to be that most of us are working more for less. In many cases, a two-income middle-class household today has trouble affording the same quality of housing and education that were available to a single-income family a generation ago. The other prediction, embodied in the *Global 2000 Report* commissioned by President Jimmy Carter, seems to have been just as wide of the mark in forecasting "a colder, hungrier, poorer world of poisoned seas and food wars," as Colvin put it. Perhaps they were only wrong in their timing; decide for yourself after reading the articles in the third section.

In the aforementioned "Can the Millennium Deliver?" Henry A. Grunwald unearths even earlier and lesser-known predictions that focused on the year 2000, beginning with the early Christians and moving to Nostradamus, Nicolas-Edme Restif de la Bretonne's 1789 play *The Year 2000*, Jules Verne's fantasy *An Ideal City*, Edward Bellamy's socialist utopian novel *Looking Backward,* John Jacob Astor's capitalist rebuttal *A Journey to Other Worlds,* and Fritz Lang's film *Metropolis.* He then moves on to consider the "next significant—and much less entertaining—phase of futurology," that which belonged to the think tanks of the latter half of the 20th century. (It is a shame that he did not consider what the science-fiction of the same period has had to offer; indeed, the entire genre seems to remain suspended in the critical no-fly zone previously reserved for certain novels of the 18th and 19th centuries, for television in its early days, and for popular music until relatively recently. Then again, perhaps most of the good science-fiction of recent times has simply been set after 2000.

One science-fiction prediction may actually turn out to be a little too close for comfort. Ann Reilly Dowd introduces her article, "Will Y2K Spark a Worldwide SOS?" (*Kiplinger's Personal Finance*), with a reminder that *The Day the Earth Stood Still* (1951) featured a simultaneous shut-off of the world's power supplies. The Y2K bug, the name given to the computer glitch that would occur if a program reads the date "00" to mean 1900 instead of 2000, is potentially more and less threatening. More so because it arguably affects more areas of life than does a power outage (after all, you don't lose all your financial data when the power lines are downed in a storm), and less so because most computer systems will, one hopes, have been certified Y2K compliant well in advance of the fateful day when the date rolls over. In this article, the author provides a rundown of what we should and shouldn't worry about. She addresses your bank accounts, the stock market, home appliances, telephones, the power supply, the nation's hospitals, air traffic, elevators, and taxes. While there are plenty of worst-case scenarios to be worried about, the likeliest effect of Y2K is some inconvenience, such as flight delays or ATMs not working properly for a while. Certainly some common-sense precautions are in order. But should you stockpile food and buy a generator? Even this sober financial magazine doesn't laugh it off entirely (although it comes close), because the sad fact is that no one can predict the potential cumulative effect that lots of small networks and foreign networks that are not Y2K compliant could have on those systems that are. "We're all connected" takes on new meaning. Her parting advice? "Don't phone home at 12:01 a.m. on January 1, 2000," just to see if the phones are working. If we all do it, they won't be.

Millennium: The Biggest Party Ever—And You Are Invited![1]

The arrival of the year 2000 will be wildly celebrated around the world. Are you ready for the party of the millennium?

Where will you be on New Year's Eve 1999?

Though most scholars insist that the third millennium won't begin until January 1, 2001, the start of the year 2000 has more popular appeal and enormous symbolism. Millennium, shmillennium: The world is ready to party! If the neighborhood gathering you had planned seems too tame for New Year's Eve 1999, there will be plenty of alternatives. Many countries will welcome 2000 with extravagant celebrations, while others are hosting ambitious fairs and exhibits to focus people's thoughts on the twenty-first century.

Some argue that Antarctica or New Zealand is the place to be for a head start on the next 1,000 years, while others say that the prime meridian gives Greenwich, England, the inside track.

A few early celebrants will be ending their Pacific cruise from Yokohama to Hawaii, crossing the international date line at midnight, December 31, for the first glimpse of dawn in 2000.

Here's a sample of what's expected elsewhere:

France: Eiffel Tower Will Lay an Egg

In Paris, the new year will be ushered in at the Eiffel Tower countdown when a huge egg descends and then cracks apart, revealing hundreds of television screens broadcasting programs from countries around the world. On the Left Bank, a 660-foot "Tower of the Earth" is being built to celebrate environmental awareness. The structure will include restaurants, a media center, and an observation deck.

The renovated Pompidou Center will reopen to host a series of art shows in 2000, focusing on twentieth century art's "outsider voices." The Louvre will feature exhibitions on the invention of time and the future of museums, while the Bibliotheque Nationale unveils books and prints on the theme of utopia. Among the Grand Palais's offerings will be a "Visions of the Future" exhibit. Dozens of other cities in France will stage millennial arts festivals.

French plans also include the construction of four gigantic clocks. One 30-ton timepiece with chimes that can be heard for 20 miles could be operating in 1999, if a site is selected in

---

1. Article by Dan Johnson from the *Futurist* Oct. 1998 v32 n7 p. 41 + . Copyright © 1998 World Future Society. Reprinted with permission. Dan Johnson is a staff editor of the *Futurist* and author of *Come Looking* (Washington Writers' Publishing House, 1995).

the near future. In Paris, work is under way to transform the Place de la Concorde into the largest sun dial in the world, to construct a clock at the Arc de Triomphe, and to build an enormous hour glass that will hold 100 tons of sand.

Italy: Vatican Expects 30 Million for Holy Year 2000

Italy's most prominent millennium event, the Great Jubilee of 2000, is a uniquely sacred celebration: a Holy Year that begins on Christmas Eve 1999 and will last through 2000. Millions of pilgrims are expected to converge on Rome. The Vatican expects 30 million visitors in 2000, while other estimates range from 18 million to 40 million people.

Many devout Catholics will visit Rome's four major basilica—St. Peter's, St. John Lateran, St. Mary Major, and St. Paul Outside the Wallsq—in order to fulfill one of the conditions required to receive indulgence. Pope John Paul II's millennial schedule will include special audiences, canonizations, and beatifications. He will also open the door of St. Peter's Basilica, which has been sealed since 1975, the last Holy Year, and then close it in 2000.

Pilgrims, tourists, and backpacking students throughout Italy in 2000 are likely to encounter more of the restrictions that some cities now use to control overcrowding. Venice, for example, sometimes limits the number of vehicles entering the city from the mainland via causeway, and officials there may require millennium tour groups to make reservations. Florence already limits the number of tour buses in its historic center to 150 at a time.

In Tuscany, officials have accelerated restoration work on the Via Francigena—a network of pilgrim routes used from the eighth through the fourteenth century—to be ready for Holy Year. Assisi, still recovering from earthquakes in 1997, is rebuilding St. Francis Basilica and restoring its frescos.

Italy's most prominent millennium event, the Great Jubilee of 2000, is a uniquely sacred celebration: a Holy Year that begins on Christmas Eve 1999 and will last through 2000.

United Kingdom: A Building Boom

Britain's most ambitious project is the Millennium Dome, a gigantic complex of exhibits in Greenwich. An urban village will be constructed adjacent to the dome and a new subway extension will connect the site to London.

Britain is also building a 500-foot-tall Ferris wheel near the Houses of Parliament; a new cinema complex with 32 movie theaters, two hotels, and two stages; and a pedestrian bridge across the Thames River from St. Paul's Cathedral to the new Tate Gallery.

The dome is by far the most ambitious British undertaking. Stationed prominently on the prime meridian for Greenwich Mean Time, the Millennium Dome is scheduled to open at midnight, December 31, 1999, and host a "celebration of time" throughout 2000. It will be the largest cable-supported domed arena in the world, big enough to accommodate two large football stadiums within its thousand-foot circumference. Twelve 330-foot pylons will support the dome's 20-acre glass-fiber canopy, and on warm days its side walls can be retracted, allowing a view of the Thames River. Gardens and parks will surround the site, along with entertainment and other amenities accessible by the Jubilee subway line and by boat from the Thames.

"It will be the biggest celebration of the millennium in the world," says Barry Hartop, chief executive of the exhibition.

Inside the dome, a central performance area will seat 12,500 people and offer a multimedia "journey through time" show that combines live performances with visual effects. Thirteen exhibit zones surround the performance space and explore the themes of society, environment, and culture. Each multilevel exhibit focuses on a different aspect of time and presents a mix of education and entertainment through performances, hands-on activities, and multimedia technology.

Project developers predict that 12 million people will visit the dome in 2000, according to Jennie Page, chief executive of the New Millennium Experience Company, which is owned by the British government. Organizers also expect the dome to host conventions and other large events during the first decades of the twenty-first century and are negotiating contracts with sports and art groups for its future use.

Meanwhile, the Millennium Ferris Wheel should be spinning early in 1999 on the banks of the Thames River at Jubilee Gardens, across from the Houses of Parliament. The 500-foot-tall structure will carry up to 960 passengers (16 people in each of 60 closed capsules) on a quiet 20-minute revolution, offering new views of London and its surroundings up to 30 miles beyond the capital. Mini-turbines will turn the wheel using tidal power from the Thames; solar cells will power cabin lights, ventilation, and communications. After five years of operation in London, the wheel will be dismantled and moved to a new permanent home.

Germany: Hanover Expo Spotlights Innovations

Germany is hosting a bimillennial world's fair called "Expo 2000" in Hanover from June 1 to October 31, 2000, and bracing for 40 million visitors. Expo 2000 will have more to do with pondering issues of the next millennium than partying into the night.

China, the United States, and 163 other countries are scheduled to participate, along with many international organizations. Attendees' exhibits will focus on the issue of sustainability and be grouped into categories such as the future of work, health, and mobility. Expo organizers are seeking projects that have succeeded in their regions and could be transferred to other parts of the world.

For example, a series of projects from the United States include Chattanooga, Tennessee's, new electric bus fleet and the city's long-term efforts to protect its environment and provide affordable housing and family-supporting jobs. Another U.S. exhibit highlights the Greenpoint Manufacturing Center in Brooklyn, New York, a community-owned industry and arts center that supports small- and medium-sized businesses, including arts cooperatives and high-quality furniture manufacturers.

Berlin's millennial celebration, "2000: In Berlin," will run from May 14, 2000, until January 7, 2001. The event follows the tradition of arts festivals, *Berliner Festspiele*, sponsored by the city beginning in 1951, when West Berlin hosted an international film festival. The millennial festival is titled "Images and Signs of the 21st Century."

More than half a million revelers are expected to spend New Year's Eve 1999 in Times Square, awaiting the countdown to midnight.

United States: Times Square Braces for 500,000 Revelers

More than half a million revelers are expected to spend New Year's Eve 1999 in Times Square, awaiting the countdown to midnight. The party will begin at 7 a.m. Eastern Standard Time on December 31 (as New Year's Day begins in the South Pacific) and continue for 24 hours. Giant TV screens in Manhattan will broadcast highlights of global celebrations from all 24 time zones, while cameras trained on Times Square send images of New York's party to millions of viewers around the world.

On the West Coast, ticket holders for a megaconcert called "Party 2000" will gather in Southern California from December 28, 1999, through January 1, 2000, to hear more than 100 rock bands and other musicians ring in the new year. Event promoters expect 2.5 million people to attend the event and 2 billion more to watch it on television. The 4,500-acre site (exact location not yet disclosed) will feature four campgrounds, 4,000 cement barbecues, five stages, 30 minutes of fireworks, and a 2,000-gun salute to close out the second millennium.

The All One Tribe Foundation of Taos, New Mexico, is organizing a worldwide welcome of the third millennium: People in selected cities will drum in unison to mark the final moments of 1999. Elsewhere in the United States, some New Year's Eve 1999 reservations are hard to find or expensive. In New Orleans, the Japanese Room of Antoine's restaurant has been booked since 1985. In Long Beach, California, a New Year's Eve room and dinner for two on the Queen Mary will cost $1,999.99. Revelers with extra money to spend may have to hurry to catch the cruise from New York to Cairo for the Millennium Society ball at Egypt's Great Pyramid.

Few seem concerned about where the last New Year's Eve 1999 celebration will take place. For the record, the Marquesas Islands of French Polynesia (latitude: 8.53 [degrees] S, longitude: 140.02 [degrees] W) have claimed that distinction and plan an arts festival and celebration of archaeological sites on the island of Nuku Hiva. All islanders will be welcome.

Contacts for Millennium Celebrations
* FRANCE—Paris will anchor France's Worldwide Observatory of the Year 2000 with street fairs, light shows, art exhibits, and a new year's countdown at the Eiffel Tower. Contact: Web site www.toureiffel.fr/an2000_uk/.
* ITALY—Rome's millennial celebration, the Great Jubilee 2000, will bring millions of pilgrims to Italy to observe the Catholic Holy Year. Contacts: Web sites www.xibalba.com/solt/jubilee/ and www.romagiubileo.it/.
* UNITED KINGDOM Britain's Millennium Exhibition in Greenwich will be housed in the world's largest domed stadium. Contact: Telephone 44-171649-1318; Web site www.greenwich 2000.com/exhibition.htm.
* GERMANY—Hanover will host Expo 2000, a world's fair with exhibits from 165 countries. Contact: Expo 2000 Hanover, D-30510 Hanover, Germany; fax 49-(511) 84-04-100; Web site www.expo2000.de/englisch/inhalt/index.html.
* UNITED STATES—The Times Square Ball for New Year's Eve 1999 will be a 24-hour celebration including New York's midnight countdown, a 93-year tradition. Contact: Times Square Business Improvement District; telephone 1-212-768-1560; Web site www.times-square-bid.org/index2.html.
The promoters of Party 2000, a three-day concert in the Southern California desert, expect several million people to attend the event and 2 billion to watch it on television. Contact: Telephone 1-805-723-5501; Web site www.party2000.com.
Attendees of the Ball at the Great Pyramid will cruise from New York to Egypt on the Queen Elizabeth II and dance at the Cheops monument. Contact: Millennium Society; telephone 1-202-332-1999; Web site www.alaskanet.com/party 1999.
Drumming in the Year 2000 is a global event for world peace in which people in each time zone will drum together as the midnight hour arrives. Contact: All One Tribe Foundation; telephone 1-505-751-0019; Web site www.allonetribedrum.com.

Making Sense of Past Visions of 2000: What Were They Thinking?[2]

So I'm at Penn Station in New York, about to board the underground train to L.A.—it takes 54 minutes, but I use the time productively—when I run into my friend Dave. I tell him I'm heading to the Coast for a couple of months' vacation. He asks what I'm doing with my other five weeks off this year, but I haven't decided; that Cruise in Orbit sounds like fun, but it's expensive. Dave's mad because the recombinant DNA treatment isn't making his hair grow, so he wants to sue his doctor. "Sue him!?" I ask. "How you gonna find a lawyer? They're rare as—"

Okay. I admit it. This didn't actually happen. It's just that for the past few weeks I've been living in the year 2000 as envisioned by various heavy thinkers of the past 40 years, and it's easy to get carried away—not just easy, but also fun and even useful at a time when foreseeing the future feels more urgent than ever.

All those zeroes have for ages enticed people to imagine 2000, but I've been immersing myself in the work of serious forecasters of just the past few decades. See, I'm looking for lessons, and business people perceive little advantage in looking out much further than a generation. The 2000 industry has boomed twice, once in the mid-'60s and again about 1980, with predictions coalescing around what we might call respectively the Good News view and the Bad News view. Both sets of forecasts were built on great big howlers—yet counterintuitive as it may seem, the older predictions were less wrong.

The biggest error in the Good News view . . . was that by now technology would have made us Americans so productive that we'd be working much, much less and might even be facing significant problems whiling away our leisure.

The biggest error in the Good News view, delicious for the sheer scope of its wrongness, was that by now technology would have made us Americans so productive that we'd be working much, much less and might even be facing significant problems whiling away our leisure. This view was widespread in the Sixties, in the wake of a book called *Cybernation: The Silent Conquest*, by social psychologist Donald Michael. (You'll still find the term "cybernation"— "the use of computers coupled with automatic machinery to control and carry out complex operations"—credited to him in the dictionary.) Exactly how it would all happen was worked out in exquisite detail in a 1967 book called *The Year 2000*, by Herman Kahn and Anthony J. Wiener of the Hud-

---

2. Article by Geoffrey Colvin from *Fortune*, Mar. 1, 1999, p236 + . Copyright © 1999 Time Inc. All rights reserved. Reprinted with permission.

son Institute. To them, predicting a leisure revolution wasn't even going out on a limb.

The "surprise-free" economic projections they assembled indeed seemed modest, merely assuming that population and productivity would keep growing as before. In that case, the authors showed, even if we all worked 20% less, the economy would at least triple in real terms by 2000; chances were fair it would quintuple. Actually one could only guess how much we'd cut back on work with so much prosperity washing over us, but the authors offered some possibilities. They showed alluringly how we could work four days a week, 7 1/2 hours a day, taking 13 weeks' vacation a year, and still be twice as well off in 2000 as in 1965. Though much was uncertain, they said, the basic outlook seemed clear: "a likely increase in leisure and a concomitant reduction of the pressures of work." And with 2000 practically here, isn't that just what you're experiencing?

Here's how wrong those surprise-free projections were: We work every bit as hard as we did in the '60s (over 2,000 hours a year for full-timers), and far more of us are employed—some 48% of the population vs. 38%. Yet the economy isn't even as big as its minimum projected size in the envisioned Barcalounger society. As for reduced work pressures, well, that's subjective. What do you think?

What went wrong is no mystery. Kahn and Wiener, like nearly everyone else, believed labor productivity would increase 2.5% to 4% a year, in line with postwar experience; some thought it would grow faster. In fact, it has increased only about 1.6% annually since 1965, and as students of compounding know, that's all the difference in the world. Why did productivity fizzle? Depends on whom you ask: It was the oil shocks and stagnation of the '70s; it was all those baby-boomers pouring into the work force, pushing down output per worker; it's because new technology always takes longer to work its magic than people expect. Bottom line, we just didn't cybernate as forecast.

The Bad News millennial view that arose circa 1980 was built around various ecodisasters and was expressed most fulsomely in a U.S. government report, ordered by Jimmy Carter, called *Global 2000*. With utter confidence it predicted a colder, hungrier, poorer world of poisoned seas and food wars. In the same spirit, other writers with plausible expert credentials foresaw that by now we'd be farming the seabeds and the moon, sending people into space colonies, and building solar energy collectors in orbit. Oil would be so rare and valuable that driving for pleasure would be restricted by the government.

How could this view have been so wrong? The world is richer, better fed, and more abundant in energy, not less. The Bad News view suffered from a common problem: It couldn't escape the gravity of the present. The troubles of the time

The Bad News millennial view that arose circa 1980 . . . predicted a colder, hungrier, poorer world of poisoned seas and food wars.

seemed so overwhelming that few could make an imaginative leap to a dramatically different future. A minority of forecasters, led by the late Julian Simon, looked at long-term trends and said flatly that the Bad News view was wrong, but the mainstream culture considered them radicals.

If both waves of millennial predictions contained huge errors, how can I say one was less wrong? Two reasons:

First, the Good News view was off in degree but not in kind. America really is much richer than it used to be, if not as rich as the double-domers of the '60s expected. We may not have more leisure than we used to, but we spend a great deal more money on it. If you had based business decisions on the Good News view, you would have had to adjust them significantly, but your company would be pointing in the right direction. The Bad News view, by contrast, pointed in the wrong direction. If you had prepared your company for a world of kelp farms and $200-a-barrel oil, you'd have been in ever deeper trouble as the years rolled by.

Major tech developments can be spotted at some distance, but the ways quirky humans will use them can't be.

Second, apart from the Good-News-vs.-Bad-News conflict, the two waves of predictions differed sharply on the most important business development of our time, the advance of technology. Serious forecasters of the '60s saw quite clearly the outlines of our infotech world: distributed computing, exponential increases in processing power, universal connectivity, bandwidth as a limiting factor, lasers as part of the solution, personal wireless communication, e-commerce. With the year 2000 so far off, these seers realized they couldn't predict how people would use this technology, so they allowed for all kinds of possibilities.

By the early '80s, with the millennium in sight, forecasters were bolder—but shouldn't have been. We were told that by 2000, teleconferencing would cut business travel dramatically, retailers would charge extra when you paid cash, and we would write fewer checks, all the opposite of what really happened. Instead of dictating letters to stenographers, we would dictate them to computers, which would print them out at the astonishing rate of a page a minute. My favorite tech prediction from this era involved a military advance that we somehow missed, the stealth blimp.

As infotech upends our world more violently than ever, the big lessons of all this are worth remembering. Major tech developments can be spotted at some distance, but the ways quirky humans will use them can't be. In ten or 20 years life can change more than we think, so dare to escape the present and imagine truly different futures. Most important, remember that at least two things in this world are infinite: human desires and human ingenuity. We'll always want more, and we'll always find new ways—unimaginable at the moment—to get it. Believing this is admittedly an act of faith, but believing otherwise has so far been a losing proposition.

Can the Millennium Deliver?[3]

The centuries of envisioning and predicting it reveal more about the hopes, dreams and fears of people in ages past than about the event itself.

The year A.D. 2000 has long hovered in an imagined sky like a distant, luminous sign. Generations have used it as a target for their dreams, hopes and fears. Since prophecies usually tell us more about the past than the future, how the millennium was envisioned—and, in a sense, invented—during earlier eras says a great deal about the successive stages of Western history, about the religious as well as secular faith of our ancestors—in short, about how we came to be what we are.

Unlike Eastern religions, Christianity saw history not as an endless cycle but as an ascent to a magnificent goal. The special significance of the year 2000 emerged from prophecies about Christ's Second Coming. By the reckoning of early Christian scholars, human history would end after 6,000 years, each thousand years corresponding to one day of creation. Some believed that there were 2,000 years between Adam and Abraham and 2,000 between Abraham and Jesus, and that after 2,000 more (constituting the Christian era) Jesus would return and reign in glory for 1,000 years—hence the millennium.

For centuries such calculations were confined to a few learned theorists. In the minds of most people, time was vague; the future was tomorrow's sunrise, the next harvest, the coming winter or the inevitability of death. The more distant future belonged to the realm of religion. The modern concept of the future did not begin to develop until the late Middle Ages and early Renaissance, with the gradual consolidation of calendars, the spread of clocks and the stirrings of new forces. Both science and commerce needed to anticipate things, whether a chemical reaction or the expiration of contracts.

But visions of the future still mixed science with superstition, as was demonstrated by Nostradamus. A successful physician in 16th century France (for years he ministered to victims of the plague), he managed to believe both in scientific Copernican astronomy and in astrology. Eventually he turned to the occult. In seven volumes he foretold "the future events of the entire world" (according to his epitaph). In one of his obscure quatrains, he prophesied that in 1999, "from the sky there will come a great King of terror." Nobody

By the reckoning of early Christian scholars, human history would end after 6,000 years, each thousand years corresponding to one day of creation.

---

3. Article by Henry A. Grunwald from *Time*, May 11, 1998 v151 n18 p84(4) Copyright © 1998 Time Inc. All rights reserved. Reprinted with permission. Henry Grunwald, former managing editor of *Time* and editor-in-chief of Time Inc., is the author of *One Man's America*.

knows what that was supposed to mean, but in recent decades many would-be prophets have used those lines to predict all manner of cataclysms, from nuclear war to global warming to the end of the world. This suggests that centuries of science have not displaced—and perhaps have even reinforced—people's desire for mystical clues to their fate.

A contemporary of Nostradamus was Sir Thomas More, whose Utopia was not so much a vision of the future as a vision of a better society and thus a reproach to present evils. But henceforth, Utopian dreams of reform invariably mingled with anticipation of tomorrow. This was particularly true in the 18th century, with the Age of Reason's belief in the perfectibility of human nature and the near inevitability of progress. Revolution was in the air, and revolution itself is a kind of prophecy—a violent prediction.

By the 19th century, visions of the future had come to be dominated by the machine, belching steam and later sparking electricity.

One symbol of this was a play, *The Year 2000*, written in 1789 by Nicolas-Edme Restif de la Bretonne, a prolific author and polemicist who functioned in the literary demimonde between the great philosophers and the pornographic hacks. In preceding years he had addressed voluminous suggestions to the Estates General for legal and constitutional reforms, including an embryonic welfare state with workers' insurance, retirement funds, free medical care and education. The play itself projected an ideal community in which marriage has been purged of all crass commercialism and bridegrooms are chosen by a council of elders according to merit, military or otherwise. Married couples are kept apart for years to ensure the survival of their passion. Society as a whole, under a benign king, is perfectly just, even though—or perhaps because—lawyers have been eliminated. The King declares, "In the year 2000, virtue never goes unrewarded!"

By the 19th century, visions of the future had come to be dominated by the machine, belching steam and later sparking electricity. This is what inspired Jules Verne, the first major prophet of technology, who was born a generation after the French Revolution and lived until 1905. A bourgeois stockbroker who became fascinated by science, he noted near the end of his life that he had been present at the birth of railroads, trams, the electric light, the telegraph, the telephone and the phonograph, not to mention postage stamps and detachable collars.

In his books, Verne always tried to stay within the limits of what he considered scientifically plausible. Apart from his major works (*Around the World in 80 Days, Journey to the Center of the Earth*), he wrote a fantasy about the year 2000 titled *An Ideal City*. The story is full of mechanical gimmicks: streets are cleaned automatically, recitals are conveyed from the artist by wire to pianos around the world, babies get their milk from steam-driven breast-feeding machines. The trains of women's gowns, having grown absurdly long, move on little wheels (one of the rare touches of humor in futurist writing). But much of the emphasis is less on physical than on social engineering: bachelors are taxed to prod them into marriage; physicians are paid for healthy patients rather than sick ones.

Social engineering became a dominant theme in the futurist imagination, and increasingly its symbol was 2000. It was the year chosen by Edward Bellamy for his projection of the future America in *Looking Backward*, published in 1888. The book instantly became immensely popular, obviously filling an emotional need in a country that was beset by strikes, battles between workers and police and proliferating industrial trusts. Bellamy, the son of a Baptist minister, was revolted by the brutality of contemporary capitalism and the misery it caused. He believed relief must come not through promises of heaven but—in the Utopian tradition—by building something like heaven on earth.

According to his vision, which he called Nationalism, America in 2000 is essentially one huge corporation. In his odd version of economics, the absence of competition means that all production is efficient and goods are cheap. Since there is enough for everybody, greed has disappeared and so has money. People are issued something like credit cards with which they can draw whatever they need from common stores. Every citizen must serve in a kind of workers' army in which all get the same pay. In lieu of financial incentives there is patriotism and "passion for humanity." People marry each other only for the finest moral and physical qualities; the race has been "purified." A minor detail symbolizes the collectivist ideal: when it rains, canopies are lowered over the streets, replacing everyone's individual umbrella.

Looking Backward not only popularized long-standing socialist ideas but also strongly influenced their further development and appeal. The Socialist leader Eugene V. Debs publicly thanked Bellamy for guiding him "out of darkness into light..." and for "fill[ing] a despairing world with hope." Not everybody shared that particular hope. Like most Utopias, Bellamy's not only was naive but also seemed to leave little room for individual freedom.

A few years after the publication of *Looking Backward*, there appeared a very different view of A.D. 2000. It was a sort of capitalist rebuttal, although by definition the free-market philosophy does not easily lend itself to Utopianism, with its regimented bliss. In *A Journey to Other Worlds* by John Jacob Astor, Socialism has hopelessly ruined Europe, while the U.S., having absorbed Canada, Mexico and most of Central and South America, virtually rules the world together with its ally, Great Britain. A great-grandson of the dynasty's founder, Astor was a playboy with a serious side. Fascinated by science, he spent much time working in machine shops and patented a number of inventions, including marine turbines. His book is filled with some of his imag-

Social engineering became a dominant theme in the futurist imagination, and increasingly its symbol was 2000.

ined inventions. Steam boilers are powered by the sun; electricity, which runs everything, is generated by tides; battery-powered airplanes traverse the sky.

At the center of the plot is the Terrestrial Axis Straightening Company, which plans to reposition the globe so that the Earth's climate will be universally benign, like everlasting spring ("Polar bears will soon have to use artificial ice"). In Astor's view, "this period—A.D. 2000—is by far the most wonderful the world has as yet seen." But the world has grown too small, which is why the book's main characters take off for Jupiter in a spaceship equipped with booster rockets. "The future glory of the human race," concludes Astor, "lies in exploring at least the solar system." Ironically, this dreamer of technical progress, especially of huge powerful ships, went down with the Titanic.

Alongside Astor's kind of optimism, the Socialist critique of society and the era's muckraking passions continued, contributing darker shades to images of the future. In 1903 William Wallace Cook, a newspaperman and free-lance writer, published *A Round Trip to the Year 2000*, in which robots known as "muglugs" displace human workers, sending them to live out a miserable existence somewhere in the Midwest (a vision not designed to cheer chambers of commerce in the heartland). Voracious capitalism has triumphed. The "Air Trust" sells the very air people breathe; the "Sun Trust" forces the public to pay even for sunshine.

World War I, with its machines that dealt death rather than hope, further darkened the view of things to come.

World War I, with its machines that dealt death rather than hope, further darkened the view of things to come. In 1927 the famous German moviemaker Fritz Lang released *Metropolis*, the idea for which came to him when he first saw, from shipboard, the glaring lights and tall buildings of Manhattan. (The film became a favorite of Hitler's.) Set in the year 2000, *Metropolis* shows plutocrats living in idle pleasure while workers slave away underground until a spectacular rebellion sets them free. This was reminiscent of H.G. Wells' 1895 dystopian fantasy, *The Time Machine*, in which a subhuman race called the Morlocks lives underground and emerges to devour the humans who live above.

In the meantime, what was not yet known as the media had enthusiastically taken up the science-fiction approach to the future. In 1910 an illustrator named Jean Marc Cote began a series of advertising cards depicting life in the year 2000: underwater croquet tournaments, men being shaved by robots, battery-powered roller skates. Later, Hugo Gernsback, who started out as a manufacturer of automotive batteries, launched the magazine *Amazing Stories* ("Extravagant Fiction Today—Cold Fact Tomorrow"). It was endlessly imitated. A typical series in *Famous Fantastic Mysteries* was titled "Crimes of the Year 2000." The crimes were not especially novel, but some of the crime-fighting devices were, for the time: tiny recorders strapped to the wrist, heli-pursuit cars, bloodhound machines that identified a perpetrator's smell. The pulp view of the millennium was dominated by gadgetry. If there was a philosophical outlook, it was patriotic and upbeat in the sense that the good guys always won.

In the next significant—and much less entertaining—phase of futurology, the year 2000 was taken over by the think tanks. Most notably there was the Academy of Arts and Sciences Commission on the Year 2000, set up in 1966 (rather rushing things). It was headed by the distinguished sociologist Daniel Bell and included 42 leading thinkers in fields ranging from science to mysticism. One of the commission's prominent members was that brilliant man-mountain Herman Kahn, who published *The Year 2000* alongside the commission's report, *Toward the Year 2000*.

In a mass of speculation and extrapolation, the reports forecast many trends that have come true: decentralization, the communications revolution, the rise of services, genetic engineering, threats to privacy, nuclear proliferation. They were optimistic about the economy, predicting huge increases in personal income and the GNP (they forecast an increase to $3.6 trillion, thus falling short of the actual figure, at latest count, by about $5 trillion). They also foresaw a rise in hedonism and a decline in the work ethic. There were the inevitable misjudgments and omissions—especially, as Bell now concedes, a lack of any reference to the dramatic change in the role of women.

As if to make up for that, a group of writers a few years later published the book *Woman in the Year 2000*. The contributions were cast in the form of fantasy and fiction but largely reflected the familiar feminist gospel. One story involved a girl born at midnight in the year 2000, appropriately named Millenny. When she goes to school, she finds that girls are no longer discouraged from fighting with one another and that boys are no longer looked down on when they weep. On television, violence and machismo have been banned. Safe pharmaceutical contraceptives are available free at banks and post offices. When and if Millenny is ready to get married, she and her partner will negotiate a contract specifying their mutual expectations and responsibilities, a document to be renegotiated from time to time and always subject to cancellation.

Other pieces in the book predicted that conception would take place in laboratories and gestation in artificial wombs, that the gender of babies would be determined in advance, that homosexuality would be universally accepted. Today, two years before Millenny's birth, it all sounds remarkably familiar.

During the 1970s, gloom spread, partly as a result of the energy crisis, and growth was demonized. At the end of Jimmy Carter's presidential term a group of federal agencies submitted *Global 2000 Report to the President*. It was strongly

In a mass of speculation and extrapolation, the reports forecast many trends that have come true: decentralization, the communications revolution, the rise of services, genetic engineering, threats to privacy, nuclear proliferation.

neo-Malthusian, predicting environmental degradation, over-population, shrinking resources and vast increases in poverty unless there were technological breakthroughs and international action. The Carter Administration passed the report on to Ronald Reagan, who ignored it. The doomsayers could not have foreseen the collapse of the Soviet Union, the retreat of the welfare state in most parts of the world, the full impact of the global market or the resurgence of the American economy.

On balance, technological forecasts have often proved remarkably accurate, in outline if not in detail. By contrast, the political forecasts—whether the dreams of brotherhood or the nightmares of Big Brother—have been far more dubious.

For decades the phrase "by the end of the century" denoted something far distant. But it is distant no longer. Millennial predictions are proliferating with increasing speed as prognosticators try to get in under the wire. The Internet, that electronic jungle drum, vibrates to the beat of prophecy. Much of it is in the religious, apocalyptic tradition. Just about any recent event, from the fall of the Berlin Wall to the assassination of Israeli Prime Minister Yitzhak Rabin, is taken by some as a sign of the impending Doomsday or the flowering of the Peaceable Kingdom. Countless secular predictions also sway between doom and hope. Socialist Utopias are out of fashion, but belief in free-market cornucopias is rivaled by nightmares of savage Blade Runner cities.

Forecasters have a problem because stunning developments in science and technology are constantly overtaking their imagination, while the most logical predictions are bound to be pushed aside by the unexpected. We also know that the millennium is an entirely artificial mark on the calendar. But beneath our preoccupation with it is a deep psychological meaning: the need to believe that we are not lost in time, that we are going somewhere and that we can glimpse where. We will feel a little forlorn having to look back to the year 2000. But soon enough, the predictions will start reaching toward A.D. 3000.

On balance, technological forecasts have often proved remarkably accurate, in outline if not in detail.

By contrast, the political forecasts—whether the dreams of brotherhood or the nightmares of Big Brother— have been far more dubious.

Will Y2K Spark a Worldwide SOS?[4]

With a year to go, the experts aren't willing to offer a reassuring "no."

In *The Day the Earth Stood Still*, the 1951 sci-fi thriller, an alien invader brazenly turns off the earth's power, bringing the industrial world to a terrifying halt. Lights flicker off. Phones go dead. Trolleys stop in their tracks. Pandemonium reigns from New York City to Tokyo.

Half a century later, doomsayers would have you believe an Information Age sequel is on the way. Only this time the alien is the millennium bug, a programming glitch that will cause some computers and products with computer chips to shut down or spaz out when they think the "00" in a date means they're back in the McKinley administration in 1900.

Could it really happen? Could the earth stand still?

"I think not," is the less-than-100%-reassuring answer from White House year 2000 czar John Koskinen, who has been spearheading an administration assessment of the risks ahead. "The problem is that no one really knows. While the big American companies are working on it, there is still great risk in some foreign countries and parts of the U.S. of serious disruptions if we can't get people to address the problem in time."

Call it the revenge of the nerds. Some 50 years ago, when early computer programmers designed hardware and software and chips, they used only the last two digits of each year in order to save memory and money. So, when the clock strikes one second past midnight next year, many date-sensitive programs will read the "00" as 1900 instead of 2000, causing them to stop or malfunction. Because such systems are integral to everything from personal computers to lifesaving medical devices to the air-traffic control system, the Information Age could grind to a screeching halt.

The good news is that most major U.S. companies have long been keenly aware of the need to eradicate this bug and are working feverishly to prepare themselves for a seamless transition to the next century. The bad news is that many small U.S. companies—and foreign firms and governments—are so far behind that some system failures are virtually inevitable. Considering our reliance on global computer networks, no one is absolutely sure to what extent the weak links could break the chain—and wreak havoc with the

No one is absolutely sure to what extent the weak links could break the chain—and wreak havoc with the economy, financial markets and life as we know it.

4. Article by Ann Reilly Dowd from *Kiplinger's Personal Finance* magazine January 1999 pp. 104-106. Copyright © 1999 *Kiplinger's Personal Finance.* Reprinted with permission.

economy, financial markets and life as we know it. Deutsche Bank Securities chief economist Edward Yardeni thinks there's a 60% chance that Y2K (shorthand for year 2000) problems will plunge us into a global recession as deep as the 1973–74 downturn that sent the Dow Jones industrial average down 42%.

With 12 months to go, the best bet is that the doomsayers will be disappointed. But while you don't need to pack your pickup for that survival camp in Montana, there will almost surely be unforeseen breakdowns that could bankrupt some companies, rattle markets and disrupt daily life, at least temporarily. Here's a practical guide to help you navigate around the hype and hysteria and protect yourself against the real risks ahead.

Banking

It's January 1, 2000. Is your money safe? Yes, but that doesn't mean we'll all be able to get at our cash with equal ease. Regulators say nearly 95% of federally insured institutions are making "satisfactory progress" in readying their computers for the year 2000. But that leaves more than 500 institutions in need of improvement and 37 dangerously behind. If your bank is one of the few that misses the deadline, your transactions could be incorrectly debited or credited. And if the bank is part of an ATM network, it could infect the entire system, causing temporary ATM errors or outages even for customers of well-prepared institutions.

Wherever your money is, ask officials if their computers will be ready for the millennium. If not, consider switching. In any case, paper records will take on added importance near the end of this year and for the first few months of 2000. Plan to hold on to your statements, just in case computer records get lost or corrupted. And although most ATMs and credit cards should work just fine, it might be wise to keep a little extra cash around. The Federal Reserve will have an extra $50 billion cash—14% more than usual—on hand at the end of 1999 for just that reason.

Investments

Bull market, bear market. Will there be a market? Not to worry. The securities industry, including the major exchanges, is far ahead of most industries in ensuring that its computer networks are up to snuff. The major mutual fund companies, including Fidelity, T. Rowe Price and Vanguard, say they will have fixed their in-house systems by this February, as do major brokers such as Merrill Lynch and Charles Schwab. A reassuring sign of progress: A four-day industry-wide test last September found no Y2K glitches that prevented trades.

If there is a problem, it's likely to be with small brokers or systems outside the industry's control. Says John Panchery, the Securities Industry Association's year 2000 expert: "The things that scare us most are problems over which we have no control, like outside data feeds, phones, elevators and utilities."

The Securities and Exchange Commission requires all public companies to report on their readiness, and posts the reports on its Web site. If your brokerage isn't forthcoming, it may signal a problem in the making. Call your broker and ask what's going on. More important, check with companies whose stock you own. The SEC requires firms to keep shareholders up to date on their Y2K preparedness. Get hold of the company's latest quarterly statement (check its Web site or call investor relations) to see if Y2K problems are anticipated and what the company is doing to avoid them.

Home

Will all those digitally correct gizmos work? Relax.   For the most part, your home appliances, including the ones with digital displays that blink mindlessly after the power goes out, are not vulnerable to the turn-of-the-century change. Your microwave, coffeepot, washing machine, stove, thermostat and lawn-sprinkling system should all be fine because their timers are based on the time of day or day of the week, not the year. With an old VCR, you may need to reset the record-ahead function, and some older fax machines may print the wrong date, though they'll still work. Also, some sophisticated security systems with programmable dates may need upgrading. But for most people, the only year 2000 problems at home will involve their personal computer.

If you bought your computer from a major manufacturer in the past year, it will probably operate just fine, says Bill Gregory of Greenwich Mean Time-UTA, a year 2000 computer consulting firm. But some cheaper clones and most older computers and software are not ready for 2000 and could shut down, corrupt files or miscalculate data when the New Year dawns. Before you freak out, check out the Internet home page of your hardware and software manufacturers. Most report their product readiness by make and model, and recommend upgrades—some of which are free—if necessary.

Phones

Will you be able to phone home? "Probably," says Michael Powell, a commissioner of the Federal Communications Commission, in another not-quite-sterling reassurance. The biggest fear for telephone executives, he says, is that everyone in the U.S. will pick up the phone on millennium morn to see if there's a dial tone. That alone could crash the system on any morning. As long as that doesn't happen, Powell is confident that the big telephone companies will be ready. But he worries about some of the nation's 1,300 small operators serving rural areas, as well as foreign telecommunications providers and the private phone systems typically found in hotels, office buildings and large retail apartment complexes. "It's not so much whether any one system is working," says Powell. "But when it all comes together, what kinds of cascading effects could cause a costly chain reaction?"

The FCC and major telephone companies are working overtime to help small companies and foreign countries get ready. But if you are served by a small phone company or private phone system, you can help yourself as well: Ask the provider whether its system will be ready. And if you're planning an important call to Bombay, Bali or some other less-developed region, you might want to make it before the first of the year.

Power

Should you stock up on candles and firewood? It isn't a bad idea," says Department of Energy spokesman Glenn Coplon. While many older power plants still operate largely without computers, the newer ones depend on them to manage both the production and distribution of electricity. What's more, a September survey by the North American Electric Reliability Council found the industry (particularly small coal- and oil-fired power plants, rural co-ops and municipal power generators) behind schedule. There's no need to worry about nuclear accidents, according to General Accounting Office chief scientist Rona Stillman. However, isolated brownouts or blackouts are real possibilities if the industry doesn't pick up the pace upgrading its systems.

Other weak links in the energy chain include natural-gas and oil suppliers.

Other weak links in the energy chain include natural-gas and oil suppliers. "Natural gas is way behind in fixing its Y2K problems," says Lou Marcoccio, year 2000 research director for the GartnerGroup, which advises companies worldwide on managing their millennium bugs. "Consumers could encounter problems in metering and billing. And because chips embedded in valves control distribution, there could also be supply problems." As for oil and gasoline, Marcoccio says there could be computer-generated problems associated with production and distribution. "We're not talking about oil and gasoline shortages like we saw in the early 1970s," he says. "But we could see modest disruptions and price increases."

Health Care

What if you end up in the ER? If your heart fails, will the defibrillator work? If you need emergency medication, will the infusion pump provide the correct dosage? Will your records be retrievable? Doctors' biggest worry about the year 2000 involves medical devices, some of which contain date-sensitive chips or rely on date-sensitive computer systems to analyze medical information. For example, while pacemakers do not contain such chips, the computers used to analyze how they are performing do. Similarly, says Department of Veterans Affairs (VA) spokesman Ken McKinnon, although defibrillators—used to resuscitate heart-attack victims—will work on January 1, 2000, printouts of the details of the procedure could be flawed if date-sensitive features are not fixed.

While the Food and Drug Administration believes most medical devices are not date-sensitive, regulators were disturbed that only 10% of manufacturers responded to a recent survey to determine which devices could have problems. In a separate inquiry, 694 manufacturers told the VA they were ready, but 136 said they were not, and 530 never responded, many because they had gone out of business. The VA identified some 855 devices that are not in compliance, such as a radiation-treatment device.

Worse yet, many health care organizations are not well prepared to identify or fix errant machines in time. Ditto for the massive computer systems that store patient records and process bills and insurance claims. A January 1998 report by the GartnerGroup concluded that doctors, hospitals and other health care providers were so poorly prepared that some failures seem "unavoidable."

What's a patient to do? Don't panic, prepare. If you're dependent on a medical device, check with your doctor and the manufacturer to make sure the product will function properly in the new year. Particularly if you are undergoing treatment for a life-threatening condition, it would be wise to ask your doctor for paper records of your medical history and treatment.

Air Traffic

No, planes won't fall out of the sky—but brace for delays.

Should you acquire a fear of flying? No, planes won't fall out of the sky—but brace for delays. U.S. airlines have been working assiduously to find and correct problems. The air-traffic control system, while initially behind, seems to be on schedule to meet the millennium without crisis. Problems are more likely to stem from the nation's 5,000 airports. A recent survey by the Air Transport Association found that roughly 40% of them have not finished identifying vulnerable systems, which include security controls, runway lighting, baggage conveyors, fire alarms, backup generators and heating systems. Add to that the likelihood that U.S. regulators will prohibit airlines from flying to unprepared foreign destinations and you have the makings of a mind-boggling backup.

If you are planning a millennium vacation to some exotic clime, check first to see if the airports there are ready for the date change. And if you're flying stateside, bring a good book or two, just in case you end up in a millennium-size holding pattern.

Elevators

Will they fall or stall? Not likely. One of the most oft-repeated millennium scare stories involves this most common of modern conveniences. The way it's told and retold, if you happen to be in the wrong elevator a second past midnight on January 1, 2000, the elevator could conclude that it hasn't been serviced since 1900, shut its doors and go immediately to the basement—with you locked inside. Fun story, bad facts. The truth is there are no date-sensitive chips in elevators, according to Peter Kowalchuk, a spokesman for Otis Elevator, the world's leading elevator manufacturer. So there is no risk that one will shut down abruptly with you in it.

The truth is there are no date-sensitive chips in elevators.

But that doesn't mean that some elevators won't seem a bit possessed on New Year's Day. If you happen to be in an apartment, office or retail complex where elevators are run by a computer that is not ready for the year 2000, the computer could send them to their starting point, usually the bottom floor. The doors won't lock, but you will have to hit the button for your desired floor again. The only serious risk to anyone riding an elevator shortly after the New Year dawns is if the power goes out, in which case you'll be stuck until it returns or a repairman shows up. So pick your midnight riding companions wisely.

Taxes

Will the IRS computers compute? Absolutely, says IRS year 2000 conversion chief John Yost, who's learned the hard way just what the date conversion could mean to the IRS. In 1996, when the IRS first began testing its systems, someone decided to turn a computer clock ahead to January 1, 2000. "It was about as serious as it could be," recalls Yost. "The computer locked everybody out, including people with security passes. It brought the entire system down."

Never again, says Yost. The IRS has already updated two-thirds of the 48.7 million lines of code that needed it, including the basic systems that record and calculate individual taxes. The rest, he says, will be ready this January. "Our intent," he says, "is for the year 2000 to have no impact on the taxpayer, and I think we're on schedule."

Of course, if the power or phone system goes down, Yost concedes, all bets are off. If you're used to getting a big refund, it makes more sense than ever to trim your withholding so that Uncle Sam isn't sitting on a bunch of your money a year from now. Likewise, be careful not to underpay. Even if the IRS computers go down, it won't change what you owe or halt the tick-tick-tick of interest and penalties mounting while the agency fixes them.

WHAT'S GOING ON HERE?

It's easy to understand why early computer designers tossed us into this millennium-bug boat. To save precious memory space, they ditched the "19" in front of every year. Not very farsighted, to be sure, but understandable.

But why on earth do all the devices threatened by Y2K care what year it is, anyway? The three real millennium threats below should help you understand what's going on here.

- Radiation therapy. The maker of one cancer-treating device has told the Department of Veterans Affairs the machine must not be used in the year 2000. An internal clock is used to measure the age of radioactive material. When it reads "00" as 1900 and assumes the material is more than 100 years old, a massive overdose could result.

- Natural gas. Inside those dark-green metal boxes on city streets or in brick buildings in the middle of nowhere are devices that monitor pressure in natural-gas pipelines, automatically releasing gas into the atmosphere to prevent the pipes from cracking. These devices care what day it is because they keep a time record of their activities that is monitored to see if a serious problem is developing. Most can't read the year 2000 and, sensing an error, will stop working on January 1, 2000, if they're not updated. Pressure in the pipes could still be relieved manually. But in a worst-case scenario, the pressure could build to the point that the pipe would burst, spewing natural gas into the air. That, in turn, could cause a massive explosion.

- ATMs. The time and date of every transaction is recorded and, as with the natural-gas valve, if the machine can't read the date, it will sense an error—just as if it couldn't read the magnetic strip on the back of the card. So if any computers in a network are not updated to read the year 2000, they will sense an error and the transaction could be interrupted. The computer would get an error message and refuse to honor your request for cash. You'd be told to try back later.

Expect the worst? the *Y2K Preparedness Catalog* offers a one-year bulk-food supply ($395); solar power system ($795); tips for underground burial of valuables ($14.95). . . . Modest proposal from economist Edward Yardeni: "nonessential" employees should consider taking off the first week of 2000. . . . Don't phone home at 12:01 A.M. on January 1, 2000.

Why on earth do all the devices threatened by Y2K care what year it is, anyway?

III. The Future of the Planet

Editor's Introduction

As if Y2K problems were not enough to worry about, we may be faced with a new ice age in the near future if global warming trends continue, according to William H. Calvin, the author of the first selection in this section. In "The Great Climate Flip-Flop" (*Atlantic*), Calvin explains how a general climatic warm-up, given the right combination of circumstances, could trigger a global cooling. "We could go back to ice age temperatures within a decade," he argues, "and judging from recent discoveries, an abrupt cooling could be triggered by our current global warming trend." There are several events that could set things in motion to trigger a global cooling, according to paleoclimatologists and oceanographers. For example, warming trends could lead to the failure of the saline flushing system of the North Atlantic Current, a process that allows warmer water to flow farther north than it otherwise would. The proper working of this flushing system, in which excess salt sinks to the bottom of the ocean and flows south, warms Europe sufficiently for it to grow food. Europe could find itself in deep trouble if the flushing system fails, whether because of the melting of Greenland's ice or increased rainfall in the northern latitudes, both of which pour too much fresh water into the North Atlantic to allow for proper flushing of heavier saline waters. The worst-case scenario Calvin posits is that the declining temperatures would drastically reduce the food supply, and Europe's armies would go marauding. But there are things we can do, both to try to prevent global cooling from being triggered and to deal with it if it does occur, and Calvin discusses our options and their probable outcomes.

If things were to become unbearable on Earth, could some of us leave the planet and survive elsewhere in the solar system? Freeman J. Dyson, author of the second selection, "Warm-Blooded Plants and Freeze-Dried Fish" (also *Atlantic*) believes that we could, sometime in the late 21st century. "My date for the beginning of cheap manned exploration and settlement," he writes, "is based on a historical analogy: from Columbus's first voyage across the Atlantic to the settlement of the Pilgrims in Massachusetts was 128 years. So I am guessing that in 2085, 128 years after the launch of the first *Sputnik*, the private settlement of pilgrims all over the solar system will begin." Dyson suggests that we start with the Kuiper Belt, a comet-filled region outside the orbit of Neptune. He argues that comets are more hospitable to life than Mars, and that biotechnological advances could someday allow us to survive on this archipelago of comets. "One of the first steps a human colony would take to establish itself in the Kuiper Belt would be to surround its cometary habitat with an extended efflorescence of mirrors in space to collect sunlight," Dyson suggests. If, after a few centuries, humans grew weary of living in the Kuiper Belt, Dyson writes that we could always move to the Oort Cloud, a collection of comets even farther from the Sun.

But never mind Kuiperville, what can we expect here on Earth in the next century? According to Stephen Baker, the author of the third selection ("Should Kurdistan Be a Nation? Scotland? How about New York City?" *Business Week*), we can expect to witness the splintering of nations at an astonishing rate of proliferation. "Imagine some of the new governments," he writes, "replete with flags, anthems, national birds, and Olympic bobsledders: Scotland. Quebec. Palestine. Kosovo. Tibet. Kashmir. South

Osseria. Kurdistan. Timor. Biafra. New York City." Despite the likelihood that, in the United States, prime candidates for independence would probably be found in Texas or Montana sooner than New York City, in this editor's opinion, the urge to break away from the motherland in the other places Baker mentions is a long-standing and enduring one. Why should it happen "suddenly" in the 21st century? Baker believes that two factors will bear primary responsibility: the spread of information via the Internet, which allows interest groups to focus and expand, and the globalization of the economy, which provides small entities with a more equal footing on the world stage than they might have enjoyed in the past. Although the desire for independence may indeed intensify in the coming decades, the determination of the parent countries to hold on to their possessions, which they see as integral parts of themselves, is likely to strengthen as well. Therefore, according to Baker, "too often in the 21st century the birth of nations will be violent…. Imagine the horror of Yugoslavia's breakup repeated over and over in the century to come."

What would the role of the United States military—indeed, that of all Western-led international coalitions—become in the event of future Kosovos? Ralph Peters addresses this question in the fourth and last selection, "The Future of War" (*Maclean's*). He perceives the recent American military action in Yugoslavia to have been not only woefully inadequate, but misdirected as well. The failure of air strikes to root out door-to-door killers became apparent to all but the politicians, it seemed, as did the futility of promising peace to a dictator who didn't want peace in the first place. If military advisers knew these things, why were they unable to convince the politicians in Washington and the policy makers in Brussels? Because, according to Peters, this was a military action conducted like much of the rest of American policy, both foreign and domestic, under the administration of Bill Clinton—by polls. The president knew that there was not enough public support for sending ground troops to Kosovo other than to keep the peace after the dirty work had been accomplished from the air. Peters argues that we can't have it both ways: we can't satisfy our consciences by "doing something" about humanitarian crises abroad while not sustaining significant casualties. "Does it matter," Peters asks us to consider, "if distant populations slaughter each other? May we close our eyes and still believe in our own decency? Our dilemma is that we want to care a little, not a lot. Peacekeeping efforts in their present form put a bandage on the wound, when the situation calls for taking away the knife. We want our humanitarianism painless and cheap."

The Great Climate Flip-Flop[1]

"Climate change" is popularly understood to mean green-house warming, which, it is predicted, will cause flooding, severe windstorms, and killer heat waves. But warming could lead, paradoxically, to drastic cooling—a catastrophe that could threaten the survival of civilization.

One of the most shocking scientific realizations of all time has slowly been dawning on us: the earth's climate does great flip-flops every few thousand years, and with breath-taking speed. We could go back to ice-age temperatures within a decade—and judging from recent discoveries, an abrupt cooling could be triggered by our current glo-bal-warming trend. Europe's climate could become more like Siberia's. Because such a cooling would occur too quickly for us to make readjustments in agricultural productivity and supply, it would be a potentially civilization-shattering affair, likely to cause an unprecedented population crash. What paleoclimate and oceanography researchers know of the mechanisms underlying such a climate flip suggests that glo-bal warming could start one in several different ways.

For a quarter century global-warming theorists have pre-dicted that climate creep is going to occur and that we need to prevent greenhouse gases from warming things up, thereby raising the sea level, destroying habitats, intensifying storms, and forcing agricultural rearrangements. Now we know—and from an entirely different group of scientists exploring separate lines of reasoning and data—that the most catastrophic result of global warming could be an abrupt cooling.

We are in a warm period now. Scientists have known for some time that the previous warm period started 130,000 years ago and ended 117,000 years ago, with the return of cold temperatures that led to an ice age. But the ice ages aren't what they used to be. They were formerly thought to be very gradual, with both air temperature and ice sheets changing in a slow, 100,000-year cycle tied to changes in the earth's orbit around the sun. But our current warm-up, which started about 15,000 years ago, began abruptly, with the temperature rising sharply while most of the ice was still present. We now know that there's nothing "glacially slow" about temperature change.

Superimposed on the gradual, long-term cycle have been dozens of abrupt warming and coolings that lasted only cen-turies. The back and forth of the ice started 2.5 million years ago, which is also when the ape-sized hominid brain began

> *We could go back to ice-age temperatures within a decade.*

1. Article by William H. Calvin from the *Atlantic* January 1998 p. 47-64. Copyright © 1998 by The Atlantic Monthly Company. Reprinted with permission.

to develop into a fully human one, four times as large and reorganized for language, music, and chains of inference. Ours is now a brain able to anticipate outcomes well enough to practice ethical behavior, able to head off disasters in the making by extrapolating trends. Our civilizations began to emerge right after the continental ice sheets melted about 10,000 years ago. Civilizations accumulate knowledge, so we now know a lot about what has been going on, what has made us what we are. We puzzle over oddities, such as the climate of Europe.

Keeping Europe Warm

Europe is an anomaly. The populous parts of the United States and Canada are mostly between the latitudes of 30° and 45,° whereas the populous parts of Europe are ten to fifteen degrees farther north. "Southerly" Rome lies near the same latitude, 42°N, as "northerly" Chicago—and the most northerly major city in Asia is Beijing, near 40°. N. London and Paris are close to the 49°N line that, west of the Great Lakes, separates the United States from Canada. Berlin is up at about 52°, Copenhagen and Moscow at about 56°. Oslo is nearly at 60°N, as are Stockholm, Helsinki, and St. Petersburg; continue due east and you'll encounter Anchorage.

Europe's climate, obviously, is not like that of North America or Asia at the same latitudes. For Europe to be as agriculturally productive as it is (it supports more than twice the population of the United States and Canada), all those cold, dry winds that blow eastward across the North Atlantic from Canada must somehow be warmed up. The job is done by warm water flowing north from the tropics, as the eastbound Gulf Stream merges into the North Atlantic Current. This warm water then flows up the Norwegian coast, with a westward branch warming Greenland's tip, at 60°N. It keeps northern Europe about nine to eighteen degrees warmer in the winter than comparable latitudes elsewhere—except when it fails. Then not only Europe but also, to everyone's surprise, the rest of the world gets chilled. Tropical swamps decrease their production of methane at the same time that Europe cools, and the Gobi Desert whips much more dust into the air. When this happens, something big, with worldwide connections, must be switching into a new mode of operation.

The North Atlantic Current is certainly something big, with the flow of about a hundred Amazon Rivers. And it sometimes changes its route dramatically, much as a bus route can be truncated into a shorter loop. Its effects are clearly global too, inasmuch as it is part of a long "salt conveyor" current that extends through the southern oceans into the Pacific.

I hope never to see a failure of the northernmost loop of the North Atlantic Current, because the result would be a population crash that would take much of civilization with

For Europe to be as agriculturally productive as it is . . . all those cold, dry winds that blow eastward across the North Atlantic from Canada must somehow be warmed up.

it, all within a decade. Ways to postpone such a climatic shift are conceivable, however—old-fashioned dam-and-ditch construction in critical locations might even work. Although we can't do much about everyday weather, we may nonetheless be able to stabilize the climate enough to prevent an abrupt cooling.

Abrupt Temperature Jumps

The discovery of abrupt climate changes has been spread out over the past fifteen years, and is well known to readers of major scientific journals such as *Science* and *Nature*. The abruptness data are convincing. Within the ice sheets of Greenland are annual layers that provide a record of the gases present in the atmosphere and indicate the changes in air temperature over the past 250,000 years—the period of the last two major ice ages. By 250,000 years ago *Homo erectus* had died out, after a run of almost two million years. By 125,000 years ago *Homo sapiens* had evolved from our ancestor species—so the whiplash climate changes of the last ice age affected people much like us.

In Greenland a given year's snowfall is compacted into ice during the ensuing years, trapping air bubbles, and so paleoclimate researchers have been able to glimpse ancient climates in some detail. Water falling as snow on Greenland carries an isotopic "fingerprint" of what the temperature was like en route. Counting those tree-ring-like layers in the ice cores shows that cooling came on as quickly as droughts. Indeed, were another climate flip to begin next year, we'd probably complain first about the drought, along with unusually cold winters in Europe. In the first few years the climate could cool as much as it did during the misnamed Little Ice Age (a gradual cooling that lasted from the early Renaissance until the end of the nineteenth century), with tenfold greater changes over the next decade or two.

The most recent big cooling started about 12,700 years ago, right in the midst of our last global warming. This cold period, known as the Younger Dryas, is named for the pollen of a tundra flower that turned up in a lake bed in Denmark when it shouldn't have. Things had been warming up, and half the ice sheets covering Europe and Canada had already melted. The return to ice-age temperatures lasted 1,300 years. Then, about 11,400 years ago, things suddenly warmed up again, and the earliest agricultural villages were established in the Middle East. An abrupt cooling got started 8,200 years ago, but it aborted within a century, and the temperature changes since then have been gradual in comparison. Indeed, we've had an unprecedented period of climate stability.

Coring old lake beds and examining the types of pollen trapped in sediment layers led to the discovery, early in the twentieth century, of the Younger Dryas. Pollen cores are still

We've had an unprecedented period of climate stability.

a primary means of seeing what regional climates were doing, even though they suffer from poorer resolution than ice cores (worms churn the sediment, obscuring records of all but the longest-lasting temperature changes). When the ice cores demonstrated the abrupt onset of the Younger Dryas, researchers wanted to know how widespread this event was. The U.S. Geological Survey took old lake-bed cores out of storage and re-examined them.

Ancient lakes near the Pacific coast of the United States, it turned out, show a shift to cold-weather plant species at roughly the time when the Younger Dryas was changing German pine forests into scrublands like those of modern Siberia. Subarctic ocean currents were reaching the southern California coastline, and Santa Barbara must have been as cold as Juneau is now. (But the regional record is poorly understood, and I know at least one reason why. These days when one goes to hear a talk on ancient climates of North America, one is likely to learn that the speaker was forced into early retirement from the U.S. Geological Survey by budget cuts. Rather than a vigorous program of studying regional climatic change, we see the shortsighted preaching of cheaper government at any cost.)

There seems to be no way of escaping the conclusion that global climate flips occur frequently and abruptly.

In 1984, when I first heard about the startling news from the ice cores, the implications were unclear—there seemed to be other ways of interpreting the data from Greenland. It was initially hoped that the abrupt warmings and coolings were just an oddity of Greenland's weather—but they have now been detected on a worldwide scale, and at about the same time. Then it was hoped that the abrupt flips were somehow caused by continental ice sheets, and thus would be unlikely to recur, because we now lack huge ice sheets over Canada and Northern Europe. Though some abrupt coolings are likely to have been associated with events in the Canadian ice sheet, the abrupt cooling in the previous warm period, 122,000 years ago, which has now been detected even in the tropics, shows that flips are not restricted to icy periods; they can also interrupt warm periods like the present one.

There seems to be no way of escaping the conclusion that global climate flips occur frequently and abruptly. An abrupt cooling could happen now, and the world might not warm up again for a long time: it looks as if the last warm period, having lasted 13,000 years, came to an end with an abrupt, prolonged cooling. That's how our warm period might end too.

Sudden onset, sudden recovery—this is why I use the word "flip-flop" to describe these climate changes. They are utterly unlike the changes that one would expect from accumulating carbon dioxide or the setting adrift of ice shelves from Antarctica. Change arising from some sources, such as volcanic eruptions, can be abrupt—but the climate doesn't flip back just as quickly centuries later.

Temperature records suggest that there is some grand mechanism underlying all of this, and that it has two major states. Again, the difference between them amounts to nine to eighteen degrees—a range that may depend on how much ice there is to slow the responses. I call the colder one the "low state." In discussing the ice ages there is a tendency to think of warm as good—and therefore of warming as better. Alas, further warming might well kick us out of the "high state." It's the high state that's good, and we may need to help prevent any sudden transition to the cold low state.

Although the sun's energy output does flicker slightly, the likeliest reason for these abrupt flips is an intermittent problem in the North Atlantic Ocean, one that seems to trigger a major rearrangement of atmospheric circulation. North-south ocean currents help to redistribute equatorial heat into the temperate zones, supplementing the heat transfer by winds. When the warm currents penetrate farther than usual into the northern seas, they help to melt the sea ice that is reflecting a lot of sunlight back into space, and so the earth becomes warmer. Eventually that helps to melt ice sheets elsewhere.

When that annual flushing fails for some years, the conveyor belt stops moving and so heat stops flowing so far north—and apparently we're popped back into the low state.

The high state of climate seems to involve ocean currents that deliver an extraordinary amount of heat to the vicinity of Iceland and Norway. Like bus routes or conveyor belts, ocean currents must have a return loop. Unlike most ocean currents, the North Atlantic Current has a return loop that runs deep beneath the ocean surface. Huge amounts of seawater sink at known downwelling sites every winter, with the water heading south when it reaches the bottom. When that annual flushing fails for some years, the conveyor belt stops moving and so heat stops flowing so far north—and apparently we're popped back into the low state.

Flushing Cold Surface Water

Surface waters are flushed regularly, even in lakes. Twice a year they sink, carrying their load of atmospheric gases downward. That's because water density changes with temperature. Water is densest at about 39°F (a typical refrigerator setting—anything that you take out of the refrigerator, whether you place it on the kitchen counter or move it to the freezer, is going to expand a little). A lake surface cooling down in the autumn will eventually sink into the less-dense-warmer waters below, mixing things up. Seawater is more complicated, because salt content also helps to determine whether water floats or sinks. Water that evaporates leaves its salt behind; the resulting saltier water is heavier and thus sinks.

The fact that excess salt is flushed from surface waters has global implications, some of them recognized two centuries

Salt sinking on such a grand scale in the Nordic Seas causes warm water to flow much farther north than it might otherwise do.

ago. Salt circulates, because evaporation up north causes it to sink and be carried south by deep currents. This was posited in 1797 by the Anglo-American physicist Sir Benjamin Thompson (later known, after he moved to Bavaria, as Count Rumford of the Holy Roman Empire), who also posited that, if merely to compensate, there would have to be a warmer northbound current as well. By 1961 the oceanographer Henry Stommel, of the Woods Hole Oceanographic Institution, in Massachusetts, was beginning to worry that these warming currents might stop flowing if too much fresh water was added to the surface of the northern seas. By 1987 the geochemist Wallace Broecker, of Columbia University, was piecing together the paleoclimatic flip-flops with the salt-circulation story and warning that small nudges to our climate might produce "unpleasant surprises in the greenhouse."

Oceans are not well mixed at any time. Like a half-beaten cake mix, with strands of egg still visible, the ocean has a lot of blobs and streams within it. When there has been a lot of evaporation, surface waters are saltier than usual. Sometimes they sink to considerable depths without mixing. The Mediterranean waters flowing out of the bottom of the Strait of Gibraltar into the Atlantic Ocean are about 10 percent saltier than the ocean's average, and so they sink into the depths of the Atlantic. A nice little Amazon-sized waterfall flows over the ridge that connects Spain with Morocco, 800 feet below the surface of the strait.

Another underwater ridge line stretches from Greenland to Iceland and on to the Faeroe Islands and Scotland. It, too, has a salty waterfall, which pours the hypersaline bottom waters of the Nordic Seas (the Greenland Sea and the Norwegian Sea) south into the lower levels of the North Atlantic Ocean. This salty waterfall is more like thirty Amazon Rivers combined. Why does it exist? The cold, dry winds blowing eastward off Canada evaporate the surface waters of the North Atlantic Current, and leave behind all their salt. In late winter the heavy surface waters sink en masse. These blobs, pushed down by annual repetitions of these late-winter events, flow south, down near the bottom of the Atlantic. The same thing happens in the Labrador Sea between Canada and the southern tip of Greenland.

Salt sinking on such a grand scale in the Nordic Seas causes warm water to flow much farther north than it might otherwise do. This produces a heat bonus of perhaps 30 percent beyond the heat provided by direct sunlight to these seas, accounting for the mild winters downwind, in northern Europe. It has been called the Nordic Seas heat pump.

Nothing like this happens in the Pacific Ocean, but the Pacific is nonetheless affected, because the sink in the Nordic Seas is part of a vast worldwide salt-conveyor belt. Such a conveyor is needed because the Atlantic is saltier than the

Pacific (the Pacific has twice as much water with which to dilute the salt carried in from rivers). The Atlantic would be even saltier if it didn't mix with the Pacific, in long, loopy currents. These carry the North Atlantic's excess salt southward from the bottom of the Atlantic, around the tip of Africa, through the Indian Ocean, and up around the Pacific Ocean.

There used to be a tropical shortcut, an express route from Atlantic to Pacific, but continental drift connected North America to South America about three million years ago, damming up the easy route for disposing of excess salt. The dam, known as the Isthmus of Panama, may have been what caused the ice ages to begin a short time later, simply because of the forced detour. This major change in ocean circulation, along with a climate that had already been slowly cooling for millions of years, led not only to ice accumulation most of the time but also to climatic instability, with flips every few thousand years or so.

Failures of Flushing

Flying above the clouds often presents an interesting picture when there are mountains below. Out of the sea of undulating white clouds mountain peaks stick up like islands.

Greenland looks like that, even on a cloudless day—but the great white mass between the occasional punctuations is an ice sheet. In places this frozen fresh water descends from the highlands in a wavy staircase.

Twenty thousand years ago a similar ice sheet lay atop the Baltic Sea and the land surrounding it. Another sat on Hudson's Bay, and reached as far west as the foothills of the Rocky Mountains—where it pushed, head to head, against ice coming down from the Rockies. These northern ice sheets were as high as Greenland's mountains, obstacles sufficient to force the jet stream to make a detour.

Now only Greenland's ice remains, but the abrupt cooling in the last warm period shows that a flip can occur in situations much like the present one. What could possibly halt the salt-conveyor belt that brings tropical heat so much farther north and limits the formation of ice sheets? Oceanographers are busy studying present-day failures of annual flushing, which give some perspective on the catastrophic failures of the past.

In the Labrador Sea, flushing failed during the 1970s, was strong again by 1990, and is now declining. In the Greenland Sea over the 1980s salt sinking declined by 80 percent. Obviously, local failures can occur without catastrophe—it's a question of how often and how widespread the failures are—but the present state of decline is not very reassuring. Large-scale flushing at both those sites is certainly a highly variable process, and perhaps a somewhat fragile one as

What could possibly halt the salt-conveyor belt that brings tropical heat so much farther north and limits the formation of ice sheets?

well. And in the absence of a flushing mechanism to sink cooled surface waters and send them southward in the Atlantic, additional warm waters do not flow as far north to replenish the supply.

There are a few obvious precursors to flushing failure. One is diminished wind chill, when winds aren't as strong as usual, or as cold, or as dry—as is the case in the Labrador Sea during the North Atlantic Oscillation. This El Niño-like shift in the atmospheric-circulation pattern over the North Atlantic, from the Azores to Greenland, often lasts a decade. At the same time that the Labrador Sea gets a lessening of the strong winds that aid salt sinking, Europe gets particularly cold winters. It's happening right now: a North Atlantic Oscillation started in 1996.

Another precursor is more floating ice than usual, which reduces the amount of ocean surface exposed to the winds, in turn reducing evaporation. Retained heat eventually melts the ice, in a cycle that recurs about every five years.

Yet another precursor, as Henry Stommel suggested in 1961, would be the addition of fresh water to the ocean surface, diluting the salt-heavy surface waters before they became unstable enough to start sinking. More rain falling in the northern oceans—exactly what is predicted as a result of global warming—could stop salt flushing. So could ice carried south out of the Arctic Ocean.

There is also a great deal of unsalted water in Greenland's glaciers, just uphill from the major salt sinks. The last time an abrupt cooling occurred was in the midst of global warming. Many ice sheets had already half melted, dumping a lot of fresh water into the ocean.

A brief, large flood of fresh water might nudge us toward an abrupt cooling even if the dilution were insignificant when averaged over time. The fjords of Greenland offer some dramatic examples of the possibilities for freshwater floods. Fjords are long, narrow canyons, little arms of the sea reaching many miles inland; they were carved by great glaciers when the sea level was lower. Greenland's east coast has a profusion of fjords between 70°N and 80°N, including one that is the world's biggest. If blocked by ice dams, fjords make perfect reservoirs for meltwater.

Glaciers pushing out into the ocean usually break off in chunks. Whole sections of a glacier, lifted up by the tides, may snap off at the "hinge" and become icebergs. But sometimes a glacial surge will act like an avalanche that blocks a road, as happened when Alaska's Hubbard glacier surged into the Russell fjord in May of 1986. Its snout ran into the opposite side, blocking the fjord with an ice dam. Any meltwater coming in behind the dam stayed there. A lake formed, rising higher and higher—up to the height of an eight-story building.

A brief, large flood of fresh water might nudge us toward an abrupt cooling even if the dilution were insignificant when averaged over time.

Eventually such ice dams break, with spectacular results. Once the dam is breached, the rushing waters erode an ever wider and deeper path. Thus the entire lake can empty quickly. Five months after the ice dam at the Russell fjord formed, it broke, dumping a cubic mile of fresh water in only twenty-four hours.

The Great Salinity Anomaly, a pool of semi-salty water derived from about 500 times as much unsalted water as that released by Russell Lake, was tracked from 1968 to 1982 as it moved south from Greenland's east coast. In 1970 it arrived in the Labrador Sea, where it prevented the usual salt sinking. By 1971–1972 the semi-salty blob was off Newfoundland. It then crossed the Atlantic and passed near the Shetland Islands around 1976. From there it was carried northward by the warm Norwegian Current, whereupon some of it swung west again to arrive off Greenland's east coast—where it had started its inch-per-second journey. So freshwater blobs drift, sometimes causing major trouble, and Greenland floods thus have the potential to stop the enormous heat transfer that keeps the North Atlantic Current going strong.

The Greenhouse Connection

Of this much we're sure: global climate flip-flops have frequently happened in the past, and they're likely to happen again. It's also clear that sufficient global warming could trigger an abrupt cooling in at least two ways—by increasing high-latitude rainfall or by melting Greenland's ice, both of which could put enough fresh water into the ocean surface to suppress flushing.

Further investigation might lead to revisions in such mechanistic explanations, but the result of adding fresh water to the ocean surface is pretty standard physics. In almost four decades of subsequent research Henry Stommel's theory has only been enhanced, not seriously challenged.

Up to this point in the story none of the broad conclusions is particularly speculative. But to address how all these nonlinear mechanisms fit together—and what we might do to stabilize the climate—will require some speculation.

Even the tropics cool down by about nine degrees during an abrupt cooling, and it is hard to imagine what in the past could have disturbed the whole earth's climate on this scale. We must look at arriving sunlight and departing light and heat, not merely regional shifts on earth, to account for changes in the temperature balance. Increasing amounts of sea ice and clouds could reflect more sunlight back into space, but the geochemist Wallace Broecker suggests that a major greenhouse gas is disturbed by the failure of the salt conveyor, and that this affects the amount of heat retained.

In Broecker's view, failures of salt flushing cause a worldwide rearrangement of ocean currents, resulting in—and this

Sufficient global warming could trigger an abrupt cooling in at least two ways—by increasing high-latitude rainfall or by melting Greenland's ice, both of which could put enough fresh water into the ocean surface to suppress flushing.

We must be careful not to think of an abrupt cooling in response to global warming as just another self-regulatory device, a control system for cooling things down when it gets too hot.

is the speculative part—less evaporation from the tropics. That, in turn, makes the air drier. Because water vapor is the most powerful greenhouse gas, this decrease in average humidity would cool things globally. Broecker has written, "If you wanted to cool the planet by 5°C [9°F] and could magically alter the water-vapor content of the atmosphere, a 30 percent decrease would do the job."

Just as an El Niño produces a hotter Equator in the Pacific Ocean and generates more atmospheric convection, so there might be a subnormal mode that decreases heat, convection, and evaporation. For example, I can imagine that ocean currents carrying more warm surface waters north or south from the equatorial regions might, in consequence, cool the Equator somewhat. That might result in less evaporation, creating lower-than-normal levels of greenhouse gases and thus a global cooling.

To see how ocean circulation might affect greenhouse gases, we must try to account quantitatively for important nonlinearities, ones in which little nudges provoke great responses. The modern world is full of objects and systems that exhibit "bistable" modes, with thresholds for flipping. Light switches abruptly change mode when nudged hard enough. Door latches suddenly give way. A gentle pull on a trigger may be ineffective, but there comes a pressure that will suddenly fire the gun. Thermostats tend to activate heating or cooling mechanisms abruptly—also an example of a system that pushes back.

We must be careful not to think of an abrupt cooling in response to global warming as just another self-regulatory device, a control system for cooling things down when it gets too hot. The scale of the response will be far beyond the bounds of regulation—more like when excess warming triggers fire extinguishers in the ceiling, ruining the contents of the room while cooling them down.

Preventing Climate Flips

Though combating global warming is obviously on the agenda for preventing a cold flip, we could easily be blindsided by stability problems if we allow global warming per se to remain the main focus of our climate-change efforts. To stabilize our flip-flopping climate we'll need to identify all the important feedbacks that control climate and ocean currents—evaporation, the reflection of sunlight back into space, and so on—and then estimate their relative strengths and interactions in computer models.

Feedbacks are what determine thresholds, where one mode flips into another. Near a threshold one can sometimes observe abortive responses, rather like the act of stepping back onto a curb several times before finally running across a busy street. Abortive responses and rapid chattering between modes are common problems in nonlinear systems with not quite enough oomph—the reason that old fluorescent lights flicker. To keep a bistable system firmly in one state or the other, it should be kept away from the transition threshold.

We need to make sure that no business-as-usual climate variation, such as an El Niño or the North Atlantic Oscillation, can push our climate onto the slippery slope and into an abrupt cooling. Of particular importance are combinations of climate variations—this winter, for example, we are experiencing both an El Niño and a North Atlantic Oscillation—because such combinations can add up to much more than the sum of their parts.

We are near the end of a warm period in any event; ice ages return even without human influences on climate. The last warm period abruptly terminated 13,000 years after the abrupt warming that initiated it, and we've already gone 15,000 years from a similar starting point. But we may be able to do something to delay an abrupt cooling.

Do something? This tends to stagger the imagination, immediately conjuring up visions of terraforming on a science-fiction scale—and so we shake our heads and say, "Better to fight global warming by consuming less," and so forth.

Surprisingly, it may prove possible to prevent flip-flops in the climate—even by means of low-tech schemes. Keeping the present climate from falling back into the low state will in any case be a lot easier than trying to reverse such a change after it has occurred. Were fjord floods causing flushing to fail, because the downwelling sites were fairly close to the fjords, it is obvious that we could solve the problem. All we would need to do is open a channel through the ice dam with explosives before dangerous levels of water built up.

Timing could be everything, given the delayed effects from inch-per-second circulation patterns, but that, too, potentially has a low-tech solution: build dams across the major fjord systems and hold back the meltwater at critical times. Or divert eastern-Greenland meltwater to the less sensitive north and west coasts.

Fortunately, big parallel computers have proved useful for both global climate modeling and detailed modeling of ocean circulation. They even show the flips. Computer models might not yet be able to predict what will happen if we tamper with downwelling sites, but this problem doesn't seem insoluble. We need more well-trained people, bigger computers, more coring of the ocean floor and silted-up lakes, more ships to drag instrument packages through the depths, more instrumented buoys to study critical sites in detail, more satellites measuring regional variations in the sea surface, and perhaps some small-scale trial runs of interventions.

It would be especially nice to see another dozen major groups of scientists doing climate simulations, discovering the intervention mistakes as quickly as possible and learning

Of particular importance are combinations of climate variations—this winter, for example, we are experiencing both an El Niño and a North Atlantic Oscillation—because such combinations can add up to much more than the sum of their parts.

from them. Medieval cathedral builders learned from their design mistakes over the centuries, and their undertakings were a far larger drain on the economic resources and people power of their day than anything yet discussed for stabilizing the climate in the twenty-first century. We may not have centuries to spare, but any economy in which two percent of the population produces all the food, as is the case in the United States today, has lots of resources and many options for reordering priorities.

Three Scenarios

Futurists have learned to bracket the future with alternative scenarios, each of which captures important features that cluster together, each of which is compact enough to be seen as a narrative on a human scale. Three scenarios for the next climatic phase might be called population crash, cheap fix, and muddling through.

Three scenarios for the next climatic phase might be called population crash, cheap fix, and muddling through.

The population-crash scenario is surely the most appalling. Plummeting crop yields would cause some powerful countries to try to take over their neighbors or distant lands—if only because their armies, unpaid and lacking food, would go marauding, both at home and across the borders. The better-organized countries would attempt to use their armies, before they fell apart entirely, to take over countries with significant remaining resources, driving out or starving their inhabitants if not using modern weapons to accomplish the same end: eliminating competitors for the remaining food.

This would be a worldwide problem—and could lead to a Third World War—but Europe's vulnerability is particularly easy to analyze. The last abrupt cooling, the Younger Dryas, drastically altered Europe's climate as far east as Ukraine. Present-day Europe has more than 650 million people. It has excellent soils, and largely grows its own food. It could no longer do so if it lost the extra warming from the North Atlantic.

There is another part of the world with the same good soil, within the same latitudinal band, which we can use for a quick comparison. Canada lacks Europe's winter warmth and rainfall, because it has no equivalent of the North Atlantic Current to preheat its eastbound weather systems. Canada's agriculture supports about 28 million people. If Europe had weather like Canada's, it could feed only one out of twenty-three present-day Europeans.

Any abrupt switch in climate would also disrupt food-supply routes. The only reason that two percent of our population can feed the other 98 percent is that we have a well-developed system of transportation and middlemen—but it is not very robust. The system allows for large urban populations in the best of times, but not in the case of widespread disruptions.

Natural disasters such as hurricanes and earthquakes are less troubling than abrupt coolings for two reasons: they're short (the recovery period starts the next day) and they're local or regional (unaffected citizens can help the overwhelmed). There is, increasingly, international cooperation in response to catastrophe—but no country is going to be able to rely on a stored agricultural surplus for even a year, and any country will be reluctant to give away part of its surplus.

In an abrupt cooling the problem would get worse for decades, and much of the earth would be affected. A meteor strike that killed most of the population in a month would not be as serious as an abrupt cooling that eventually killed just as many. With the population crash spread out over a decade, there would be ample opportunity for civilization's institutions to be torn apart and for hatreds to build, as armies tried to grab remaining resources simply to feed the people in their own countries. The effects of an abrupt cold last for centuries. They might not be the end of *Homo sapiens*—written knowledge and elementary education might well endure—but the world after such a population crash would certainly be full of despotic governments that hated their neighbors because of recent atrocities. Recovery would be very slow.

It is possible that solutions could turn out to be cheap and easy, and that another abrupt cooling isn't inevitable.

A slightly exaggerated version of our present know-something-do-nothing state of affairs is know-nothing-do-nothing: a reduction in science as usual, further limiting our chances of discovering a way out. History is full of withdrawals from knowledge-seeking, whether for reasons of fundamentalism, fatalism, or "government lite" economics. This scenario does not require that the shortsighted be in charge, only that they have enough influence to put the relevant science agencies on starvation budgets and to send recommendations back for yet another commission report due five years hence.

A cheap-fix scenario, such as building or bombing a dam, presumes that we know enough to prevent trouble, or to nip a developing problem in the bud. But just as vaccines and antibiotics presume much knowledge about diseases, their climatic equivalents presume much knowledge about oceans, atmospheres, and past climates. Suppose we had reports that winter salt flushing was confined to certain areas, that abrupt shifts in the past were associated with localized flushing failures, and that one computer model after another suggested a solution that was likely to work even under a wide range of weather extremes. A quick fix, such as bombing an ice dam, might then be possible. Although I don't consider this scenario to be the most likely one, it is possible that solutions could turn out to be cheap and easy, and that another abrupt cooling isn't inevitable. Fatalism, in other words, might well be foolish.

A muddle-through scenario assumes that we would mobilize our scientific and technological resources well in advance of any abrupt cooling problem, but that the solution wouldn't be simple. Instead we would try one thing after another, creating a patchwork of solutions that might hold for another few decades, allowing the search for a better stabilizing mechanism to continue.

We might, for example, anchor bargeloads of evaporation-enhancing surfactants (used in the southwest corner of the Dead Sea to speed potash production) upwind from critical downwelling sites, letting winds spread them over the ocean surface all winter, just to ensure later flushing. We might create a rain shadow, seeding clouds so that they dropped their unsalted water well upwind of a given year's critical flushing sites—a strategy that might be particularly important in view of the increased rainfall expected from global warming. We might undertake to regulate the Mediterranean's salty outflow, which is also thought to disrupt the North Atlantic Current.

Only the most naive gamblers bet against physics, and only the most irresponsible bet with their grandchildren's resources.

Perhaps computer simulations will tell us that the only robust solutions are those that re-create the ocean currents of three million years ago, before the Isthmus of Panama closed off the express route for excess-salt disposal. Thus we might dig a wide sea-level Panama Canal in stages, carefully managing the changeover.

Staying in the "Comfort Zone"

Stabilizing our flip-flopping climate is not a simple matter. We need heat in the right places, such as the Greenland Sea, and not in others right next door, such as Greenland itself. Man-made global warming is likely to achieve exactly the opposite—warming Greenland and cooling the Greenland Sea.

A remarkable amount of specious reasoning is often encountered when we contemplate reducing carbon-dioxide emissions. That increased quantities of greenhouse gases will lead to global warming is as solid a scientific prediction as can be found, but other things influence climate too, and some people try to escape confronting the consequences of our pumping more and more greenhouse gases into the atmosphere by supposing that something will come along miraculously to counteract them. Volcanos spew sulfates, as do our own smokestacks, and these reflect some sunlight back into space, particularly over the North Atlantic and Europe. But we can't assume that anything like this will counteract our longer-term flurry of carbon-dioxide emissions. Only the most naive gamblers bet against physics, and only the most irresponsible bet with their grandchildren's resources.

To the long list of predicted consequences of global warming—stronger storms, methane release, habitat changes, ice-sheet melting, rising seas, stronger El Niños, killer heat waves—we must now add an abrupt, catastrophic cooling. Whereas the familiar consequences of global warming will force expensive but gradual adjustments, the abrupt cooling promoted by man-made warming looks like a particularly efficient means of committing mass suicide.

We cannot avoid trouble by merely cutting down on our present warming trend, though that's an excellent place to start. Paleoclimatic records reveal that any notion we may once have had that the climate will remain the same unless pollution changes it is wishful thinking. Judging from the duration of the last warm period, we are probably near the end of the current one. Our goal must be to stabilize the climate in its favorable mode and ensure that enough equatorial heat continues to flow into the waters around Greenland and Norway. A stabilized climate must have a wide "comfort zone," and be able to survive the El Niños of the short term. We can design for that in computer models of climate, just as architects design earthquake-resistant skyscrapers. Implementing it might cost no more, in relative terms, than building a medieval cathedral. But we may not have centuries for acquiring wisdom, and it would be wise to compress our learning into the years immediately ahead. We have to discover what has made the climate of the past 8,000 years relatively stable, and then figure out how to prop it up.

Those who will not reason
Perish in the act:
Those who will not act
Perish for that reason.
—W. H. Auden

Warm-Blooded Plants and Freeze-Dried Fish[2]

When emigration from Earth to a planet or a comet becomes cheap enough for ordinary people to afford, people will emigrate.

About twelve years ago I visited the Johnson Space Center, in Houston, and climbed around in the space shuttle that is kept there for visitors to examine. That was before the *Challenger* disaster, when the shuttle was advertised as a safe ride for congressmen and schoolteachers. What impressed me about the shuttle was the immense quantity of stuff on board for the care and comfort of human passengers. It felt more like a hotel or a hospital than a rocket ship. I made rough calculations of how many tons of material were needed to keep seven passengers alive and well for a couple of weeks. I was thinking, Why don't we rip all this out and fly the thing from the ground by remote control?

At that time most of the shuttle missions were carrying unmanned satellites into orbit for various purposes—some scientific, some commercial, and some military. These launching jobs could just as well have been done automatically. Only a few of the shuttle missions really need people on board, to do experiments or to repair the Hubble Space Telescope, for example. It would have made sense to reserve two shuttle ships with all their hotel equipment for missions in which people were essential and to use the other two for satellite-launching jobs. A freight-only version of the shuttle could carry bigger payloads for less money than the passenger version, without risking any lives. Unfortunately, when I suggested this to people at Houston, they did not think it was a good idea. Their whole existence is centered on the training of astronauts and the operation of manned missions.

After failing to eviscerate the shuttle, I wandered into the museum of the Johnson Space Center, where there is a collection of rocks that astronauts brought back from the Moon. Many of the Moon rocks have been lent to scientists in other places, but a large number remain in Houston. Scientists who are interested in Moon rocks are usually also interested in meteorites: their tools for analyzing meteorites work on Moon rocks as well. The space-center museum has a fine collection of meteorites, too, some of which were sitting in glass cases next to the Moon rocks. Among them were two from Mars.

---

2. Article by Freeman J. Dyson from the *Atlantic*. Nov. 1997. Copyright © 1997 the Atlantic Monthly Company. Reprinted with permission.

It seemed like a miracle. Here I was, in the museum in Houston, twelve inches away from a piece of Mars, with only a thin pane of glass to stop me from grabbing hold of it. In those days the National Aeronautics and Space Administration was talking seriously about grandiose missions to Mars, costing many billions of dollars. One of the reasons for going to Mars was to bring back samples of rock for scientists to analyze. And here were samples of Mars rock already in Houston, provided by nature free of charge. I found it odd that nobody seemed to be studying them. As far as I could tell, I was the only person in Houston who was excited about the Mars rocks. I stood and gazed at them for a long time. Nobody else came to look at them. I remarked to the NASA people that they might usefully spend some time studying the Mars rocks they already had, instead of planning billion-dollar missions to collect more. At that time the administrators in Houston seemed little interested in anything that did not cost billions of dollars.

Things have changed since then. Now NASA is interested in cheap missions, and many more scientists are interested in Mars rocks. Last year some of the rocks were examined more thoroughly than ever before. Two contain chemical traces that might be interpreted as evidence of ancient life on Mars, and scientists have also found microscopic structures that might be relics of ancient microbes. The evidence that these traces have anything to do with biology is highly dubious; we cannot say on the basis of it that life must have existed on Mars. These traces are important for two other reasons. First, if we are seriously interested in finding evidence of life on Mars, we now know that Mars rocks on Earth are the most convenient place to look for it. Instead of waiting for many years for an expensive sampling mission to land on Mars and return a few small chips of rock to Earth, we can find a supply of bigger chips lying in Antarctica, where meteorites accumulate on the ice and are freely available. Second, these rocks show that if life was established on Mars at any time in the past, it could have been transported to Earth intact. In the first billion years after the solar system was formed, when Mars had a warm climate and abundant water, asteroid impacts were much more frequent than they are now. Mars rocks fell on Earth in great numbers, and many Earth rocks must also have fallen on Mars. We should not be surprised if we find that life, wherever it originated, spread rapidly from one planet to another. Whatever creatures we may find on Mars will probably be either our ancestors or our cousins.

We should not be surprised if we find that life, wherever it originated, spread rapidly from one planet to another.

The Europa Ocean

Another place where life might now be flourishing is in a deep ocean on Jupiter's satellite Europa. Jupiter has four large satellites, discovered almost 400 years ago by Galileo:

Of all the worlds that we have explored beyond Earth, Mars and Europa are the most promising places to look for life.

Io, Europa, Ganymede, and Callisto, in order of their increasing distance from Jupiter. The *Galileo* spacecraft now orbiting Jupiter is sending back splendid pictures of the satellites. The new pictures of Europa show a smooth, icy surface with many large cracks but very few craters. It looks as if the ice is floating on a liquid ocean and being fractured from time to time by movements of the water underneath. The pictures are strikingly similar to some pictures of the ice that floats on the Arctic Ocean; it would not be surprising if Europa had a warm ocean under the ice. Io is blazing hot, with active volcanoes on its surface; Ganymede's surface is icy like Europa's but not so smooth; and Callisto looks like a solid ball of ice covered with ancient craters. All four satellites are heated internally by the tidal effects of the huge mass of Jupiter, but the internal heating falls off rapidly with distance from Jupiter. We should expect that below the surface Europa is much cooler than Io and much warmer than Ganymede and Callisto. Since Io is hot enough to boil away all its water, and Callisto is cold enough to freeze solid, Europa might well have a warm liquid ocean. Ganymede might also have a liquid ocean, but it would be covered by a much thicker layer of ice. Of all the worlds that we have explored beyond Earth, Mars and Europa are the most promising places to look for life.

To land a spacecraft on Europa, with the heavy equipment needed to penetrate the ice and explore the ocean directly, would be a formidable undertaking. A direct search for life in Europa's ocean would today be prohibitively expensive. But just as asteroid and comet impacts on Mars have given us an easier way to look for evidence of life on that planet, impacts on Europa give us an easier way to look for evidence of life there. Every time a major impact occurs on Europa, a vast quantity of water is splashed from the ocean into the space around Jupiter. Some of the water evaporates, and some condenses into snow. Creatures living in the water far enough from the impact have a chance of being splashed intact into space and quickly freeze-dried. Therefore, an easy way to look for evidence of life in Europa's ocean is to look for freeze-dried fish in the ring of space debris orbiting Jupiter. Sending a spacecraft to visit and survey Jupiter's ring would be far less expensive than sending a submarine to visit and survey Europa's ocean. Even if we did not find freeze-dried fish in Jupiter's ring, we might find other surprises— freeze-dried seaweed, or a freeze-dried sea monster.

Freeze-dried fish orbiting Jupiter is a fanciful notion, but nature in the biological realm has a tendency to be fanciful. Nature is usually more imaginative than we are. Nobody in Europe ever imagined a bird of paradise or a duck-billed platypus before it was discovered by explorers. Even after the platypus was discovered and a specimen brought to London, several learned experts declared it to be a fake. Many of nature's most beautiful creations might be dismissed as wildly improbable if they were not known to exist. When we are exploring the universe and looking for evidence of life, either we may look for things that are probable but hard to detect or we may look for things that are improbable but easy to detect. In deciding what to look for, detectability is at least as useful a criterion as probability. Primitive organisms such as bacteria and algae hidden underground may be more probable, but freeze-dried fish in orbit are more detectable. To have the best chance of success, we should keep our eyes open for all possibilities.

A similar logic suggests warm-blooded plants as a reasonable target in the search for life on the surface of Mars. By "warm-blooded" I do not mean that the plant will have a circulatory system or a precise temperature control. I mean only that the plant will be able to keep its internal temperature within the normal range of a cool greenhouse, roughly freezing to 80° Fahrenheit. Any form of life that survived on Mars from the early, warm and wet era to the present, cold and dry era had two alternatives: either it adopted an entirely subterranean lifestyle, retreating deep underground to places where liquid water could be found, or it remained on the surface and learned to protect itself against cold and dryness by growing around itself an insulating greenhouse to maintain a warm and moist environment. The first alternative is more likely but would be much more difficult to detect. Organisms living deep underground, without sunlight, would probably be microscopic, like the bacteria that live deep in the earth. To find such organisms would require deep drilling and heavy machinery. The second alternative, though less likely, would be easier to detect. The two missions that arrived at Mars this year—the *Pathfinder*, landing on the surface, and the *Global Surveyor*, remaining in orbit— are not intended to detect living greenhouses or other possible forms of life. Their purpose is to explore the planet in a general way and to raise questions that later missions could answer.

Many species of terrestrial plants, including the skunk cabbage that sprouts in February in the woods of Princeton, New Jersey, where I live, are warm-blooded to a limited extent. For about two weeks the skunk cabbage maintains a warm temperature by rapidly metabolizing starch stored inside the part of its anatomy known as the spadix, which contains the hidden flowers with their male and female structures. According to folklore, the spadix is warm enough to melt snow around it. The evolutionary advantage of warm-bloodedness to the plant is probably that it attracts small beetles or other insects that linger in the spadix and pollinate the flowers. The spadix is not a greenhouse, and the supply of starch is not sufficient to maintain a warm temperature year-round. No terrestrial plants are able to stay

A similar logic suggests warm-blooded plants as a reasonable target in the search for life on the surface of Mars.

*Human coloniza-
tion of the solar
system would
not be primarily
a scientific
enterprise; it
would be driven
by motivations
that go far
beyond science.*

warm through an Arctic winter. On Earth polar bears can flourish in colder climates than trees can. It seems to be an accident of history that warm-blooded animals evolved on Earth to colonize cold climates, whereas warm-blooded plants did not. On Mars plants might have been pushed to yet more drastic adaptations.

Plants could grow greenhouses (so far the idea remains a theory) just as turtles grow shell and polar bears grow fur and polyps build coral reefs in tropical seas. These plants could keep warm by the light from a distant Sun and conserve the oxygen that they produce by photosynthesis. The greenhouse would consist of a thick skin providing thermal insulation, with small transparent windows to admit sunlight. Outside the skin would be an array of simple lenses, focusing sunlight through the windows into the interior. The windows would have to be small, to limit the loss of heat from outward radiation. The plant would also need deep roots, to tap water and nutrients from warmer layers underground. Inside the greenhouse the plant could grow leaves and flowers in an oxygen-containing habitat where aerobic microbes and animals might also live. Groups of greenhouses could grow together to form extended habitats for other species of plants and animals. An attendant community of microbes and fungi might help the plants to extract nutrients from the local ice or soil. Pores in the outer skin of the greenhouse might open to admit carbon dioxide from the atmosphere outside, with miniature airlocks and cold traps to keep losses of oxygen and water to a minimum.

If warm-blooded plants exist on Mars, they may or may not be easy to see. We cannot predict whether they would stand out from their surroundings in a visual or photographic survey. Two clues to their presence would almost certainly be detectable: leakage of heat and leakage of oxygen. Neither thermal insulation nor atmospheric containment is likely to be perfect. If we looked for heat radiation from anomalously warm patches on the Martian surface at night, or for anomalous local traces of oxygen in the atmosphere in daytime, we might find places where warm-blooded plants are hiding.

That we might find warm-blooded plants living wild on Mars or elsewhere in the solar system, it must be admitted, is only a remote possibility. It is much more likely that we will find Mars to be sterile, or inhabited only by subterranean microbes. In that case warm-blooded plants could be important in a different way—as a tool for human settlement. I now leave the subject of science to talk about human space travel and colonization. Human colonization of the solar system would not be primarily a scientific enterprise; it would be driven by motivations that go far beyond science.

Confusion of Aims

The space-shuttle program was in trouble even before the *Challenger* accident, because it was based on a confusion of aims. It was trying both to open the way to human adventure in space and to serve as a practical launch system for scientific, commercial, and military missions. As I saw when I climbed into the shuttle at Houston, the two aims were never compatible. The shuttle was the result of a political compromise between people who wanted a reliable freight service into space and people who wanted to keep alive the tradition of the manned *Apollo* missions to the Moon. No single vehicle could do both jobs well. The shuttle tried, but it was too expensive for the first and too limited in its performance for the second.

In the future the two aims of the space program will be pursued separately. The twenty years since the birth of the shuttle have seen spectacular progress in the technologies of data processing, remote sensing, and autonomous navigation. With these technologies almost all the practical needs of science, commerce, and national security are now better served by unmanned missions than by the shuttle.

The future shape of a manned program pursuing idealistic aims is the great unknown. The shuttle is inadequate as a vehicle for human adventure. It resembles a Greyhound bus rather than a Land Rover. Another spending spree like the one for *Apollo* would be inadequate, even if it were politically possible. Does the manned space program have a future?

Does the manned space program have a future?

The confusion of aims afflicting the space program from the beginning was in essence a confusion of time frames. The practical aims of scientific and military activities in space made sense in a time frame of ten years; the basic technology for unmanned space missions took only ten years to develop. The aim of opening the skies to human exploration and adventure makes sense in a time frame of a hundred years—what it will probably take to develop the technologies needed for significant numbers of human explorers to roam space at a price that earthbound citizens will consider reasonable. The *Apollo* missions, tied to a ten-year time frame, gave a false start to human exploration. They were far too costly to be sustained, and at the end of the ten-year program they had reached a dead end. If it had been made clear from the beginning that manned exploration would be a hundred-year program—one with a stable and affordable budget—we might by now have a light two-passenger spacecraft instead of the shuttle. We might already have a few people learning how to live permanently on the Moon, using only local resources.

We are now at the beginning of a revolution in space technology, when for the first time cheapness will be mandatory. Missions that are not cheap will not fly. This is bad news for space explorers in the short run and good news in the long run. Finally cheapness has a chance. Missions to the planets have been few and far between in the past ten years because

The chief problem for a manned mission is not getting there but learning how to survive after arrival.

they became inordinately expensive; they were expensive because of an imbalance in funding between ground-based and space-based science. For thirty years it was easier politically to obtain ten dollars for a space-science mission than to obtain one dollar for astronomy on the ground. The unfair competition injured both parties, starving ground-based astronomy and spoiling space science. The injury to space science was greater: ground-based astronomy flourished in spite of starvation, while planetary missions almost came to a halt in spite of big budgets. The rules are now changing, in the direction of fair competition between ground and space. This means that in the future space missions will be cheap. Once the barrier of high cost is broken, missions will be more frequent and the pace of discovery will be faster.

The essential first step in making either unmanned or manned operations cheap is to eliminate the standing army of people at Mission Control who take care of communication with spacecraft day after day. Spacecraft and the instruments they carry must become completely autonomous. The second step is to develop new technologies for launching payloads into space cheaply. The current Mars missions are making only small steps toward these goals. The coming era of cheap space operations will begin with unmanned missions, which will exercise the new technologies of propulsion and operation. Cheap manned missions will come later. Cheap unmanned missions require only new engineering; cheap manned missions will require new biotechnology. The chief problem for a manned mission is not getting there but learning how to survive after arrival. Surviving and making a home away from Earth are problems of biology rather than of engineering.

No law of physics or biology forbids cheap travel and settlement all over the solar system and beyond. But it is impossible to predict how long this will take. Predictions of the dates of future achievements are notoriously fallible. My guess is that the era of cheap unmanned missions will be the next fifty years, and the era of cheap manned missions will start sometime late in the twenty-first century. The time these things will take depends on unforeseeable accidents of history and politics. My date for the beginning of cheap manned exploration and settlement is based on a historical analogy: from Columbus's first voyage across the Atlantic to the settlement of the Pilgrims in Massachusetts was 128 years. So I am guessing that in 2085, 128 years after the launch of the first *Sputnik*, the private settlement of pilgrims all over the solar system will begin.

Learning to Live in the Universe

The main lesson I draw from the history of space activity in this century is that we must clearly separate short-term from long-term aims. The dream of expanding the domain of life from Earth into the universe makes sense only as a long-term goal. Any affordable program of manned exploration must be centered in biology, and its time frame tied to the time frame of biotechnology; a hundred years, roughly the time it will take us to learn to grow warm-blooded plants, is probably reasonable. The people who decide to go to Mars or Europa will know whether or not indigenous life exists there. If it does exist, they will know how to nurture and protect it when they come to build their own habitats. If it does not, they will bring new life to make good nature's lack.

The most important part of their baggage will be the seeds of plants and animals genetically engineered to survive in an alien climate. On a world that has only a thin atmosphere, like Mars, or no atmosphere at all, like Europa, the most useful seeds will be the seeds of warm-blooded plants. After a hundred years of development of genetic engineering, we will know how to write the DNA to make plants grow greenhouses. Plants as large as trees could grow greenhouses big enough for human beings to live in. If the human settlers are wise, they will arrive to move into homes already prepared for them by an ecology of warm-blooded plants and animals introduced by earlier, unmanned missions.

Why should anybody wish to live on Mars or Europa?

Warm-blooded plants will not by themselves solve all our problems. The essential requirement for a successful human colony will be a deep understanding of the local ecology, so that human beings can become a part of it without destroying it. The Biosphere 2 experiment in Arizona, in which eight people tried unsuccessfully to live in a closed ecology for two years, was not a failure but a valuable object lesson. It taught us how human beings without sufficient understanding of their habitat could unexpectedly run out of oxygen.

Why should anybody wish to live on Mars or Europa? The only answer we can give to this question is the answer that George Mallory gave to the question why he wanted to climb Mount Everest: "Because it is there." There may be economic, scientific, or sentimental reasons attracting people to remote places; people always have a variety of reasons for moving from one place to another. One of the few constant factors in human history is migration, often over huge distances for reasons that are difficult to discern. I have little doubt that as soon as emigration from Earth becomes cheap enough for ordinary people to afford, people will emigrate. To make human space travel cheap, we will need advanced biotechnology in addition to advanced propulsion systems. And we will need a large number of travelers, to bring down the cost of a ticket. These are the reasons human space travel will not be cheap until fifty or a hundred years have gone by.

The most important fact about the geography of the solar system is that the habitable surface area is almost all on small objects—asteroids and comets—rather than on planets. Planets have most of the mass but very little of the surface area. Asteroids are usually rock, and orbit in the inner part of the solar system, inside the orbit of Jupiter. Comets are usually ice, and orbit in the outer part of the solar system, farther from the Sun than Neptune. Comets of average size are visible from Earth only on the rare occasions when gravitational perturbations cause them to fall close to the Sun and their volatile surfaces boil off to form bright tails in the sky.

Comets are more significant than asteroids in the ecology of the solar system, and a huge swarm of them can be found in a ring-shaped region called the Kuiper Belt, outside the orbit of Neptune. Only in the past few years have some of the largest Kuiper Belt objects been seen, first with ground telescopes in Hawaii and more recently with the Hubble Space Telescope. According to my rough estimate, the total surface area of the trillions of objects in the Kuiper Belt is about a thousand times the area of Earth.

Why are comets of greater ecological interest than asteroids? First, they are vastly more numerous. Second, ice is better than rock as a basis for life, and comets contain not only ice but also most of the other chemical elements that are essential for biology. Third, the orbital speeds of comets are much slower than the speeds of asteroids. The Kuiper Belt may seem to us today to be a cold and inhospitable place, but it is probably less inhospitable to life than Mars. It has the advantage of being an archipelago—a collection of small, habitable islands not too far apart from one another. Because their relative speeds are slow, communication and travel between islands would be easy. If you were living on a mile-wide comet in the Kuiper Belt, another mile-wide object would pass by within a million miles about once a month, on average. Objects a hundred yards wide would pass by within this distance every day. It would take only a few days, using a small spacecraft with a modest propulsion system, to hop over and visit neighbors or replenish supplies. If you were bored by the scenery or unhappy with your family, you could move permanently and try your luck on another comet, just as colonists moved to Providence and places west.

If a community occupying a Kuiper Belt object outgrew its habitat and wished to expand, it could increase its living space by attaching tethers to neighboring objects as they floated by.

If a community occupying a Kuiper Belt object outgrew its habitat and wished to expand, it could increase its living space by attaching tethers to neighboring objects as they floated by. A metropolis could grow in the twenty-second century by the accretion of objects as rapidly as Chicago or San Francisco grew in the nineteenth by the accretion of real estate. A Kuiper Belt metropolis would probably be a flat, disk-shaped collection of cometary objects, linked by long tethers and revolving slowly around the center to keep the tethers taut. To continue the accretion of desirable properties while avoiding destructive impacts, a metropolitan border patrol would engage in an interesting game of celestial billiards, tracking approaching objects with telescopes, nudging them gently with space tugs, and hooking them with tethers.

Recently the inhabitants of Earth have become aware that our planet is exposed to occasional impacts of asteroids and comets that may cause worldwide devastation. The most famous such impact occurred 65 million years ago, in Mexico, and may have been responsible for the demise of the dinosaurs. During the next hundred years, as the technologies of astronomical surveillance and space propulsion move forward, it is likely that active intervention to protect Earth from future impacts will become feasible. We may see a mutually profitable merger of the space-science enterprise with the business of planet protection. The cost of protection would be modest, provided that the warning time before an impact was as long as a hundred years. To deflect an orbiting object enough to cause it to miss Earth, a slow, steady push applied by a solar-powered engine would be much more effective than a nuclear explosion. With a hundred-year warning time the power required for the steady push would be only about two kilowatts for an average-size comet, with a mass of a billion tons. Two kilowatts is power on a human, not an astronomical, scale. Even as far from the Sun as the Kuiper Belt there is enough power in sunlight to supply two kilowatts with a solar collector of reasonable size. Once human communities were established in the Kuiper Belt, their border patrol would be in a position to offer its services to Earth, to detect objects that threatened to collide with Earth and deflect them in timely fashion at minimal cost.

Another service that Kuiper Belt communities might provide for human beings on Earth is scientific exploration. The belt contains enough unknown objects to keep explorers busy for thousands of years. The comets are cold and ancient enough to preserve detailed records of the formation and early history of the solar system. It is likely that we would find objects there that are older than the Sun. It should be possible to trace the history of our system back into the pre-solar era.

It could well happen that within a few hundred years most of the inhabitants of the solar system will be living in the Kuiper Belt. Accustomed as we are to living on a high-gravity planet close to the Sun, it is difficult for us to imagine what it would be like to live with low gravity far away. One of the first steps a human colony would take to establish itself in the Kuiper Belt would be to surround its cometary habitat with an extended efflorescence of mirrors in space to collect sunlight. An array of mirrors sixty miles in diameter could collect a steady thousand megawatts of energy anywhere in the Kuiper Belt, out to three times the distance of Neptune from the Sun. That is enough energy to sustain a considerable population of plants, animals, and human beings with all modern conveniences. The mirrors would not have to be optically perfect. The material out of which to construct them, a few thousand tons of metal or plastic, would proba-

One of the first steps a human colony would take to establish itself in the Kuiper Belt would be to surround its cometary habitat with an extended efflorescence of mirrors in space to collect sunlight.

bly be available on any Kuiper Belt object. After a century of progress in biotechnology we would not need to manufacture the mirrors. We would teach our plants to grow them.

Life in the Kuiper Belt would be different from life on Earth, but not necessarily less beautiful or more confined. After a century or two there would be metropolitan centers, cultural monuments, urban sprawl—all the glories and discontents of a high civilization. Soon restless spirits would find the Kuiper Belt too crowded. But there would be an open frontier and a vast wilderness beyond. Beyond the Kuiper Belt lies a more extended swarm of comets—the Oort Cloud, farther away from the Sun and still untamed.

Should Kurdistan Be a Nation? Scotland? How about New York City?[3]

In 1950, there were 58 nations in the U.N. Today, there are 185. If that rate of proliferation continues for another century, the U.N. or its successor will have nearly 2,000 members. Imagine some of the new governments, replete with flags, anthems, national birds, and Olympic bobsledders: Scotland. Quebec. Palestine. Kosovo. Tibet. Kashmir. South Ossetia. Kurdistan. Timor. Biafra. New York City.

Countries are fractured into new nations by two global forces that were supposed to pull everyone together: the Internet and the global economy. The Net, often seen as a force for universalism, actually makes nationalism easier to express and share. Basque or Quebecker Web pages abound, concentrating the power of breakaway elements.

Too often in the 21st century, the birth of nations will be violent.

At the same time, the globalization of the economy enables small fry to go it alone. With open trade, countries with something valuable to sell can break away from bigger neighbors and support themselves. They don't even need their own money supplies. Even old-time powers like France and Germany are dropping their national currencies. And with regional security umbrellas, small countries needn't bother with their own armed forces.

If the Basques of northern Spain won independence, for instance, they would promptly file for membership in the European Union, adopt the euro as a currency, and maintain virtually open borders with neighboring Spain and France. Little would change. In fact, the clamor for independence is intensifying. Already, the Basque language, after being suppressed by dictator Francisco Franco, is flourishing.

NEW BALKANS. The problem is that Spain won't let them go. If the Basques are allowed to break off, the Spanish government argues, then the Catalonians (centered in Barcelona) and the Galicians will want out, too. Suddenly, Spain could be torn from top to bottom by ethnic rivalries.

Too often in the 21st century, the birth of nations will be violent. The same welling up of nationalism that gives rise to new countries also produces a reaction from mother countries that don't want to give up parts of themselves. China refuses to cede Taiwan. Israel hangs on to the West Bank, Indonesia to East Timor. Imagine the horror of Yugoslavia's breakup repeated over and over in the century to come. If every would-be nation in the world were to assert indepen-

---

3. Article by Stephen Baker from *Business Week* Aug. 30, 1999. Copyright © 1999 *Business Week*. Reprinted with permission.

dence, the bloodbath would be "unimaginable," says Boston University international relations professor David Fromkin, author of *The Way of the World: From the Dawn of Civilizations to the Eve of the 21st Century.*

All this talk of blood and soil seems irrelevant to globe-trotting multinationalists, whose world revolves around conference tables, laptop computers, frequent-flier miles, and stock options. These globalists speak the cool, rational language of money. But such people are in the minority. Nationalists, like Yugoslavia's Slobodan Milosevic, speak of ancient loyalties and grievances, and theirs is the language that stirs the blood among people whose allegiances are local and tribal.

It may be possible to accommodate nationalistic fervor in a relatively civilized fashion. Great Britain, for instance, has granted a form of home rule to the Scots and Welsh without undue trauma. But even in Britain, there are fears that one effect of the semisplit will be to isolate Scotland and Wales from the world economy.

The poor nations of the world could break, like vases on the floor, into thousands of pieces.

The risk is that as advanced information societies such as the U.S. and Western Europe form transnational confederations, regions that are left out of the confederations will go in the opposite direction. They may become even more nationalistic, more torn by violence. The poor nations of the world could break, like vases on the floor, into thousands of pieces.

The Future of War[4]

As the conflict in Kosovo makes clear, war is still a fact of human life. But NATO's strategy in Yugoslavia has also demonstrated the limits of high-tech warfare. Those issues are only too familiar to Ralph Peters, a recently retired U.S. army lieutenant-colonel who has visited more than 40 countries examining conflict and security threats. The author of eight novels with geopolitical themes, including his latest, Traitor *(Avon Books), published this month, Peters has also written widely on military issues. Last month, he produced his first non-fiction book,* Fighting for the Future: Will America Triumph? *(Stackpole Books). In this essay, he argues that peace can only be won with strong force—and lives lost.*

In much of this troubled world, only blood persuades. War and conflict have an enduringly human face. For all of the technological wonders available to Western militaries, we cannot defeat the man with the knife unless we are willing to take a knife—or gun—into our own hands. The basic human dilemmas, of which the urge to violence is one, still require a human response. That is the lesson of our Kosovo misadventure, and it is the fundamental principle of warfare that will endure throughout our lifetimes.

The air campaign against Slobodan Milosevic's Yugoslavia offers a better paradigm for Western folly than a novelist could invent. NATO and its first-among-equals, the United States, imagined that the military instrument could be used successfully without shedding blood, and that technological superiority would define the terms of a brief conflict. Homegrown myths live a long time in the Balkans, but foreign myths perish rapidly.

A new generation of Western political leaders, their views shaped by the blithe idealism of the Sixties and the increasing comfort of subsequent decades, long imagined that mankind might settle its differences peacefully. Confronted with the reality of hatred and bloodlust in this uncooperative decade, they next convinced themselves that war could be waged on the cheap, at least in terms of human lives—not only the lives of their own soldiers, but enemy lives as well.

Canada turned its military into global babysitters, and the United States sought to turn war into a computer game. Now, the myths of the peaceable kingdom and of bloodless techno-war are dead, murdered in the Balkans.

Military technologies are important. But they only matter if they are appropriate and properly used. In Kosovo, NATO chose not the instruments that might do the job, but the

Now, the myths of the peaceable kingdom and of bloodless techno-war are dead, murdered in the Balkans.

The paradox of the next century is that it will be one of fabulous wealth for us, but of bitter poverty for billions of others.

instrument of least risk. But war is risk. A month into the first yuppie war, the Kosovar Albanians are homeless and shattered, a discount Hitler has defied the world, and the NATO states wring their hands and look for absolution. That is the price of wishful thinking.

We have, indeed, entered a new age of conflict. It will not be an age of duelling computers, however, but of fundamental brutality: ethnic cleansing, religious pogroms, genocide, terrorism and international crime on a grand scale.

In a sense, we are going backward. The enemies who will confront our soldiers appear between the pages of the Bible and the *Iliad*, in Thucydides and Herodotus, Tacitus, Caesar and Gibbon. The model of war cherished by general staffs, with well-ordered army pitted against well-ordered army, is largely gone. Conventional war remains a threat, but a diminishing one. Today's—and tomorrow's—enemies are half-trained killers in uniform, tribesmen, mercenaries, criminals, children with rusty Kalashnikovs, shabby despots and gory men of faith. The most dangerous enemy will be the warrior who ignores, or who does not know, the rules by which our soldiers fight, and who has a gun in one hand, a cell phone in the other, and hatred scorching his heart.

The paradox of the next century is that it will be one of fabulous wealth for us, but of bitter poverty for billions of others. The world will not "come together," but has already begun to divide anew between open and tradition-bound societies, between rule-of-law states and lawless territories with flags, and between brilliant postmodern economies and cultures utterly unequipped for global competition. We will be envied and hated by those without a formula to win. In the 20th century, we had to worry about successful industrial states and the militaries they produced. In the next century, the threats will arise from the realms of failure.

Apart from terrorism involving weapons of mass destruction, none of the broad violence of the coming decades will threaten the existence of Canada or the United States. Rather, it is our economic interests and, even more often, our humanitarian instincts that will be challenged, and our soldiers who will pay the bills of blood. At the end of a century of slaughter, from Vimy Ridge and the Somme to Auschwitz and Cambodia, we in the West have taken refuge in the utterly irrational conclusion that mankind is fundamentally good and lacks only opportunity to demonstrate that goodness. In the next century, we will learn otherwise.

To behave effectively in tomorrow's conflicts, we need to back away from the daily tumult and dig deep into root causes. As with Kosovo, we cannot wish away horror. At least a minority of human beings—primarily male—thrive on violence, both psychologically and practically. Some men acquire a taste for killing. We ache to believe otherwise, but the cultural genocide and brutalities of Kosovo are not being committed by reluctant hands. Love withers, but hatred endures and inspires. Where is the tribe that loves its neighbour selflessly?

The slaughters in Rwanda, Sierra Leone and elsewhere in Africa were not laborious chores, but descents into intoxication and even ecstasy. The atrocities and dispossessions of Chechnya, Nagorno-Karabakh, Abkhazia, Bosnia and Croatia, of southern Iraq and the Kurdistan that does not exist (except in flesh and blood), of Afghanistan and fractured Indonesia, of Algeria and Northern Ireland were not executed by men steeled to a despised task, but by enthusiastic hands. Until we face Man as he is, we will have no end of Kosovos and Rwandas, of well-intentioned failures, refugees and bones. Man remains a killer, and we cannot wish the killer away.

In broken states and territories beyond state control, from the African bush to American slums, violence is empowering. Privileged and insular with our college degrees and good prospects, we of the reading class hope to solve crises of blood and hatred with diplomatic niceties, failing to recognize the addictive nature of violence (genocidal murderers and spouse abusers don't do it just once). Worse, we reconstruct our opponents in our own image, imagining that all men want peace. But for the hard-boy gunman of Ulster or the Balkan bully, peace is the least desirable state of affairs—unless he can dictate the terms of the peace. We thrive on order, but our enemies prosper from disorder. The end of the violence means the end of the good times for the local warlord or black-market king.

Most human beings do not thrive on violence, nor do they wish it, despite the resentments they may feel towards their neighbours. But it takes only a fraction of one per cent of a population, armed and determined, to destroy a fragile society. That is another lesson of the collapse of Yugoslavia, where even now, after years of organized brutality, under five per cent of the population has a hand in the business of death and ethnic cleansing.

The object of our interventions cannot be treaties alone. Ours is a strategy of self-satisfaction, not of meaningful change. If we wish to rescue or help reconstruct troubled societies, our first military action upon intervention must be to disarm the violent actors—and to fight those who resist. The worst offenders must be captured (or killed) and tried for their crimes before they slip into the criminality that has paralyzed many a "peace." We failed to do so in Bosnia, and the peace endures only because of the presence of foreign troops. Advocates of disarmament have pitched their programs too high. It isn't the decaying nuclear arsenals that threaten the world, but the pistol in the pocket of the killer.

Back in the 1960s, one of the original alternative-rock groups, the Fugs, recorded a satirical song about the Vietnam War entitled "Kill for Peace." That is exactly what we must be prepared to do.

What kind of militaries will we need in the next century? Not those which we have. Canada's military is unprepared to fight, and the U.S. armed forces are prepared to fight the wrong war. The first is under-equipped, the latter improperly equipped. Ottawa has pinched pennies, relying on the American defence umbrella, while Washington continues to lavish money on systems and organizations designed to fight the forces of the vanished Soviet Union. For Canada, the question is whether or not it will pull its weight (peacekeeping efforts matter, but they don't matter as much as the willingness to use a rifle in a good cause). For the United States, the issue is whether it can fight in a lower weight class than it has trained for.

Canada's military is unprepared to fight, and the U.S. armed forces are prepared to fight the wrong war.

Consider the American military today. The inability of air power to win wars by itself is on display as I write. What we attempted to do in Yugoslavia is equivalent to telling a metropolitan police department they can control crime only from the air—we cannot even find the little bands of butchers at large in Kosovo, let alone strike them. Yet, air power remains the glutton of U.S. defence dollars, the promised miracle cure for conflict.

The U.S. navy is structured to defeat foreign fleets that do not and will not exist, and the U.S. army, while potent, is so ponderous it cannot get to crises promptly with sufficient hitting power. Despite deep cuts to its forces during the '90s, the U.S. military could "do" Desert Storm again—if the enemy again allowed half a year for our preparations. But the U.S. army cannot even get to Kosovo, let alone sustain itself there, without a lengthy buildup that would guarantee the levelling of the last ruins in Pristina. If America's goal is to avoid meaningful interventions, its armed forces are perfectly structured to that purpose.

And yet, there is an exception. The U.S. Marine Corps, long regarded as thick of muscle and thick of head, has grasped the future with both hands. In a sense, the Marines lucked out, since the dirty little non-wars of the future are the same sort of fights they faced throughout their history. The corps felt the Cold War least, and has cast off its legacy with relative ease.

The centrepiece of innovation in the marine corps is a focus on urban warfare, the ugly fight that all want to avoid. Urban warfare is the growth area for Western militaries. Other services do not want to face it (despite some lip service), since fighting in cities and industrialized terrain threatens traditional organizations and weapons-buying habits. Worse, it is warfare at its most savagely human and dangerous.

No sensible soldier wants to fight in a city. But in a grossly urbanizing world, conflict inevitably becomes urbanized.

The fight follows the population. Cities have long been the object of military campaigns—today, they are increasingly the battlefields as well. It is not a matter of choice. Demographics, wealth concentration, sources of power, and even our military effectiveness in other environments drive our enemies into urban jungles. Mogadishu in Somalia was an elementary version of the problem—this is war in-close and deadly without neat lines on the planning map, surrounded by non-combatants, and fought in three dimensions, from multi-storey buildings down into sewers. There is no more difficult form of combat. For a military in love with technology, urban warfare's demands for large numbers of well-trained infantry come first as a shock, then as a critical shortage. City fighting produces casualties.

Western militaries will continue to operate in other environments, from rainforests to oil-rich deserts. But the days of ordered battles on green fields are behind us. Even were we to dispatch ground troops to Yugoslavia, the ethnic Serb military would not come out to duel with tanks in a grand battle. We would face guerrilla tactics and snipers, terror attacks and local armoured skirmishes—but, above all, we would have to go door-to-door in villages and half-burned cities, to root out the hard-core killers in uniform. What began as an exercise in technological prowess and war waged at a sterile remove may end in a gunfight in a darkened cellar.

Another instructive feature of the current debacle in the Balkans is the matter of initiative. In any fight, high-tech or bare knuckles, whoever can seize and retain the initiative has a tremendous advantage. Despite NATO's air attacks against empty buildings, Milosevic has done a brilliant job of forcing NATO to react, instead of allowing NATO to set the rules. He pulls the strings and Brussels jumps (while Washington spins).

NATO bombed and tried not to shed blood. In response, Milosevic accelerated a stunning campaign of ethnic cleansing and cultural genocide without impediment. He manipulated the refugee issue savagely and brilliantly. NATO must spend time and energy maintaining a fractious alliance, while Milosevic works to pry the alliance apart—though unsuccessful at rupturing it thus far, his efforts have ensured that the bombing campaign remains a tentative, nervous affair. Prior to the Orthodox Easter holiday, Milosevic declared a unilateral ceasefire, knowing that, should NATO accept, Brussels would find it nearly impossible to resume the bombing. With NATO's refusal, he was able to portray himself to his people and to receptive audiences abroad as a willing peacemaker. Thus far, Milosevic has managed to reduce NATO to a frustrated, impotent giant, unable to protect those it pledged to defend. Even if he loses in the end, Milosevic has outmanoeuvred NATO thus far. He made NATO's primary concern the care of refugees, not the mili-

Milosevic has done a brilliant job of forcing NATO to react, instead of allowing NATO to set the rules. He pulls the strings and Brussels jumps (while Washington spins).

tary campaign, and cast himself as hero to his people. Kosovo is destroyed, the mission a failure, and any eventual NATO victory will be as hollow as it is belated.

This ability of our enemies to set the terms of the conflict already had cost the West dearly in this decade, in Somalia and in Iraq. The reasons are twofold. First, for a variety of reasons, the West has been unable to muster and sustain the determination, the strength of will, that is the basis of all effective military operations; second, we consistently underestimate our enemies. Fighting on his own turf, the illiterate tribesman may prove wiser than the well-trained officer who does not speak the local language, know the local customs or understand the layout of the streets. Pride and its handmaiden, ignorance, have crippled our efforts, from the Horn of Africa to the Balkan fringes of Europe.

No better example is needed than the American administration's conviction that they knew Milosevic, and that he would back down at the threat of force. The American leadership failed to understand the man, his people or his goals. Then, NATO and the United States each took pains to assure Milosevic that ground troops would not be deployed, should the air campaign fail. All he had to do was hunker down, with his fingers in his ears. Bill Clinton and Javier Solana of NATO wrote the epitaph of the Kosovar Albanians in advance.

How do we prepare for the future of conflict? There are numerous practical measures that should be taken, from resisting the blandishments of defence contractors peddling weapons that are marvelous but irrelevant, to streamlining military units for swift deployment and buying the transport aircraft to carry them. But such steps do not address the core of the problem: we must decide what is worth fighting for.

Our problems lie with a generation of leaders who deemed themselves of too much worth to serve in uniform, and who arrived at the pinnacle of power ignorant of what militaries can and cannot do.

Our militaries, despite structural problems and materiel deficiencies, can do the ugly jobs the world presents. But they cannot do it bloodlessly, or instantly, or without injury to each last noncombatant. Our problems lie with a generation of leaders who deemed themselves of too much worth to serve in uniform, and who arrived at the pinnacle of power ignorant of what militaries can and cannot do. It is a generation accustomed to easy success, and it cannot understand why bloody-minded foreigners behave so badly. For all its international studies and travels, it is a generation sheltered from much of the world's reality. It knows how to win elections, but not how to lead.

And leadership is crucial to the effective use of the military. Whether the squad leader at the lowest level of combat, or the president or prime minister, the leader is the most important factor in deciding between victory or defeat (witness the unequal contest between the namby-pamby Mr. Clinton and the ruthless Mr. Milosevic). This has not changed since the battle of Jericho, or the fall of Troy—the fundamentals of the military art are so timeless they haunt our myths. The best leaders, of course, are not shoot-from-the-hip sorts, but thoughtful and resolute, knowledgeable and inspiring. The best-trained, best-equipped soldiers in the world are parade-ground toys unless their nation's leaders possess the vision to use them wisely, and the determination to support them fully and enduringly.

Wars and military interventions cannot be waged according to opinion polls. While the public's views matter, the citizenry is fickle and sometimes wrong in the short-term. The public speaks, in our privileged societies, through elections. Foreign and military policies managed by polling make a mockery of institutional democracy, reducing it to instant pudding.

Finally, we must decide whether or not we are our brother's keeper. The truth is that most of the world's atrocious conflicts will not threaten daily routines in Montreal or Milwaukee, let alone the survival of our nations. We do not feel the axe that falls a continent away.

Yet, we must watch that axe fall, on television. Perhaps the media is a fierce tool in the cause of justice, one that will not let us look away. Does it matter if distant populations slaughter each other? May we close our eyes and still believe in our own decency? Our dilemma is that we want to care a little, not a lot. Peacekeeping efforts in their present form put a bandage on the wound, when the situation calls for taking away the knife. We want our humanitarianism painless and cheap.

The great issues of conflict in the coming decades will be moral ones. The signs that we will solve them well are few. We choose the rights of governments over the rights of man, and the sanctity of borders over the sanctity of life. We want to stop the killing with reason and kindness, or with promises of a peace the butcher despises. We have lost our sense of perspective, and even our sense of reality.

If we want a better world, we shall have to fight for it. Until we rise to the task, the Kosovos will continue. The future of conflict is here.

The best-trained, best-equipped soldiers in the world are parade-ground toys unless their nation's leaders possess the vision to use them wisely, and the determination to support them fully and enduringly.

IV. The Economic Outlook

Editor's Introduction

Having examined the future of the planet's environment, our role in space exploration, prospects for the sustainability of the current global political arrangement dominated by powerful nations, and the strategy, tactics, and conduct of a military force that was trained and equipped to fight World War III but that must contemplate engaging primarily in hand-to-hand urban warfare, we now turn to the economic outlook. The future of the global and national economy is influenced by many factors, including an aging population, technological advances, and lifestyle trends that affect career patterns and consumer habits. We will consider each in turn.

In "The World Turns Gray: How Global Aging Will Challenge the World's Economic Well-Being" (*U.S. News & World Report*), Phillip J. Longman notes how quickly we have had to switch from worrying about a global population explosion—just a generation ago—to taking stock of the needs of an aging population due to plummeting fertility rates. The author of this article does not address the possible non-economic causes of women having fewer children worldwide. Economics is certainly a strong factor in places where jobs are scarce, leading to financial insecurity and smaller families. Government policy is also a factor, as in China. But in this editor's opinion one should not overlook the transformation of women's roles the world over. It is possible that women have decided en masse that endless childbearing is not to be their lot in life. Even if this were a factor, however, there would certainly be significant exceptions. The most important point to keep in mind is that global trends of any sort are created by a complex interplay of multiple factors, none of which alone can be credited with the new direction except in the rarest of circumstances. First you have your necessary preconditions, themselves the products of long-term trends. Then you have your catalysts, which may be several. Then you have the additional factors of timing and individuals, such as Bill Gates and George Soros, whose activities exert a greater influence on global events than do those of the faceless multitudes to which most of us belong. But ultimately, a trend does not become anything more than a short-lived fad unless the teeming throngs take part. Because it is difficult to accumulate hard data on the reasons for millions of individual decisions, such factors as women's changing concepts of their roles often go unreported, whereas it is relatively easy to conclude that rational people will have fewer offspring in the face of constricted opportunities. And yet this reasoning may be nothing more than a spurious extrapolation of the factors behind the American postwar baby boom to the rest of the world. There are plenty of places, in America and elsewhere, in which dwindling opportunities produce more, not fewer, children. But the fact remains that the population on the whole is aging as women in general have fewer children. The focus of Longman's article is the economic impact this trend may have on the current and future generations of workers who must support an increasing elderly population.

Considering this burden that society faces, it is imperative that the economy remain strong. High growth rates and increased productivity are essential components of many of the plans, both economic and political, that have been put forward as methods of dealing with this looming crisis. Some nations will try to finance their way out of the problem by increasing the national debt. Others will force workers to delay their retirement, which may feel like a huge cheat to people who have worked all their lives in the expectation of enjoying a long and healthy retirement. And yet it also makes some sense to extend the retirement age, considering that the average life expectancy has increased. The question is, are people living longer, *healthier* lives that will allow them to continue to contribute to the GNP? Or are our "extra" years spent in ill health that taxes the system even longer?

Whatever the case, the economy will need to expand. Therefore one hopes that Michael J. Mandel, the author of the second selection ("You Ain't Seen Nothing Yet," *Business Week*), is right when he writes, "There is growing evidence that the U.S. economy is in the early stages of a powerful new wave of innovation.... From the Internet to biotech to cutting-edge technologies that are just now nearing commercialization, the U.S. is riding a groundswell of innovation that could carry it well in the next century." That's all well and good for Americans, but what about the rest of the world? One theme that is expressed over and over again in these pages is that the gap between rich and poor, not only in the United States but in the world, is likely to continue its long-term expansion. Just as Ralph Peters asked in the previous section whether we should be our brother's keeper militarily, one might well ask should we fill that role economically as well, despite our dependence on foreign capital. We may fill it unwittingly, without being compelled by policy makers, simply by virtue of globalization. As the Internet makes national borders less relevant and confounds the labyrinthine laws of international trade and commerce, technological progress is no longer just a national phenomenon for any nation.

Fueling the economic boom is a surge in entrepreneurialism and self-employment that is paradoxically "born of fright," note Daniel McGinn and John McCormick in the third selection ("Your Next Job," *Newsweek*). "Despite stunning prosperity, companies still face ferocious cost pressures.... Last year corporations laid off 103,000 workers, the highest level in five years, according to outplacement specialists." Armed with a set of transferable skills and a personal computer, many workers are choosing to go it alone rather than return to the corporate environment. Former labor secretary Robert Reich estimates that 20 percent of the labor force is self-employed. Acknowledging that this option is less available to the blue-collar workers laid off from manufacturing jobs, many of which have been transferred to Asia, the authors assert that for them, "the news isn't all bleak. The explosion of new technologies is creating opportunities for America's newest skilled worker: the trained techie who lays the cable and repairs the chips that connect our wired world."

Another factor contributing to economic growth is consumer spending, itself driven, in this case, by technology. Annetta Miller writes in the fourth selection, "The Millennial Mind-set: It's Here, It's Clear, Get Used to It!" (*American Demographics*), that according to the Bureau of Labor Statistics, Americans in 2006 are projected to spend 84 percent of the money they spend on food and drink on computers, up from 0.32 percent in 1986. Since the prices of computers are trending down, this means that more people—a greater percentage of the population—are buying computers, not just that the same people are going to buy more computer hardware, software, and accessories. Miller cites "several fundamental demographic changes [that] will serve as the underpinning for this new consumer mind-set: the aging of the baby boom generation, the increasing importance of children as consumers, a growing chasm between society's haves and have-nots, and the country's increasingly diverse population."

The World Turns Gray: How Global Aging Will Challenge the World's Economic Well-Being [1]

From his office high above Park Avenue, Peter Peterson surveys a booming city of leveraged deals and paper profits that, almost every day, add to his bounty. As the Dow rallies once again beneath the fading winter sky to the south, this son of Greek immigrants can only count his blessings, which range from a summer home in the exclusive Hamptons whose inflating value he can scarcely believe, to a secure position as the chairman of the Blackstone Group, a prestigious New York investment bank.

Yet Peterson, 72, is worried about the future. These days, as most, he's thinking about aging—and not just his own. The world is going gray, and one day soon, the implications of that trend could unnerve today's boom psychology. "The scenario I see is that one or more developed countries, say Italy, is going to decide that the political cost of reforming their pension systems is just too high," says Peterson. "Then they will try running high deficits—much higher than limits set by the European Union's monetary authorities—in an attempt to finance their way out of the problem. When the financial markets wake up to this news, there will be a broad realization that we have a global aging crisis that is going to be unrelenting in its economic consequences."

The bull brought to its knees by too many Italian retirees? In some ways, the world should be so lucky. Not long ago, experts worried not about how to finance a world going gray but about a cresting wave of kids. And for good reason. Worldwide, as recently as 1972, a woman gave birth to an average of 5.6 children over her lifetime. Global population, as a result, was doubling every generation. Citing the trend, a hoary group of intellectuals known as the Club of Rome issued an influential study, titled "The Limits to Growth," that told what it all meant. The 21st century, said the club, would inevitably be marked by declining standards of living as human population exceeded the "carrying capacity" of the Earth, leading to mass famine and energy shortages.

But in the years since this Malthusian prophecy, a change has occurred in human behavior that is as revolutionary as it is unheralded: Around the world, fertility rates are plummeting. Today, women on average have just half the number of children they did in 1972. In 61 countries, accounting for 44

Around the world, fertility rates are plummeting.

---

1. Article by Phillip J. Longman from *U.S. News & World Report* Mar. 1, 1999. Copyright © 1999 *U.S. News & World Report*. Reprinted with permission. With Elise Ackerman, Don Boroughs in Zimbabwe, Bay Fang in China, Daniela Hart in Brazil, and Bill Myers in Spain.

percent of the Earth's population, fertility rates are now at or below replacement levels.

That doesn't mean the Earth's population will fall anytime soon. Thanks to the high fertility rates of the past, a large percentage of the world's population is still of childbearing age. Life expectancy is also up. Globally, the average life span has jumped from 49.5 years in 1972 to more than 63 years. Consequently, according to projections by the United Nations, the world's population will slowly increase at an average rate of 1.3 percent a year during the next 50 years, and it could decline by midcentury if fertility continues to fall.

BIRTH DEARTH. So there is a new problem for mankind. Global aging. Next year, for the first time in history, people over 60 will outnumber kids 14 or younger in industrial countries. Even more startling, the population of the Third World, while still comparatively youthful, is aging faster than that of the rest of the world. In France, for example, it took 140 years for the proportion of the population age 65 or older to double from 9 percent to 18 percent. In China, the same feat will take just 34 years. In Venezuela, 22. "The developed world at least got rich before it got old," notes Neil Howe, an expert on aging. "In the Third World the trend is reversed."

And that means trouble. For one thing, the cost of supporting a burgeoning elderly population will place enormous strains on the world's economy. Instead of there being more workers to support each retire—as was the case while birthrates were still rising—there will be fewer. Instead of markets growing, they will shrink, at least in large parts of the globe. Economists define a recession as two or more consecutive quarters of declining gross domestic product. Yet as Peterson points out in his new book, Gray Dawn, in the world's richest and most productive countries, the number of working-age people will be dropping well over 1 percent a year within 20 years. Even assuming healthy increases in productivity, such a continuing contraction in the work force could mean decades of declining economic output.

For Selina Gonzalez, that world has already arrived. In her store in Mieres, a once prosperous town in northern Spain, Gonzalez sells baby clothes at a discount, but turnover is slow. As she sews a button onto a tiny, lacy blouse, she admits that the garment has been in the shop for some time. "Many young people move away from here to look for work," she says. "And the ones who stay don't have any financial security, so they don't have children."

Mieres could be ground zero of the global aging phenomenon. It lies in the least fecund province of the least fertile nation on Earth. Spanish women now have an average of just 1.15 children in their lifetimes. In Asturias, the province containing Mieres, the lifetime fertility rate is just 0.79 children. The implications of the birth dearth are abundantly

Next year, for the first time in history, people over 60 will outnumber kids 14 or younger in industrial countries.

clear. After making allowances for premature death, at least 2.1 children per woman are needed to replace the population. This means that Spain's population will very likely shrink from 39 million to less than 30 million over the next 50 years in the absence of a dramatic increase in immigration.

Certainly a lackluster economy partly explains why young adults in this part of the world have suddenly become so wary of parenthood. Spain's unemployment rate, long the highest in Europe, hovers around 20 percent. And Asturias, which has been buffeted by the decline of its coal-mining industry, has one of the highest jobless rates in Spain.

PRODUCTIVITY PROBLEM. Yet economics alone are not enough to explain people's reproductive behavior. After all, in general the world's highest birthrates are in the poorest countries. Teresa Castro, a fertility expert at the Spanish government's Superior Council for Scientific Research, points to diffuse cultural factors at work. In Spain, she says, the Roman Catholic prohibition against birth control is now widely ignored. The church, she says, "lost all influence in family matters years ago and now serves only as a setting for rites of passage," such as weddings, baptisms, and funerals. Another key factor is the incorporation of a majority of women into the work force. This change, says Castro, "has come about so rapidly that there are not enough day-care facilities for working women who would like to have children."

Spain may lead the world in its diminishing fertility, but there are plenty of runners-up. Italy is in the midst of a bambini bust that will cause it to lose more than half its native younger workers with each new generation. The Czech Republic, Romania, and Bulgaria all are producing children at a rate of just 1.2 per woman. Germany, Japan, Greece, Russia, Portugal, Hungary, and Ukraine have similar fertility rates. American women, though still not producing enough babies to replace the population, are fertility goddesses by comparison, with a lifetime average of two children each.

For the developed world, fiscal consequences of these trends are dire. Over the next 25 years, the number of persons of pensionable age (65 and over) in industrial countries will rise by 70 million, predicts the Organization for Economic Cooperation and Development (OECD), while the working-age population will rise by only 5 million. Today, working taxpayers outnumber nonworking pensioners in the developed world by 3 to 1. By 2030, absent increases in retirement ages, this ratio will fall to 1.5 to 1. In Italy and other places, it will drop to 1 to 1 or lower.

Of course, there will be fewer children to feed and educate. But most experts agree that while aging societies may be able to divert some resources that now go to the young, the increasing cost of supporting the elderly is almost certain to

American women, though still not producing enough babies to replace the population, are fertility goddesses by comparison, with a lifetime average of two children each.

consume these savings many times over. Throughout the developed world, total public spending per old person is two to three times as great as public spending per child. And in the future, that gap will probably widen. The elderly consume far more health care resources than do children, and new technologies to extend life are bound to escalate health care costs.

Who will pay the bills? One option is to raise taxes on the diminishing number of workers. But according to official projections, doing so would require increasing the total tax burden on workers by the equivalent of 25 to 40 percent of their taxable wages, an unthinkable prospect in industrial countries, where payroll tax rates already sometimes exceed 40 percent. Another option would be to cut benefits, but given the political and ethical obstacles, this approach is likely to be put off for as long as possible.

That leaves borrowing. As aging nations attempt to avoid hard choices, they are likely to rack up mountains of debt. And, at some point, that could destabilize the world economy. For example, with neither tax increases nor benefit cuts, Japan will have to increase its public-debt levels from a little more than 20 percent of gross domestic product today to over 100 percent by 2050, according to OECD. In Europe, public indebtedness would have to rise from under 60 percent of GDP to nearly 110 percent.

Despite today's talk of budget surpluses, the OECD forecasts that population aging will force the United States to increase its national debt from just over 40 percent of GDP today to 70 percent by the mid-21st century.

The United States faces less of a challenge, thanks mostly to its comparatively high fertility and immigration rates. But the nation is still woefully unprepared for the coming age wave. Despite today's talk of budget surpluses, the OECD forecasts that population aging will force the United States to increase its national debt from just over 40 percent of GDP today to 70 percent by the mid-21st century. The long-term debts of America's public pension systems come to about $10 trillion. With a savings rate near zero, the United States is already highly dependent on foreign capital. The aging of its population will only make it more so.

LOOK TO BRAZIL. But will the world's investors continue to pour money into aging nations with mounting pension debts? A forewarning comes from Brazil, which is currently undergoing a financial meltdown so perilous it periodically scorches Wall Street. "There are important lessons to learn from what's been going on in Brazil," says Bradley Belt of the Center for Strategic and International Studies in Washington. "Quite frankly, a large chunk of their fiscal distress right now is attributable to an overgenerous, one might even call lavish, public pension system."

The last time most Americans bothered to look, Brazil was a youthful nation whose most pressing social problem appeared to be a growing army of glue-sniffing street urchins. But a recent report by the Ministry of Social Security concludes that the aging of the population is now the nation's most important challenge, and that if the government doesn't take urgent action, "we may be faced in the coming years with the problem of street elders without having solved the problem of street children."

Like all Latin American countries, Brazil has seen a dramatic decline in its fertility rate over the last generation. In 1960, a Brazilian woman on average had more than six children over her lifetime; today, her counterpart has just 2.3 children. As a result, in a land once known for its celebration of dental-floss bikinis and youthful "carnaval" exuberance, pension debt has become the public's central preoccupation.

The growing ranks of the aged have rendered the cost of Brazil's once generous public pensions far higher than the country can afford. "Our social security system was planned for a young country," says Luiz Roberto Ramos, head of the geriatrics department at the Paulista Federal University in Sao Paulo. "Now it has become unfeasible."

Global capital markets couldn't agree more. Under pressure from the International Monetary Fund and other creditors, Brazil recently increased the age at which most Brazilians become eligible for benefits and raised contribution rates. Yet the country still faces huge dislocations as it adjusts to its new status as an aging nation. Says Ramos: "The public-health system is not equipped to deal with the problems of the aged, which tend to be chronic illnesses, often involving sophisticated and expensive procedures."

China also is struggling with pension and health care bills it can't afford.

China also is struggling with pension and health care bills it can't afford. The large generation born in the first half of the 1950s (when Chairman Mao Zedong urged citizens to help build the country by having babies) will become elderly within the next two decades. Yet because of China's one-family/one-child policy, begun in the late 1970s, the number of workers is shrinking dramatically. Increasingly, the typical family pattern in China today is the "one-two-four household," with one child supporting two parents and four grandparents.

PENSION PROTESTS. As in Eastern Europe and the former Soviet Union, the failures of communism go a long way toward explaining the dismal plight of today's Chinese elderly. Thousands lost their pensions in recent years when state-sponsored enterprises folded. In some cities, such as Changchun, demonstrations by outraged elders are now a daily occurrence. But even if China succeeds in building a more market-based economy, unfavorable demographics will still hobble the country's productive potential.

For example, last year the government established a new pension plan designed to force workers to contribute to their own retirement. But that still leaves the problem of how to find the money necessary to pay off today's retirees. To quell protests by pensioners, municipal governments have assumed some of the pension debts of defunct state-owned enterprises, but the central government has refused to bear responsibility for the mess. Increasingly, China's elderly aren't even able to count on care from their children. Says Li Yanhua, a nursing home operator in Changchun, "It's a market economy now, and people have no time to take care of their parents."

Other parts of Asia are aging even faster than China. Over the next decade, Japan, for example, will suffer a 25 percent drop in the number of workers under age 30. In 1985, only 28 percent of the world's elderly lived in Asia; by 2025, Asia's share will increase to 58 percent. Though many other factors are at work, Asia's current economic woes stem in part from inadequate consumer demand, which is itself largely a function of population aging. Not only is the working-age population growing more slowly, but consumer demand also is constrained by high levels of retirement savings by a middle-aged generation that knows time is running out.

Aside from the Muslim countries of North Africa and the Middle East, it's hard to find any part of the world that isn't aging. For many Third World countries, the challenge of supporting a growing elderly population is compounded by huge out-migrations of younger people. The nations of the Caribbean, for example, have lost 5.6 million mostly working-age citizens to emigration since 1950. This trend, combined with falling fertility rates and increasing life expectancy among the elderly, has given countries like Martinique, Barbados, and Aruba populations that are nearly as old as that of the United States.

Even Africa, the world's youngest continent, is more and more burdened by aging issues.

Even Africa, the world's youngest continent, is more and more burdened by aging issues. Indeed, because of migration and the ravages of the AIDS epidemic, the number of working-age persons in sub-Saharan Africa available to support each elder is shrinking, causing enormous societal strains.

The plight of Grace Ngondo provides a good case study. Sitting in her thatch-roofed, rondavel hut along a dusty road in Epworth, Zimbabwe, Ngondo reflected recently on the good life she had expected in old age. When her late husband, a farm worker, first retired, Ngondo counted on her children for the same reverence and support she had once given her own aging parents, and for a while she received it. Her eldest son provided clothing and food. There was chicken stewing in the pot and meat hanging from a long wire. "I lived like a white person in those days," she recalls.

But now the wire is rusty and bare, and like millions of aging Africans these days, Ngondo must work to eat. Two of her sons have died of diseases Ngondo says had AIDS-like symptoms. A third son has moved away. Following the death of her husband and a brother-in-law, Ngondo now finds herself responsible for supporting more than a dozen grandchildren, nieces, and nephews. To make ends meet, she toils in the fields until the heat of the day overcomes her. Then she walks to the local school to sell ice cream to the departing children.

In Zimbabwe alone, a country of 12 million people, AIDS will leave behind an estimated 910,000 orphans by the year 2005. Most will be raised by their grandparents. To help these grandparents cope, the Zimbabwean government has asked rural headmen in some areas to set aside one plot of land to be farmed jointly by the community. Private charities, such as HelpAge Zimbabwe, are also trying to set the elderly up with small businesses and collective farms. Outside Ngondo's hut is a chicken coop where she and 11 of her elderly neighbors jointly raise up to 50 chickens at a time, a cooperative business started with a HelpAge grant. Every six weeks, when the chickens have been fattened and sold, the group splits its profits of as much as $9.

ABANDONED ELDERS. Even when they are fortunate enough not to lose their children to AIDS, many Zimbabwean elders nonetheless find themselves abandoned. Says Madi Mitchelle, one of Ngondo's elderly neighbors: "When we were looking after our children, we gave them good manners, thinking they would look after us one day, but now it's nothing like that. Either they die or they run away from you." In days gone by, the ties between the generations were strengthened through "Ekupira mudzimu," a ritual of ancestor-pleasing. "If you did not look after your parents, you could be cursed by your ancestors; you might lose your job," explains Edwell Kaseke, who heads the University of Zimbabwe's School of Social Work. But with the widespread acceptance of Christianity, says Kaseke, the threat of such curses has lost its effectiveness.

Accommodating the new realities of 21st-century aging will take a lot more than ritual incantations; even hocus-pocus trust-fund accounting won't pay the bills coming due. Most senior citizens in the West probably won't have to hoe weeds or raise chickens to make ends meet in the next century. But like their African counterparts, the elderly in even the richest countries will most likely be called upon to work much later in life and to take more of a role in rearing the next generation. That may dash some people's dreams of an early retirement to the golf course or fishing hole, but in exchange for longer lives in a less crowded world, it may be a fair price to pay.

Like their African counterparts, the elderly in even the richest countries will most likely be called upon to work much later in life and to take more of a role in rearing the next generation.

You Ain't Seen Nothing Yet[2]

We're just at the start of a powerful surge in technology that will boost economic gains into the next century.

In our society, "mature" is a euphemism for getting old. Consultants deride a mature market as one without much potential. And a mature economy, as economists use the term, can no longer sustain the high growth rates of younger, spryer economies. Indeed, as growth slowed in the 1970s and 1980s, mature was exactly the term that many economists applied to the U.S.

Boy, were they wrong. There's nothing old about the U.S. economy today. Instead, there's been an explosion of creativity and entrepreneurial vigor that puts U.S. competitors to shame. Seven years into the expansion, growth is running at a 3.5% rate over the last year, and despite a small dip in the second quarter, productivity is rising at a strong 1.9% rate.

From the Internet to biotech to cutting-edge technologies that are just now nearing commercialization, the U.S. is riding a groundswell of innovation that could carry it well into the next century.

There is growing evidence that the U.S. economy is in the early stages of a powerful new wave of innovation. The leading edge is the information revolution, which permeates every sector of the economy. Over the last year, for example, high tech has taken half a percentage point off inflation and added almost a full point to growth.

But there is much more to come. From the Internet to biotech to cutting-edge technologies that are just now nearing commercialization, the U.S. is riding a groundswell of innovation that could carry it well into the next century. "We've never had a period in which innovation has so permeated our lives as in the 1990s," notes Joel Mokyr, an economic historian at Northwestern University who studies innovation. "We have acquired knowledge in at least three or four areas that will be truly revolutionary." Adds Arnold B. Baker, head economist at Sandia National Laboratories: "There's going to be a fundamental change in the global economy unlike anything we've had since cavemen began bartering."

WAGE SURGE. Welcome to the 21st Century Economy. Historically, periods of major innovation have brought profound increases in living standards. The last one, which started with railroads in the 1890s and lasted through the advent of television and jet travel in the 1950s and 1960s, saw a quadrupling of real per capita incomes, propelled by rising productivity.

The 21st Century Economy could see similar income gains, if the latest innovative wave can boost long-term growth to 3%, rather than the 2.3% that most forecasters predict. Even over a period as short as the next ten years, faster growth dramatically changes the economic and financial landscape.

---

2. Article by Michael J. Mandel from *Business Week* Aug. 31, 1998. Copyright © 1998 *Business Week*. Reprinted with permission.

Rather than remaining almost flat through 2008, real wages would actually rise by 9%, according to projections prepared for *Business Week* by Standard & Poor's DRI.

Corporations and investors would prosper as well in this scenario. In the 21st Century Economy, corporate earnings, adjusted for inflation, would rise by 54% over the next ten years, compared with 25% in the slow-growth case. Combined with 30-year interest rates below 4%, that's spectacular news for the stock market.

The innovation boom, and the faster growth rate it could ignite, could make it much easier to address some of the vexing social and environmental problems of the 21st century. For example, a 3% annual growth rate will more than cover the needs of baby boomer's retirement, since it will lead to a 25% bigger economy in 2030. And expensive solutions to global warming, such as cutting carbon emissions, will become easier to bear if the economy is growing faster.

Are such gains really possible? Certainly, the U.S. economy has done far better in recent years than most economists expected, coming close to its spectacular performance of the 1960s. The single best measure of this is the productivity of nonfinancial corporations, which includes 75% of the business sector, from Microsoft Corp. to General Motors Corp., while omitting small businesses and financial companies. Since 1990, the productivity of nonfinancial corporations has risen at a strong 2.1% rate, far above the 1.5% seen from 1973 to 1990, and approaching the 2.4% of the 1960s and early 1970s. Manufacturing has done even better: Since 1990, factory productivity has been soaring at 3.6% annually, the fastest rate in the post-World War II era.

In the long run, the success of the 21st Century Economy will depend on whether technological progress will continue to drive growth, as it has so far in this decade. That would be a big change from the 1970s and 1980s. In those decades of economic stagnation, technology contributed almost nothing to growth, according to calculations by the Bureau of Labor Statistics. The computer revolution had yet to take off, and earlier innovations such as jet travel were no longer new.

But in the 1990s, the innovations have been coming thick and fast. This has changed the calculus of policymakers, enabling Fed Chairman Alan Greenspan to hold down interest rates even in the face of low unemployment. "Signs of major technological improvements are all around us," he observed in his July 21 testimony to Congress. "The benefits are evident not only in high-tech industries but also in production processes that have long been part of our industrial economy."

PAYBACK TIME. In part, the sudden re-emergence of technological progress is the culmination of years of research in disparate fields that are finally reaching critical mass. The Internet, which only became a commercial proposition in the

The innovation boom, and the faster growth rate it could ignite, could make it much easier to address some of the vexing social and environmental problems of the 21st century.

mid-1990s, is the direct descendant of ARPANet, which was based on research funded by the Defense Dept. in the 1960s. The first successful gene-splicing experiment was done in 1973, but biotechnology is only now set to explode. Moreover, different parts of the innovation wave are starting to feed and reinforce one another, as fast computers greatly accelerate the ability of scientists to understand and manipulate genes. Conversely, biological techniques now seem the best foundations for developing tomorrow's new generation computers.

The innovation wave is also being given more force by the globalization of the economy. Bright ideas developed in Israel or India quickly find world markets. Technologically savvy immigrants propel high-tech companies in Silicon Valley and elsewhere. And the ever-expanding markets offer the lure of mammoth profits for a successful product that can be sold worldwide. The result: It becomes far more attractive to speed up R&D in hopes of getting a competitive edge.

To be sure, the emergence of the 21st Century Economy does not put an end to recessions, financial crises, or the other ills that afflict market economies. Quite the contrary: Times of intense technological change are often volatile, as corporations and workers try to adjust to new technologies. Indeed, some of the deepest downturns in American history have come during periods of rapid productivity growth such as the first half of the 1900s. And, as the Asian crisis shows, the global economy exposes countries to risks that they did not face before.

Skeptics believe that today's hot technologies— the Internet, biotech, and so forth—are inconsequential, in economic terms, compared with past breakthroughs.

Many economists are skeptical of claims that the sustainable growth rate has permanently increased. For one thing, they argue that the low inflation of recent years may simply be the result of a few lucky events, including falling oil prices, rather than any permanent structural change. Most important, they say, government economic statistics do not yet present a clear-cut case that technological progress has accelerated. The biggest productivity gains have come only since 1995, which means that a few bad years could still easily wipe them out.

Skeptics believe that today's hot technologies—the Internet, biotech, and so forth—are inconsequential, in economic terms, compared with past breakthroughs. Fundamental innovations such as electricity and the internal combustion engine, argues Robert J. Gordon of Northwestern University, one of the most articulate critics of the New Economy, "made possible a half-century of rapid growth in productivity that far exceeds what occurred before, what has occurred since, or what is likely to occur in the foreseeable future." And Paul Krugman, a Massachusetts Institute of Technology economist who has consistently attacked the New Economy, recently wrote: "The truth is that we live in an age not of extraordinary progress but of technological disappointment."

Other economists echo Krugman and Gordon's sentiment. "A lot of the easy wins have already been had," says Martin N. Baily, a productivity expert at the McKinsey Global Institute and a former member of Clinton's Council of Economic Advisers. "It's harder to push out the frontier." Adds Robert M. Solow, Nobel laureate from MIT: "You can't expect the great old days to come back."

The experience of the 1970s and 1980s gives some weight to this lack of faith in technology. The productivity slowdown was caused in large part by the failure of some innovations to live up to their early promise. Nuclear energy was supposed to be the big breakthrough of the postwar era—a source of cheap and limitless power. If the so-called Atomic Age had worked out as expected, the oil price rise of the 1970s would have been far less damaging. Indeed, the utility industry was one of the biggest contributors to the productivity slowdown of the 1970s.

Meanwhile, the space program—identified by President John F. Kennedy in 1961 as America's top scientific priority—absorbed a stunning 25% of the nation's civilian R&D dollars in the 1960s. But even though it reached its goal of putting a man on the moon, the program has not yet generated the economic benefits to justify the huge investments—though the increasing importance of communications satellites may change that.

These flamboyant flameouts may be leading the skeptics to underestimate the power of today's technological changes—just as the Great Depression created a generation of economists and investors who worried that another crash was just around the corner. But today's innovations have a better chance of succeeding because they are being developed by the private sector in response to the profit motive, which automatically gives an incentive to seek out technologies that are economically viable. Nuclear power and the space program, by contrast, were creatures of government and of heavily regulated industries, which had no such incentive.

In information technology, profits motivate both buyers and sellers. Businesses are devoting more of their investment spending to computers and information technology, something that would make sense only if managers thought they were getting a real payoff. Over the last four years, business spending on computers has risen by 86%, far outpacing the 40% rise for all other types of investment. Certainly the productivity impact of computers is starting to show up in the numbers. For example, a new analysis from two Conference Board economists, Robert H. McGuckin and Kevin Stiroh, argues that manufacturing industries that use computers heavily have shown a brisk acceleration in productivity growth, from an annual rate of 3.2% in the 1980s to 5.7% in the 1990s.

These flamboyant flameouts may be leading the skeptics to underestimate the power of today's technological changes.

Biotech, now beginning to take off, will have a strong influence on health care, agriculture, and the output of nondurables, such as chemicals and petroleum products— and these things account for a further 15% of the economy.

Even so, much of the benefit of the information revolution is not being captured in the productivity data. Beyond manufacturing, the computer and communications explosion is totally transforming industries that move and process information, such as finance, media, entertainment, communications, and business services. Together, these industries make up about 25% of the economy—yet they are also very poorly measured by government statisticians. After all, how can you count the gains from having 24-hour access to your money at ATMs, or from being easily able to make calls from your cellular phone?

TINY WONDERS. New technologies coming to market will have equally pervasive and radical effects on other parts of the economy. Biotech, now beginning to take off, will have a strong influence on health care, agriculture, and the output of nondurables, such as chemicals and petroleum products— and these things account for a further 15% of the economy. And while many of today's biotech products are expensive, the history of technological innovation suggests that their prices will rapidly fall as production ramps up. Especially in health care, pharmaceutical companies will be under heavy pressure to find treatments that cut costs.

Just ahead are a set of innovations that could transform the economics of a wide range of industries. Microelectromechanical systems (MEMs)—a commercial toddler—will enable tiny sensors, motors, and pumps to be built right into microprocessors, which could have a big impact on transportation, food processing, and home appliances. And scientists are learning how to build up new materials atom by atom, which could transform the entire manufacturing sector, among others. What is exciting, says Peter M. Will of the Information Sciences Institute at the University of Southern California, is the "potential to fundamentally change matter, to create things and materials that can never exist otherwise."

Of course, it's hard to predict which innovations will succeed and which won't. Technologies that look good in the laboratory or on the drawing board can fizzle out due to unforeseen complications, as did nuclear power.

But history says that the odds are good. Out of the last 10 decades, eight have been periods of strong innovation. In the end, the slow-growth 1970s and 1980s will look like the exceptions, not the rule. On the edge of the 21st century, the U.S. economy is anything but mature.

What Will Drive the 21st Century Economy... And How It Will Define the Coming Decades?

WHAT WILL DRIVE THE 21ST CENTURY ECONOMY...

- The information revolution will continue to boost productivity across the economy. Over the next 10 years, such information-dependent industries as finance,

media, and wholesale and retail trade will change the
most.

- A surge of major technology breakthroughs, including
biotechnology and MEMs, will begin to create entire new
industries over the next 10 years.
- Increasing globalization will simultaneously provide
much larger markets and tough foreign competitors. The
result: Companies will have even more incentive to inno-
vate while cutting costs.

...AND HOW IT WILL DEFINE THE COMING DECADES

- The economy will grow substantially faster than most
economists expect—perhaps 3% or more per year.
- Inflationary surges and large budget deficits will become
less likely.
- Despite all the scare talk, the next generation will enjoy a
rising standard of living, even while baby boomers are
able to retire comfortably.
- Countries that follow policies that encourage innovation,
free trade, and open financial systems will enjoy a competitive edge.
- Businesses that master the new technologies will be able
to count on better profits and bigger market share.

THE DOWNSIDE

- Major dislocations and uncertainty for workers and businesses will be inevitable as new technologies are
adopted.
- Technology shocks will increase economic and financial
volatility, both in the U.S. and globally.

Your Next Job [3]

Workers of the World, Untie: Get Ready for the New American Career

We're living through the tightest U.S. labor market in three decades—a hiring bonanza that is transforming the nature of work.

Gary Barnett looks out for number one—and we aren't talking national football championships. Late in 1997 the talented coach of the Northwestern Wildcats told the world, "I'm here, and I will be here for the next 10 years of my contract ... I stand by my promises." Never mind that his naked grab for the head-coaching job at the University of Texas had just flopped. This year, in a mid-January e-mail to his Northwestern players, Barnett pledged that "I will be back to take us to Pasadena" for another Rose Bowl—even as he was still under consideration for the top job at the University of Colorado. Sure enough, last week Barnett bolted out of Evanston, Ill., for Boulder, where he'd coached as a young assistant. So what if his national reputation took a hit, with one columnist writing that Barnett's restaurant in Evanston is running a special on snake. Barnett told *Newsweek* he behaved ethically, and that "everything I said I totally believed at the time." But on his way out the door, Barnett taught his Wildcats a lesson about the economy they'll join after graduation: in a job market as hot as this one, it's Me First!

Coaches on the make aren't a new species. But the cheekiness of Barnett's move is one small sample of what employers face across the country: a newly emboldened American work force. We're living through the tightest U.S. labor market in three decades—a hiring bonanza that is transforming the nature of work. The current hypergrowth in jobs can't last forever; fast-food restaurants won't be paying signing bonuses during the next recession. But the most remarkable changes in the workplace—and our attitudes toward it—will redefine careers well into the 21st century. Just as the Great Depression produced a generation of frugal worrywarts, those of us benefiting from the long jobs boom of the 1990s sport an often brazen self-confidence about how we connect to our jobs. Former Labor secretary Robert Reich, now writing a book on "The Work of the Future," sees signs of the shift in the exploding number of self-employed workers (up to 20 percent of the labor force, he figures) and in corporate employees' newfound willingness to hopscotch among jobs. "Loyalty is dead," Reich says.

What's behind the shift? Paradoxically, this new self-reliance is partly born of fright. Despite stunning prosperity,

---

3. Article by Daniel McGinn and John McCormick from *Newsweek*, v133, i5 p42–45 Feb. 1, 1999. Copyright © 1999 Time Inc. Reprinted with permission.

companies still face ferocious cost pressures—from Wall Street analysts who'll punish them for missing earnings estimates, from overseas rivals using cheaper labor and from a fear of raising prices in an inflation-free economy. Sadly, one thing hasn't changed: employees are usually the first costs that get cut.

Despite the boom economy, last year corporations laid off 103,000 workers, the highest level in five years, according to outplacement specialists. Economists at the Federal Reserve Bank of Chicago estimate that in 1995, the most recent year for which they have data, workers faced a small but chilling 3.4 percent chance of being laid off. That risk has increased anxiety and forced workers to constantly re-evaluate options. If you can't count on Coca-Cola to keep providing your paycheck, why not consider that offer from Pepsi? Or just place a big bet on You Inc., selling your services to companies that are increasingly eager to give people work without giving them a job.

This shifting notion of how we work has twinned with the blazing economy to render the old ways of career planning obsolete. Once it made sense to talk of hot industries and hot cities. If your fortunes as, say, a bank supervisor in Phoenix looked dim, it might have been worth knowing that good jobs awaited pharmaceutical salesmen in Florida. That information is less valuable today: nearly every industry in every city is short of workers. What is worth knowing? That more Americans are creating entirely new styles of employment. They're found in the expanding ranks of self-employed Free Agents who find financial and professional independence in everything from personal training to urban planning. Or they are the new Nomads, workers who never seem to stop job hunting. There's an emerging class of Globalists, too—those have-laptop will-travel workers who straddle time zones in today's borderless economy. Even the more traditional denizens of Corporate America are getting a makeover. Bosses are learning how to manage, retain and motivate this demanding, footloose work force. And despite reports to the contrary, the Organization Man—or, increasingly, Woman—isn't dead, either. But instead of conforming and running scared, they're designing new entrepreneurial ventures inside the corporate nest.

The most striking—and frightening—feature of this new landscape is how much it demands of us. Once expertise in a single discipline, like marketing, was enough to ensure a secure corporate future. But today's free agent needs skills in selling himself (how else to drum up business?), finance (to win that bank loan) and technology (is this computer upgrade a wise investment?). Even folks who opt for life in the corporate fold face new pressures to gain experience that's transferable to other companies or industries. Workers will also have to master a series of new technologies during

Despite the boom economy, last year corporations laid off 103,000 workers, the highest level in five years, according to outplacement specialists.

their careers. Nomads face a different kind of calculus: do my current stock options and 401(k) plan outweigh the raise I'd get if I left? The new career styles also create anxiety because many people will spend a lifetime migrating among them. Maybe in the future you're a job-hopping Nomad in your 20s, a rock-solid Organization Person in your 30s and a self-employed soloist in your 40s or 50s, when your skills peak.

It's also clear that most of these styles haven't evolved from the old smokestack industries and may not offer much solace to blue-collar workers. By 2006 manufacturing jobs will account for just 12 percent of the labor force, down 5 percentage points in the last 20 years. Still, for people who don't aspire to—or who lack the means to enter—the college-educated white-collar world, the news isn't all bleak. The explosion of new technologies is creating opportunities for America's newest skilled worker: the trained techie who lays the cable and repairs the chips that connect our wired world.

The explosion of new technologies is creating opportunities for America's newest skilled worker: the trained techie who lays the cable and repairs the chips that connect our wired world.

That technology isn't just changing what work we do, but how and where we do it. Just as the Industrial Revolution brought people together in factories, the Information Revolution is pulling us apart. The ability to work at home, day or night, gives us more flexible careers but also blurs the line between company time and family life. That line is a big deal to younger workers, many of them children of divorced parents. As a solid economy gives them more choices, many simply won't surrender their lives to any job.

The Millennial Mind-set: It's Here, It's Clear, Get Used to It![4]

Once upon a time, understanding consumer motivations seemed so simple. He was John Q. Typical; she was Jane Doe Average. They held down full-time jobs with good benefits, loved to shop at the mall, used their computer mostly for e-mail and their VCR to tape *ER* once a week. They thought a good value was paying 6 percent below manufacturer's list for their sport utility vehicle.

That was 1998.

But some curious things are happening on the way to the millennium. John Q. and Jane D. lost their jobs and started their own businesses. Now they're working in a home office, getting gray around the temples and stiff in the knees. They're stocking up on herbal remedies, spending more time in the bathroom Jacuzzi, and less time at the mall. They use one of their computers to track their Individual Retirement Accounts and another to program the VCR. They think a good value is buying an SUV through an online shopping service.

Welcome to the world of consumerism in the early 21st century, when what once seemed a New-Age fairy tale is now an emerging reality. If you think you've figured out the consumer agenda for the year 2000 and beyond, you may need to reconsider. Experts say consumers in the new millennium will throw some surprising twists and turns into the business of target marketing, turning upside down some of the traditional thinking about what we'll buy, how we'll live, and where we'll work.

"The 21st century will be the century of the consumer," says Roger Blackwell, a professor of marketing at Ohio State University and the author of *From Mind to Market: Reinventing the Retail Supply Chain* (Harperbusiness). "Marketers will have to push their understanding beyond knowing what people buy to knowing why they buy."

An analysis of government spending data indicates that some startling changes are already underway. Calculated with 1992 dollars, Americans spent $2.1 billion on computers in 1986, just 0.32 percent of the $614 billion they spent on food and beverages that year. But look ahead to 2006: According to the latest projections from the Bureau of Labor Statistics, computer expenditures will soar to $666 billion— 84 percent of the $794 billion Americans will shell out for food and drink. So if the 1970s were the "Me Decade," the

"The 21st century will be the century of the consumer," says Roger Blackwell.

---

4. Article by Annetta Miller from *American Demographics* p 60-5 Jan. 1999. Additional reporting by Joan Raymond. Copyright © PRIMEDIA Intertec, a PRIMEDIA Company. All rights reserved. Reprinted with permission.

2010s will be the "Linked Decade," defined by a busy, mature, ethnically heterogeneous group of consumers who are confident in their ability to read anything, buy anything, and experience anything.

Several fundamental demographic changes will serve as the underpinning for this new consumer mind-set: the aging of the baby boom generation, the increasing importance of children as consumers, a growing chasm between society's haves and have-nots, and the country's increasingly diverse population. According to projections by the U.S. Census Bureau, non-Hispanic whites will comprise 62.4 percent of the U.S. population by the year 2025, down from 72.5 percent in 1998. Says futurist Watts Wacker, founder of FirstMatter, a business think tank in Westport, Connecticut, the day of the "Aryan from Darien" is over.

The cry of the needy in the new millennium may well be "Brother, can you spare some time?"

Given that demographic backdrop, what will be the most powerful values shaping the consumer mind-set? Below, four of the key motivational forces that will drive consumerism in the Century of the Consumer:

THE SHRINKING AMERICAN DAY

The cry of the needy in the new millennium may well be "Brother, can you spare some time?" Harried baby boomers will create a time famine for themselves by working more hours and committing to more family and community obligations. How will they cope with their time-crunched lifestyles? In general, says Blackwell, "people will decrease the amount of time they spend on things they find unpleasant." That means doing less housework and home maintenance, and doing more dining out. It also means paying more attention to brand names—not in search of status, but to make buying decisions quicker and easier. "In effect, brand loyalty helps reduce people's shopping time," says Blackwell.

To prosper in the new millennium, companies must study how consumers like Cleveland resident Donna Miller, 37, and her husband have come to view their most precious commodity. An Internet content manager with a multinational consulting firm, Miller is relentless in her pursuit of free time. With a two-hour commute to and from work, an eight- to ten-hour workday, a company laptop that keeps her connected to a never-ending stream of e-mail requests, and a seemingly endless to-do list of household chores and personal errands, Miller has finally cried "uncle!"

"I want to spend more time with my family and friends, and I want to find time to cultivate my interests," says this one-time comparison shopper. "I'm not looking for the best price anymore—I'm not looking for deals. All I'm looking for is the best service."

Miller is not alone in her "damn the torpedoes" approach to time hoarding. It seems the majority of time-challenged Americans are willing to pay "whatever" to scale down their lives. Thus, in the 21st century, value will no longer be a matter of price, but a matter of freedom, including the freedom to rest. A 1998 survey by the National Sleep Foundation found that nearly one-third of all Americans get by on six hours of sleep or less. Why? A clue comes from the 1997 Monitor survey of American social values by Yankelovich Partners: 81 percent of employed consumers feel the need to simplify their lives and create more time for home and family, and about 37 percent are making up lost time by getting less sleep; 38 percent just skip the housekeeping.

None of this is surprising to Marjorie Valin of the Washington, D.C.-based American Advertising Federation. Valin says advertisers of the future will need to capitalize on what she calls "the frenetic sense of lost time" and the life-out-of-control angst that permeates modern culture.

"What we [will] value in terms of products and services is time and convenience," says Valin. Technology—everything from television to the microwave to the Internet—has already changed our expectations, Valin says. "We won't be a wait-in-line culture anymore. We're used to getting what we want [and getting it] now."

Consumers on a constrained time budget will likely favor small shops over large ones, spend less time comparing prices, use technology to reduce transaction time, and patronize businesses that make life easier.

No company has learned this better than Kinko's, the copy-shop empire. A few years ago, Kinko's noticed that busy customers in their stores didn't just want to do their photocopying and head home. They wanted to pop in a store, create a computer document, print it out, staple it, glue it, hole-punch it, and gussy it up in a three-ring binder. In response, Kinko's has added computer workstations to many of its stores, along with sophisticated technical support, and basic supplies that turn each of their copy centers into home offices away from home.

Thus, say marketers, businesses that cater to consumer motivations, rather than simply looking at consumption patterns, are the ones that will succeed in the next millennium. How to become a 21st century market leader? Says Edward B. Keller, president of Roper Starch Worldwide, the market research and consulting firm: "Simplify life for consumers and solve their problems."

THE CONNECTEDNESS CRAZE

In the 21st century, the phrase "we're all connected" won't just be part of a telephone company jingle. This urge to connect will pervade all aspects of consumers' lives. But it will be particularly evident in the way they embrace technology. Increasingly, customers will turn to the World Wide Web for a sense of community—between buyers and sellers, information suppliers and consumers, friends and family.

While they will use the Web to socialize and search, to shop and sell and invest, they will also become far choosier

Consumers on a constrained time budget will likely favor small shops over large ones, spend less time comparing prices, use technology to reduce transaction time, and patronize businesses that make life easier.

about the sites they visit and use, predicts Evan Schwartz, author of *Webonomics* (Broadway Books). "Once a site succeeds in hooking thousands, or even millions, of eyeballs, it has to deliver something special," Schwartz writes. "Otherwise, it's just the digital equivalent of an accident on the side of the road. Everyone wants to see it as they pass by, but the commitment ends there."

Contrary to what most people believe, Schwartz says, consumers will not make the Web a mass medium, but rather a niche medium. "There may be tens of millions of people surfing the Web, but unlike network television during prime time, you'll never find a significant portion of them in any given place. The name of the game for any content creator is to find a unique niche, then use the interactive features of the Web to cater to a very specific and loyal group of individuals."

The quest for connectedness will extend into other areas of consumers' lives as well. Even their household appliances will be accessible from remote locations, if consumers have anything to say about it. "What I really want is a computer that monitors your refrigerator, finds out you've just used up the last drop of orange juice, and calls the store and orders it for you," says Michael Miller, editor-in-chief of *PC Magazine*.

William Barr, executive director of information networking for Bellcore and president of the Smart Card Forum, a non-profit consortium, predicts that by the 21st century, consumers will be able to consolidate all the information they need on just four smart cards in their wallets. Consumers will demand, however, that all the information those cards contain be useful for their everyday activities. One example: Several universities, including the University of Michigan in Ann Arbor, are already beginning to issue smart cards that contain information on students' identification, dorm meal plan, Internet access account, bus pass, and dorm-access codes, as well as cash for the bus or the laundry. In the 21st century, Barr says, "people won't want to carry 16 cards, like we do today." Forrester Research of Cambridge, Massachusetts, projects that financial firms will issue 4.7 million smart cards in the United States and Canada by 2002, up from 429,000 in 1997.

Consumers will also be looking for more efficient ways to connect with their money. Because greater numbers of Americans will be self-employed, rather than working for large corporations, more people will find themselves managing their own, increasingly complicated investment portfolios. Where to turn? For many, it will be to an online broker. Internet access to financial information and the ability to make Web-based stock purchases or trades is the fastest-growing segment of the financial services industry. Charles Schwab & Company reports that its number of online accounts increased from 300,000 in 1996 to more than two

> *"The name of the game for any content creator is to find a unique niche, then use the interactive features of the Web to cater to a very specific and loyal group of individuals."*
> —*Evan Schwartz*

million by the end of October 1998. "Four years ago, the words 'online' and 'investing' were not used in the same sentence," says Tom Taggart, director of corporate communications for Schwab. Predicts Andrew Whinston, director of the Center for Research in Electronic Commerce at the University of Texas at Austin, "The days of people calling their broker are numbered."

THE BODY VS. SOUL CONUNDRUM

The 21st century will be the era of the paradox. Americans will continue to stuff themselves with junk food while at the same time exercising to the point of obsession. They will eat no-fat cookies and enjoy their scoop of Häagen-Dazs at the same time. They will increasingly stay home to shop, meditate, and pamper their bodies, but they'll also expect more from the outside world in terms of entertainment. That's why the 21st century will see the continuation of the trend toward the "entertainmentization" of retailing, says Ira Mayer, president of EPM Communications in New York City. More than ever before, he says, stores will stage events, show videos on large screens, and use CDs as premiums in an attempt to add an entertainment overlay to the everyday shopping experience. Twenty-first century marketers may follow the lead of Wal-Mart, for example, which last November hosted a live Garth Brooks concert that was videocast on televisions in the retailer's electronics departments nationwide.

Another paradoxical force will be an effort by shoppers to transform the ordinary into the extraordinary. This might come in the form of "turning a bath or shower into luxury time [or] making the movie house a multientertainment destination," says Mayer. Marketers have already begun to capitalize on the trend. Example: Magic Johnson's ambitious plan to develop elaborate theater complexes in urban neighborhoods, complete with game areas and a cluster of youth-oriented retailers.

Consumers in the 21st century will likely continue their obsession with fitness, while at the same time consuming record amounts of takeout food. According to the National Restaurant Association, a little more than one fifth (21 percent) of consumers now order food to-go at least once a day, and another 26 percent do so every other day. No manufacturer seems better poised to reconcile the push-and-pull between holistic health concerns and the American appetite for an epicurean quick fix than the Campbell Soup Company, which claims its products can not only save us time, but renew our souls. The new motto: "M'm! M'm! Good for the Body. Good for the Soul." Explains Patrick Murphy, professor and chair of marketing at the University of Notre Dame, "As our lives are getting busier, we're starting to place a higher value on the spiritual. Advertisers have always been able to capitalize on what we consumers place value on."

The 21st century will be the era of the paradox. Americans will continue to stuff themselves with junk food while at the same time exercising to the point of obsession.

THE TRIUMPH OF INDIVIDUALISM

Older, wiser, and plumper around the middle, fin-de-siècle baby boomers know what they want. They want to be treated and catered to as individuals. A woman is no longer simply a woman for marketing purposes. She is, for example, a single mom, an ethnic minority, a bicycling enthusiast, a buyer of petite-sized clothing, and a wine connoisseur.

But while baby boomers will continue to drive many trends, the importance of children as consumers in the new millennium has only begun to be recognized, says Ohio State professor Blackwell. Many of today's parents have only one child—as opposed to two or three—and can afford to indulge them in ways parents a decade or two ago could not. Even though those children don't sign checks or earn salaries, they have an enormous influence on spending. On average, Blackwell says, children now influence 17 percent of family spending in product categories ranging from cars to vacation packages, and they control as much as 80 percent of the decisions regarding some food purchases. "By age ten, a child visits stores 270 times per year. Their opinions on brands, types of products and retailers are formed early on, and these preferences stay with them throughout their lives," Blackwell explains.

In the 21st century, individualism will have its biggest impact on the world of work.

The ethnic market, too, will benefit from the rush to market individualism. Marketers have recognized that members of ethnic groups don't respond to pitches targeted too broadly, says EPM Communications' Mayer, whose company publishes the "Minority Markets Alert" newsletter. "Ad agencies will have to know that Argentineans respond differently than people from the Dominican Republic, and that Asians who speak Mandarin have different preferences than those who speak Cantonese. There are no more homogenous groups."

Nowhere does the importance of the individual come into play more than in the fashion world. Aging baby boomers want comfortable, classic styles—not necessarily with a designer label. "It used to be that 25-year-old women drove the fashion industry; now it's 45-year-old women," says Blackwell. "Because when you're 45, you already know what you look good in. If a designer says, 'Crepe is in,' this group may confidently answer that 'crepe is crap'."

As society becomes less pluralistic, ethnic groups will contribute to drive fashion trends. The African-American clothing design company FUBU (For Us By Us), for example, has taken its baggy pants and other designs popular in ethnic neighborhoods and created a crossover market for them in the society at large.

But in the 21st century, individualism will have its biggest impact on the world of work. If you work in a factory today, you will be much more likely to work in an office job tomorrow. And you will be far more likely to work as a free agent, rather than as a salaried employee. Often, that will mean working from home, without perquisites like health and life insurance or printer paper from the company supply cabinet.

Brock Hinzmann, a technology navigator with SRI Consulting, believes it's not unlikely that we'll see a work future that mimics Hollywood: independent contractors coming together in teams to work on a specific project. "It's amazing sometimes to see all those names at the end of a movie and realize that all those disparate people worked as a one-time team to create a production," Hinzmann says. "It wouldn't be surprising to see the same thing happen in business."

As employment becomes more individualistic, what you once called your office is likely to become far more portable, and ineluctably linked to your private life. Like the tortoise who carries his house on his back, workers in the new millennium will carry parts of their digital homes and offices wherever they go. "If you're taking a vacation in Montana, you'll probably be taking your children and your laptop, as well," says Wacker. In the 21st century, the lines between consumers' work lives, their financial lives, and their home lives will become not just blurry, but almost invisible.

Like the tortoise who carries his house on his back, workers in the new millennium will carry parts of their digital homes and offices wherever they go.

V. The Society of the Future

Editor's Introduction

The confluence of an aging population and advances in biotechnology has led to increased funding for research on aging, as Heidi Evans explains in the first selection, "Your Second Century" (*Newsday*). This research has led to discoveries that give rise to claims that we may be able to live longer, healthier lives in the 21st century. A leading "biodemographer" at Duke University, James Vaupel, predicts that half the girls and a third of the boys born in 1999 will live to be centenarians. Experts credit advances in curing and preventing the diseases of childhood and youth with having increased the average life expectancy, but they say that future increases of more than a few years—say, of more than a decade—will only be made possible by new forms of biotechnology such as gene therapy and cellular regeneration.

Another important demographic trend that will affect the lives of Americans is the shrinking of the white population and the increase in the populations of African Americans, Hispanics, and Asian Americans. In the second selection, "Gen-Millennium's View of Color" (*Wisconsin State Journal*), Scott Shepard finds hope in a recent CBS News poll (of Americans under the age of 18) for a future fraught with less racial tension. The findings show that, with some exceptions, the attitudes of youth toward race are "more relaxed" than those of adults. But students of statistics will want to take note that the poll of youth is being contrasted with a poll of adults taken two years earlier by another organization. No information is provided about the sample size of either poll, nor about the error margin. While attitudes are hard to pin down, projected population changes are not, and it is clear that at some point after 2050 white Americans will be in the minority, according to experts. But that is true only if we think of the other groups that are counted in these studies—blacks, Asians, and Hispanics—as one big nonwhite majority. It would be more accurate to say that all groups will be numerical minorities in the late 21st century. Another distinction that should be kept in mind is the concept of numerical majority vs. social majority. Extrapolating from current statistics, it is likely that white Americans will continue to have a number of advantages over other Americans—such as income, education, housing, and political representation—even as the white population decreases relative to other populations. It is hoped that this deplorable situation will be alleviated by greater racial understanding in the future, but not everyone Shepard interviewed is optimistic. Demographic changes and interracial marriages are not enough to do the job; better race relations will take hard work on everyone's part. Shepard ends his piece by quoting Yvonne Scruggs-Leftwich, executive director of the Black Leadership Forum: "We must go on with the business of racial reconciliation, we must dump the useless concept of color-blindness, and we must value each other for exactly who we are, not who we are fading into."

In the third selection, "The Clocks Ahead Will Have Our Own Faces" (*Business Week*), Diane Brady speculates about the effects of "unrooted living" and "timeless schedule[s]" on our psyches: "By loosening the constraint of time, are we liberating ourselves—or submitting to a kind of 21st-century enslavement?" The blurring of the line between work and "home" or "private" life can be seen everywhere, she notes, from the ubiquitous presence of cell phones (in concert halls, churches, and, this editor would like to add, on the hiking trail) to the laptop-toting beachgoer. People in the fast-paced worlds spawned by Silicon Valley talk in terms of cyberweeks and Webdays, referring to the extraordinary pace of change and the efforts of our workloads to keep up with it. The ups and downs of this way of living are discussed.

Just as our relationship to time is changing, so is our relationship to entertainment. In the past (read "today" for most of us), Joshua Quittner reminds us in the fourth selection ("Future Shocks," *Time*) that entertainment was consumed passively by couch potatoes, but in the near future (read "today" for some of us) we will have the ability to direct the action. "The descendants of video games, interactive TV, online environments like MUDs and MOOs (where Net folks cavort in text-based worlds) and hypertext will vest the power to create in the viewers' hands." But as with space colonization and living until age 150, how many of us will want to take advantage of the brave new worlds of multimedia entertainment? "Lots of people like just watching," Quittner notes.

Another innovation many of us may be slow to embrace is the eradication of the distinction between machine vs. human life envisioned by Ray Kurzweil, author of *The Age of Spiritual Machines.* In the fifth selection ("Pundit Forecasts Portable, Praying PCs in *The Age of Spiritual Machines*," *Fortune*), Richard A. Shaffer argues that "such fanciful speculations, while entertaining fiction, shouldn't be taken too seriously," but he finds much to respect in Kurzweil's shorter-term predictions, among them that "music, software, and books will be distributed wirelessly, never assuming a physical form," and that "many business transactions will take place between a human and what the author calls a 'virtual personality.'"

Having examined the future from the perspective of thousand-year and hundred-year time frames and from the largest scope imaginable—that of the universe—to the progressively smaller worlds of the planet, nations, economies, and societies, we turn now to the smallest scale addressed in these pages: person-to-person intimacy. (That is, if you discount the even smaller scale of individual consciousness and spirituality touched upon in the previous article.) In the sixth and final selection, "The Future of Intimacy: A Search for Soul in the New Machines" (*Maclean's*), Mark Kingwell discusses the various ways in which we imagine the future, and he notes that most prognosticators fall into one of two camps: "Advocates would have us believe that the question of life a hundred years hence is one either of utopia or dystopia,…a form of bipolar thinking that is particularly prevalent at cultural-limit times like the much-discussed, entirely arbitrary and yet immensely compelling millennium." Whatever may-change, he asserts, "the base-level facts of existence" will not: "that we must rise and face each day, and that at some point this circadian cycle will cease for each one of us." Therefore, he concludes, "intimacy will continue to play its joyful, vexing, complex role in our lives, and the subtle dialectic of private and public will continue to dominate our institutions, occupations, entertainments and most of all, our sense of ourselves."

Your Second Century [1]

Can We All Live to Be 100, 150 . . . or More? And Can Science and Society Make a Long Life a Good Life?

Sometime around her 115th birthday in 1990, Jeanne Calment was asked how she saw her future. "Short," the French woman replied. "Very short."

Calment actually had more of a future than she imagined. She died seven years later, at 122, by which time the world had come to regard her as the ultimate Guinness record.

Calment may have been regarded as a medical marvel, but scientists studying the biological process of aging think she will eventually be just one of many in the world to breeze far past the century mark and still have a future. Maybe even a long future.

As we enter a new age of biology, experts say the most profound effect may ultimately be a stunning ability to slow the aging process—perhaps allowing the healthiest and strongest among us to one day live 125 years or more. Even the most cautious scientists now believe that in the coming decades, new drugs and genetic and cellular engineering may well make many people biologically capable of surpassing Calment's record.

Some say that a very select few—the Jeanne Calments of the 21st Century—may even reach 150. And for others, seeing 95, even 100, may become routine. A leading Duke University demographer, James Vaupel, projects that half the girls and a third of the boys born this year in developed countries will live more than a century.

A leading Duke University demographer, James Vaupel, projects that half the girls and a third of the boys born this year in developed countries will live more than a century.

What's more, "many people alive now will live through the next century and on to the next one," said Dr. Roy L. Walford, a researcher on aging at the UCLA School of Medicine.

"There is no doubt that over the next century, lifespan is going to increase further," said Andrew Monjan, chief of neurobiology at the National Institute on Aging. "How much, we don't know."

Researchers see two distinct but parallel trends that may soon provide some answers. In the near term, advances in disease prevention and health care promise to push up average life expectancy faster and help more people reach the century mark.

Meanwhile, experts envision breakthroughs further in the future in genetic therapies that could build on work being done today aimed at slowing the aging process in individual

1. Article by Heidi Evans from *Newsday* Feb. 28, 1999. Copyright © 1999, Newsday, Inc./Heidi Evans. Reprinted with permission.

human cells. Such developments could have more effect on life expectancy and maximum lifespan than even the eradication of cancer and heart disease.

Moreover, many researchers believe it will be possible not only to extend life, but to make those extra years largely healthy and productive—expanding what longevity experts have dubbed "healthspan." The consequences could be exhilarating, and overwhelming.

Federal agencies are already struggling to figure out what the right life expectancy projections will be, since the wrong guess could have powerful consequences if they underestimate the number of people who will need Social Security and Medicare in the decades ahead. Adding millions of people in their 100s would also raise serious questions about employment, housing and many other public issues.

"If we think we can't handle the number of people we have in the workplace now, how will we do it when people are around for 150 years?" asked Richard Sprott, head of the nonprofit Ellison Foundation in Bethesda, Md., which funds aging research. "Useful worklives will be five times as long as what we have now. Think of the prospect of your boss sitting in the same chair for 30 extra years while you want to move up and into it."

Rose Dobrof, a professor of gerontology at Hunter College in New York, added: "With people in their 90s and 100s still active and working, we would have to educate and re-educate. People would have to go back to school a number of times in their lifetime to retool themselves. With 90 years of work, you'd also have to have sabbaticals, not just for academics but for all people in the work force."

The change in family structure as we know it would also be extraordinary, with up to six generations alive at the same time, and half the people in many families older than 65.

One piece of the picture is already clear: the growth in the number of people reaching 100. The Census Bureau estimates that today there are 66,000 Americans older than 100—20 times the number in 1960—and their ranks are growing every year. The bureau projects there will be 214,000 centenarians by 2020 and 834,000 by 2050.

"This will happen without any amazing breakthroughs, just if we keep continuing to do well in bringing death rates down as we have in the last half-century," said Duke demographer Vaupel, who is a leader in an emerging field known as "biodemography."

"More people will be living to [their] genetic maximum," agreed Mark Lane, a researcher at the National Institute on Aging who is studying longevity in primates. "The goal of all of us is . . . enjoying life for the longest amount of time. And there will be some potential intervention that will push lifespan a lot further."

The Census Bureau estimates that today there are 66,000 Americans older than 100—20 times the number in 1960—and their ranks are growing every year.

Among those "interventions" now under serious scientific investigation are several that would reset our biological clocks. In one case, researchers are trying to devise a way to repair a specific kind of damage that causes cells—and us—to age. Others are working on an enzyme called telomerase, which has been shown to help cells stay young by causing them to divide many more times and over a longer period than they might on their own.

"We can now envision in five to 10 years taking someone's cells, rejuvenating them and giving them back to the person to treat genetic diseases and some of the degenerative conditions of aging," said Dr. Woodring Wright, the lead scientist on the team of researchers who discovered that telomerase could extend the lifespan of human cells.

Once a backwater of scientific inquiry, longevity has become one of the hottest areas of research. The National Institute on Aging, created in 1974, has seen its budget grow from $19.2 million to $595.5 million—for research into aging and the effect of increased lifespan on society. Locally, the New York-based American Federation for Aging Research, a private nonprofit group, has funded more than 2,000 investigators to date, and more are joining the ranks each year. Many of them are emboldened by the emerging possibility that the aging process can be altered at the genetic or molecular level.

Once a backwater of scientific inquiry, longevity has become one of the hottest areas of research.

The leading avenue of aging research intersects with the coming age of gene therapy, in which replacing defective or deteriorated genes may become commonplace. "Few of us think that controlling one or a few human genes will stop aging," said Steven Austad, author of *Why We Age* and a University of Idaho zoology professor. "But a measurable slowing down seems within the realm of possibility."

Some of the answers may start to come soon, with the expected completion in 2003 of the Human Genome Project, a $4 billion effort started in 1991 that will identify all of humanity's 80,000 genes. Among many other things, the genome project will reveal whether there are "longevity genes"—and if so, how many there are and whether they interact with other genes.

At the same time, scientists will try to learn what roles environment, lifestyle and gender play. Men die at higher rates than women throughout life and throughout the world. In the United States there is a gender gap in life expectancy of about seven years that is projected to continue. Why are women the biologically stronger sex—is it simply hormones, as popular scientific wisdom goes, or hormones and something else?

"There is definitely a protection in women and it has been quite constant," said Dr. Nir Barzilai, a molecular biologist at the Albert Einstein College of Medicine in the Bronx who is conducting a large-scale study on longevity genes in people

95 and older. "The gap is even worse in centenarians," he added, noting that for every three or four women who reach 100, there is only one man who makes the mark. "So clearly, the answer to women's increased longevity is not estrogen alone. These women have been post-menopausal for 50 years."

Equalizing life expectancy—a development not yet on the horizon—would have important consequences, says Richard Suzman, associate director of Social and Behavioral Research at the National Institute on Aging. Men's earlier deaths are a major cause of poverty among older women, he said, and a contributing factor to their decline and having to live in nursing homes.

For men and women, the centenarian trend is being driven by advances in public health. Far fewer people now die of infectious childhood diseases than earlier in the century, so more people with the genes to live to 100 have been able to fulfill their genetic promise. And in the past 20 years, scientific advances and markedly improved geriatric medicine have been able to delay many age-related diseases, such as heart disease and osteoporosis, allowing older people to get even older.

Men's earlier deaths are a major cause of poverty among older women . . . and a contributing factor to their decline and having to live in nursing homes.

"We are seeing a lot of people living to 100 with good mental and physical health," said Margery Hutter Silver, a Harvard neuropsychologist and age researcher who is 66. "It makes you rethink your perceptions of aging. Personally, it has made me realize that I can really plan for another 35 years."

Most people aren't planning quite so far in advance. Only 8 percent of 1,092 Long Islanders surveyed by *Newsday*'s Future Poll, for instance, said they expected to reach 100, based on current advances in medicine. Another 17 percent hoped to make it to 90. The median answer was 85.

"I don't see that we are going to make that much advance in the future," said one of the skeptics, Carolyn Schiller, a 44-year-old secretary from Levittown. "I would be happy to take 80 good years and call it quits."

Daniel Haber, 64, a retired New York City Housing Authority manager from Oceanside, has his sights set higher. "The pharmaceutical industry has come up with these fantastic pills—I know it will get me to at least 99," said Haber, who takes a cholesterol-lowering drug to reduce his chances of having a heart attack.

Average life expectancy—which takes into account everything from childhood diseases to fatal accidents—has been on the rise over the past centuries. For example, in 1776, average life expectancy at birth was just 35 years—largely because childhood mortality brought down the average. It still was only about 47 in 1900, though people who survived to adulthood could expect to live into their late 60s.

But in the 20th century, there has been a great leap forward. By 1950, average life expectancy at birth among Americans was 68 years. The average female child born today is expected to live to 80, the Census Bureau says, and a male child to 73.

We have gotten this far largely by eliminating diseases of childhood and midlife, by living in safe environments with clean water and food, and because of immunizations and obstetrical care—by conquering diseases of the young, not of the old. In fact, the great jump in average life expectancy has all been done without understanding much about the process of aging.

That's what has many researchers excited: Never before have so many scientists been focused not on why we get sick but why we age—and what can be done about it. That, they say, is the only hope for significantly expanding both lifespan and life expectancy.

According to Austad and others, if all cancer were eliminated tomorrow, human life expectancy would be extended only by about two years; eliminate heart disease and we would get about three to four years more. "If we can add only six years to our lives by eliminating these two diseases—which together kill more than half of all people in industrialized societies—we are clearly pushing the limits of lifespan increase by normal medical progress," Austad wrote in his book. Beating diseases back one by one, he argues, will have progressively less effect in the future. (Government projections have women and men living on average only to 84 and 79 years respectively by 2075 because they are based only on what has happened in the past, and don't take into account any dramatic findings in the future.)

The key to slowing the aging process, many believe, is in understanding—and manipulating—the most basic levels of life. Emerging as the leading line of inquiry is one focused on repairing the damage and deterioration that causes our cells to age—commonly referred to as "oxidative stress." Oxygen, though necessary for life, is also a very damaging and toxic molecule. When oxygen is broken apart to help provide our energy, we create "oxygen radicals" that damage everything that they bump into. Our bodies can repair a lot of that damage, but not quite all. To slow the aging process, researchers are trying to figure out how to slow down that damage.

Even now, researchers say there may be ways to counteract the effects of oxidative stress the old-fashioned way. Many studies have shown the life-extending benefits of eating fruits, vegetables and whole grains that are rich in the antioxidant vitamins E, C and beta-carotine, a form of vitamin A.

In another hot area of aging research, scientists are exploring whether an enzyme called telomerase can stop or reset the biological clock that ages cells. Telomeres are protective end caps—like the plastic tips of shoelaces—designed to stop

We have gotten this far . . . by conquering diseases of the young, not of the old. In fact, the great jump in average life expectancy has all been done without understanding much about the process of aging.

the chromosomes from "fraying" when cells divide. After a certain number of cell divisions, the telomeres eventually shorten too much and render the cells incapable of dividing further, making the cell act "old."

Scientists from the Geron Corp. in Menlo Park, Calif., and the University of Texas Southwestern Medical School in Dallas have been able to extend or relengthen telomeres in the laboratory with the telomerase enzyme. The enzyme can make cells continue to divide at least 250 times more than the normal limit and show no signs of stopping in the laboratory. Researchers who reported these findings in the journal *Science* in 1997 cautioned that extending the life of cells is not the same as extending the life of an entire human being. However, the scientists wrote, lengthening the lifespan of cells might someday be used to treat a number of health problems associated with aging, such as macular degeneration of the eye, clogged arteries and skin ulcers.

Other researchers are pursuing a theory that long-term restrictions in calorie-intake may retard aging. Hundreds of studies have already shown that rodents live 25 percent to 40 percent longer and healthier when they consume less food. Similar studies are now in progress in primates and already show improvements in lowering monkeys' risk for age-related diseases such as hardening of the arteries and diabetes.

With these theories being pursued, the burgeoning world of the biology of aging includes a growing number of believers—and true believers.

"There is little doubt that we will retard the rate of aging in the next decades—it can be cut in half," said Roy Walford, the UCLA researcher and pathology professor. "If you retard the rate of aging, you stretch out middle age and youth. If you stretched that out to 150, the frail years are still the last 20. The gain is in vital years."

Ronald Klatz, an osteopath who is the founder and president of the American Academy of Anti-Aging Medicine based in Chicago, takes 60 different pills a day, including HGH, a controversial human growth hormone to restore muscle mass and strengthen bones, and DHEA, a hormone that anti-aging enthusiasts believe boosts the brain, immune system and fights cancer. Klatz, 43, is convinced he will live beyond 120—way beyond. Ultimately, the only causes of death will be "homicide, suicide and aerospace accident," he predicts only half in jest. "You will live until you feel like giving Dr. Kevorkian a call."

Dr. Michael Fossel, a clinical professor of medicine at Michigan State University and editor of the *Journal of Anti-Aging Medicine*, goes so far as to predict that in 20 years, we will know so much about what makes us age that our lifespan will increase to 200 or 300 years. Fossel's predictions are based entirely on the promise of telomerase.

Ultimately, the only causes of death will be "homicide, suicide and aerospace accident," [Ronald Katz] predicts only half in jest. "You will live until you feel like giving Dr. Kevorkian a call."

But Klatz and Fossel clearly have little company—even in a field that has traditionally been full of out-there thinkers.

Caleb Finch, a professor of gerontology and director of the Alzheimer's Center at the University of Southern California, calls aging a "a remarkable set of puzzles." He gives little credence to Fossel's notion that humans will one day live for 300 years, though he thinks a 150-year lifespan is certainly possible.

"I look at aging as the sum of all of the diseases," Finch said. "Each one is a world of science on its own with genes, environment and lifestyle playing a role. You put them all together and it's a much more complicated landscape."

Some aging experts caution that to dwell too much on living to 120 and beyond is a mistake. What's more important, they say, is to increase a person's "healthspan" rather than lifespan, meaning living most of one's years in excellent health and a short period of disability at the very end of life.

"Many more mainstream gerontologists are interested in healthspan than lifespan," said Sprott of the Ellison Foundation, who headed the National Institute on Aging's biology of aging programs from 1980 until 1998. "Most of us would rather live to 85 in good health than live to 150 with 10 or 15 years of disability."

Otto Walter, 91, who still works full time as an international tax lawyer, is intrigued by the notion that people might one day be able to live both longer and healthier. "More power to the future generations if that can be pulled off," said Walter, as he sipped sherry in the elegant Manhattan apartment he shares with his 83-year-old wife, Fran. "It would be a political and economic disaster for the world if we all lived that long. But my main concern would be not to live the life of an invalid."

Finch of USC thinks the extra years would indeed be healthy ones—mainly an extension of middle age. "We are slowing the years after we have matured, when a lot of aging has already happened," Finch said. Jeanne Calment, he suggested, is a good guide: "She probably felt like 50 or 60 forever."

Dr. Thomas Perls, a Harvard Medical School physician and director of a large study of some of America's oldest people, is one of many aging experts who believe the older years, however many we will have in the future, do not have to be depressing or debilitating ones.

Since 1994, he and Silver have been analyzing the mental, physical and emotional health of 106 centenarians in the Boston area. Fully 30 percent of those in the study had no cognitive impairment. About 70 percent of them had only "mild or moderate" impairment. The researchers found that all these 100-plussers were mentally intact and lived completely independently to their mid-90s. Perls and Silver found significance in these numbers because, Perls said, "Mental

Some aging experts caution that to dwell too much on living to 120 and beyond is a mistake. What's more important, they say, is to increase a person's "healthspan" rather than lifespan.

function is by far our strongest predictor of how a person is going to do." Their onset of dementia was considerably delayed compared with the rest of the population.

In addition to their good mental functioning, Perls said, the key to his subjects' achievement was markedly delaying or completely escaping the fatal diseases of aging: heart attack, stroke, cancer and Alzheimer's disease.

"They are the gold standard of aging well," Perls said. "They demonstrate this phenomenon, where you live the vast majority of your life in excellent health and have a short period in poor health."

Personality also played a role in their longevity, said Silver—a view shared by those who study the oldest old up close. The common thread among them was how well they handled stress. Although many centenarians have had hard lives and all have suffered loss—many have outlived their spouses and children—they were upbeat and generous, could roll with life's punches and had a cheerful spirit.

"I sure am happy I have lived this long and I'm looking forward to being 105," said Catherine J. McCaig of Marshfield, Mass., who at 103 lives in her own apartment where she cooks, plays piano and shares laughs with neighbors and her baby 94-year-old sister, Winifred Whynot. Both sisters—who are part of Perls and Silver's New England Centenarian Study—say they would love to live many more years so long as they stayed healthy. "That would be wonderful," Winifred said. "As long as I can walk and talk. But I have lived a long life. Whenever God opens the door for me, I will be ready."

Until that door opens, 95-year-old George Seltzer knows how he would plan a longer life. The New Jersey dentist and widowed grandfather travels by bus and subway to New York University twice a week to teach dental students, and two nights a week he plays poker with his much younger cronies. Suppose, at 95, he was suddenly the equivalent of today's middle-aged person?

"I'd pick a new career," he said. "Sixty years of dentistry is enough. And then I'd look for a nice dame."

Gen-Millennium's View of Color[2]

Most Diverse Generation May Be One to Erase Race Line

"The problem of the 20th century is the problem of the color line," educator W.E.B. DuBois wrote in 1903. Will that still be true in 21st century America, when whites are no longer a majority and Hispanics replace blacks as the country's largest ethnic minority?

The answer may lie in the attitudes of the "Millennium Generation," Americans under the age of 18. This demographic tidal wave has already eclipsed the baby boomers in numbers, and there is no end in sight.

"This generation is going to redefine American society in ways much more profound than the boomers," said Ronald Franklin, a Detroit advertising executive who is analyzing the generation for Connecticut-based Yankelovich Partners Inc., one of the foremost trackers of changing American lifestyles.

There are already signs that race relations are changing. White kids want to "be like Mike." "Urban attitude" colors the music and fashion favored by "Millenniums" of all races. Colin Powell and Oprah Winfrey are consistently among the most admired Americans.

"Millenniums" are the most racially and ethnically diverse generation in the country's history, with a proportion of non-whites 60 percent larger than that of the two preceding generations. Polls show that its members are more relaxed in their attitudes about race and more optimistic about the future of race relations than previous generations were.

"This generation is re-creating America's racial identity every single day," said Farai Chideya, an ABC News correspondent and author of *The Color of Our Future*, a new book about individuals coping with the country's changing racial terrain. "And if anybody is going to erase the color line, it's going to be them."

SOBERING DATA

Such optimism is tempered by government data suggesting that even after a century of civil rights progress, deep problems remain.

Black families still earn 40 percent less than comparable white families and have 90 percent less family wealth. Less than half own their home, compared to 70 percent of whites. Blacks are half as likely to attend college as whites. A major-

Polls show that [Americans under 18] are more relaxed in their attitudes about race and more optimistic about the future of race relations than previous generations were.

---

ity of black births occur out of wedlock. Black men are incarcerated at a rate of nearly 8 times that of whites. And blacks' life span averages six years less than whites'.

"That's what it costs to be black in America in 1999," said Joe Feagin, a sociologist at the University of Florida. "That is what 400 years of oppression means today."

Even with the "Millennium Generation" leading the way, it's far from clear that future Americans will live as "neighborly citizens of a common country," as Frederick Douglass, the runaway slave turned abolitionist leader, predicted just five months after President Abraham Lincoln signed the Emancipation Proclamation in 1863.

Along with their wealth, whites enjoy disproportionate political power that gives them a great deal of control over the pace of social change. For example, while blacks make up 12 percent of the population, they hold only about 8 percent of the seats in the U.S. House and none in the U.S. Senate.

"All the talk about demographics really obscures a more basic point—that for all the gains of minorities, there is very little sharing of power by the white establishment," said [Farai] Chideya.

"All the talk about demographics really obscures a more basic point—that for all the gains of minorities, there is very little sharing of power by the white establishment," said Chideya. "Already, we see a backlash against racial diversity in an attempt to keep America fixed in time."

At the heart of the battle is affirmative action, the concept that the victims of discrimination should be given special consideration in employment and college admissions. Political conservatives counter with a call for a "color-blind society" that grants racial preferences to no one.

This struggle will affect race relations well into the next century, complicated by the growing number of Americans who have no personal knowledge of state-imposed segregation of blacks through most of the 20th century.

"As new generations of whites are born and raised, the memories of Jim Crow will fade, along with the guilt," said Richard Kahlenberg, a researcher at the Center for National Policy in Washington and author of *The Remedy: Class Race and Affirmative Action.*

And despite its experience with integrated schools and neighborhoods, the "Millennium Generation" is not some racial utopia. In a "Class of 2000" poll of 11th graders by CBS News, one-fourth admitted having made racist remarks, and the group was less likely to approve of interracial dating than older Americans are of interracial marriage.

TURNING POINT?

According to experts, "ground zero" for the future of race relations will come after the year 2050, when the youngest of the "Millennium Generation" will be 70 years old. Not long after, race in America will have been turned upside down, with whites in the minority and blacks, Hispanics and Asians constituting a majority.

Paula D. McClain, a civil rights expert at the University of Virginia, sees two prospects: one of increased racial tensions, the other of unprecedented racial understanding.

"Whites who have never experienced minority status will battle to maintain their privileged position in the face of changing demographics," McClain said.

"On the other hand," she added, "it is possible that the reversal in status for many white Americans will eventually bring about improved race relations as they begin to understand the situation in which black Americans have found themselves for the last 400 years."

Feagin is in the pessimistic camp.

The "most likely choice" for whites in the second half of the next century is "building more private schools, more guarded, gated communities, moving to 'white states' in the Rocky Mountains and Midwest, buying guns and more police—basically the old South African apartheid system," he said.

Table 1: U.S. Population by Race

RACE	NOV. 1, 1998*	JULY 1, 2050**
White	72.1%	52.8%
Black	12.1	13.6
Hispanic	11.4	24.5
Asian/Pacific Islander	3.7	8.2
American Indian, Eskimo, Aleut	0.7	0.9

*Estimated   **Projected

Once the color line begins to evolve into a color matrix, whites may also try to co-opt some lighter-skinned, more assimilated Asians and Hispanics into "honorary white" status, another tactic used in South Africa, Feagin said.

Mary Thornberry, an expert on racial politics at Davidson University, is suspicious of any predictions about the second

POLL INDICATES YOUNG PEOPLE HAVE BRIGHTER VIEW OF RACE RELATIONS

- View the state of race relations as good in own community Youth: 76% Adult: 72%
- Believe racial prejudice will always be a problem in the United States Youth: 50% Adult: 56%
- Believe there should be special laws protecting ethnic minorities Youth: 64% Adult: 46%
- Believe there should be affirmative action programs Youth: 72% Adults: 37%
- Have close friendships with people of another race Youth: 78% Adult: 67%
- Approve of interracial dating/marriage Youth: 46% (dating) Adult: 69% (marriage)

SOURCE: Youth—"Class of 2000" poll of 11th graders, CBS News, January 1999. Adult—"Black/White Relations in the U.S.," poll of Americans 18 and older, the Gallup Poll, June 1997. Cox News Service

half of the next century. But she believes two trends will signal whether "race is disappearing as a central factor in identity": the level of support for public education and the frequency of interracial dating and marriage.

A number of experts, noting the increase in interracial marriages over the past decade, have suggested that this trend will ultimately break down America's color line.

But Yvonne Scruggs-Leftwich, executive director of the Black Leadership Forum, an umbrella group for dozens of civil rights groups, notes that "out-marriages" occur more often among Hispanics, who can be of any race, than African Americans.

Only 8 percent of black men and 4 percent of black women marry outside their race, while 31.6 percent of native-born Hispanic men and 31.4 percent of Hispanic women do, according to an analysis of Census Bureau data by the Russell Sage Foundation.

Calling the process of racial convergence to beige "a myth," Scruggs-Leftwich said that "it will be a very long time before the overwhelming number of African Americans will appear to be anything other than African Americans."

She added, "We must go on with the business of racial reconciliation, we must dump the useless concept of colorblindness, and we must value each other for exactly who we are, not who we are fading into."

"We must go on with the business of racial reconciliation, we must dump the useless concept of color-blindness, and we must value each other for exactly who we are, not who we are fading into."—Yvonne Scruggs-Leftwich

The Clocks Ahead Will Have Our Own Faces[3]

Unrooted living is spawning the timeless schedule—with restaurants simultaneously serving breakfast cereal and martinis because people's stomachs are running on different internal clocks.

Time was, people rose with the sun. And they set with it, too. Nobody cared if it was sunny somewhere else. Voices didn't carry across the planet. Time was local: time to milk the cows, time to get in the corn, time to sit and rest. World time zones were ordained in 1884 but didn't catch on until right before World War I. Fifty years ago, few even imagined night skiing.

Increasingly, though, the andante beat of time will be juked and jazzed. The reliable rhythms of days and seasons will yield to the Constant Now.

The changes have already begun. Commerce and communications never cease. On cable-TV news shows, things happen at "half past the hour." You don't ask which hour, because local time is no longer the meaningful marker. Great events unfold in the electronic ether.

In the U.S., fewer than one-third of Americans now have a workweek of standard 9-to-5 days, and that share is shrinking, according to the U.S. Census Bureau. Women and minorities are the most likely to work late shifts or irregular hours—as cashiers, clerks, or orderlies. White-collar workers are doing more work at home, inviting the urgency of the business world into what was once a refuge. Wall Street, for instance, is becoming a red-eye profession as round-the-clock markets make "closing prices" an obsolete concept. Unrooted living is spawning the timeless schedule—with restaurants simultaneously serving breakfast cereal and martinis because different people's stomachs are running on different internal clocks.

The question is, how will all this timeshifting affect people's lives in the next 100 years? The Internet never sleeps, but people do. They must. By loosening the constraint of time, are we liberating ourselves—or submitting to a kind of 21st century enslavement? As science fiction writer Bruce Sterling points out, "3 a.m. is still the midnight of the human

By loosening the constraint of time, are we liberating ourselves—or submitting to a kind of 21st century enslavement?

---

3. Article by Diane Brady from *Business Week* Aug. 30, 1999. Copyright © 1999 The McGraw-Hill Companies, Inc. Reprinted with permission.

Instant access to information at all hours of the day could fill elevators and waiting rooms with "newszak" that numbs the brain.

soul. And there are metabolic problems like seasonal affective disorder if you never see daylight."

On the good side, allowing people to live by their own clocks is profoundly democratic. The Ritz-Carlton Hotel in Kuala Lumpur, Malaysia, doesn't even trouble its corporate guests to acknowledge local time. A "one-night stay" consists of any 24-hour span of the guest's choice. The program has already been extended to other properties in Asia, where flights often come and go at odd hours.

Quite a convenience. Yet, the death of shared daily routines will shake society to its core. A Los Angeles resident who routinely gets up in the middle of the night to telephone Tel Aviv is living in L.A. in body only. If your neighbors are on different clocks from yours, then who will be part of your community? Perhaps the people on your E-mail list. Perhaps no one.

To see where this is headed, take the trends that killed Sunday store-closings—demand for convenience, odd work hours—and move them into warp speed. Almost every service, from lawyers to marriage counselors to golf pros, will operate 24 hours or risk death. Work will start at 4 a.m. or 4 p.m., depending on your preference. What will matter is what's delivered, not when it's done. Units of time will become fungible, like dollar bills: each moment fully interchangeable with each other moment.

Timelessness can become a kind of tyranny. Remember when the image of a portable computer at the beach signaled freedom? Now, it's a sign that the office never goes away. People bring their cell phones into concert halls and churches because, to them, rudeness is a lesser sin than missing an important call.

The problem comes down to movement vs. meaning. Longer trading hours, for instance, will mean more trades—but not necessarily better trades. James C. Ackerman, president of online brokerage Sloan Securities Corp., complains that 24-hour trading "won't give anybody time to sit and breathe and think." Instant access to information at all hours of the day could fill elevators and waiting rooms with "newszak" that numbs the brain. Increased efficiency is supposed to mean doing more things in the same time, not the same thing in less time. "Humans have not evolved to move at supersonic speeds," says Howard Rheingold, a West Coast commentator on technology.

A reaction is already building. Stewart Brand, environmental pundit and author of the *Whole Earth Catalog*, is leading a project to create a giant clock that will run without winding for 10,000 years, ticking once a year. He hopes "The Clock of the Long Now," as he calls it in a new book, will remind people of the planet's continuity and their responsibility for it. In Silicon Valley, birthplace of hyperspeed "Internet time," executives such as Amazon.com's Jeffrey P. Bezos and Netscape

Communications Corp. co-founder Marc Andreessen have taken to bragging about how much sleep they get. For them, the ultimate status symbol is the power to live by nature's clock rather than the Net's.

There is no going back to the agrarian past, of course. But some people will learn to dip in and out of the 24-hour flow, living by routines that suit them rather than chasing after a sun that never sets. Elizabeth DeMotte is one. As a Singapore-based employee of America's Ritz-Carlton Co., DeMotte says she gets her work done in "a very natural ebb and flow" over any 24-hour period. "I think a contemporary global executive who tries to conform to traditional ideas of workdays and time off is not only ineffective, but burning the candle at both ends," she says. Interesting—it was the candle, illuminating the night, that started us down this road.

Future Shocks[4]

The future promises to liberate us from the tyranny of artists who would suck us into the swirling maw of their moving pictures, music and books.

Stately, plump Cyberswine gazes out across a cartoon world, ready to kick some serious toon butt. Cyberswine is both the name and the protagonist of a full-length animated movie, "Part machine. Part cop. Full boar," according to the trailer. You won't find it (him) on film, though—the movie is 100% digital bits, burned onto CD-ROMS and downloadable from the Net, and now showing at a computer near you.

This is not just old pork cooked up in a new kitchen, however. Cyberswine, produced by Los Angeles-based Brilliant Digital Entertainment, is one of the first "Multipath Movies"—animated stories that let the viewer direct the action. You get to stroll down a narrative path of your choosing: stick with Cyberswine, or peel off and follow the action from the perspective of one of his pals. Don't dig the pig's vibes? Click on an icon in the corner of the screen, and tweak his character to make him more clever, anxious, aggressive or caring. You can also change the camera angle. Or not—one of the options in a Multipath Movie is to just say no to interactivity: you can sit back and watch.

But just watching . . . that's s-o-o Bi-Millennial, don't you think? We're about to close a century in which two of the biggest advancements in entertainment—movies and television—defined the passive, couch-potato experience. The future promises to liberate us from the tyranny of artists who would suck us into the swirling maw of their moving pictures, music and books. If we can extrapolate from cyber-cave-wall stuff like Cyberswine, the next thousand years of storytelling will put us in the director's seat. The descendants of video games, interactive TV, online environments like MUDs and MOOs (where Net folks cavort in text-based worlds) and hypertext will vest the power to create in the viewers' hands.

It's already happening, albeit in the crudest of ways. Boot up a computer program called the Axe, for instance, and you can jam along with Stevie Wonder's hit song "Superstition." "Anyone can play music and have a really satisfying experience," says Eran Egozy, co-founder of Harmonix Music Systems Inc., a Cambridge, Mass., software company specializing in "jamware." By moving your mouse around on a compass-like grid, you can play faster, slower, higher and lower notes—but never out of tune. "You're always in time, in key and playing the right notes," says Egozy, who admits that, mellifluous as it is, "it's not John Coltrane." Still, like flight simulators that let you pilot a jumbo jet, Harmonix's music simulator, he says, "takes the hard part away from music, the mechanical part. We're giving you the fun of it

---

4. Article by Joshua Quittner from *Time,* v151, h22, p. 1211 + June 8, 1998. Copyright © 1998 Time Inc. Reprinted with permission.

without having to work for it." Who says you have to suffer if you want to sing the blues?

Or consider the completely nonlinear narrative of your average shoot-'em-up "twitch" game, such as Quake II or Tomb Raider. (Twitch games test reflexes rather than brains.) Players are dropped down in a game and proceed, level by level, learning the skills they need to survive in this new place and acquiring knowledge that leads them to the end, to closure that is as satisfying and complete as the epilogue to a 500-page thriller. Why watch *The Terminator* when you can be the Terminator, tapping into your own fight-or-flight feedback loop and blasting and stun-gunning your way to the happily ever after? Imagine when more cerebral entertainments such as Riven (the sequel to the best-selling CD-ROM game Myst) are the program equals of TV. Instead of sitting back and watching the Seinfeld characters interact with one another, you could hang out with them. Follow Kramer around until you get bored, then hook up with George.

Artists too will emerge stronger and better in the 2K Millennium. Entertainment in this century has been mass-produced and broadcast, rigidly controlled and protected. Media have centralized into the hands of the few; Hollywood studios, television networks and recording companies carefully distribute the stuff, cranking out a relatively modest amount of material that will be seen by everyone on the globe. But in the next century anyone will be able to create a movie, music, literature, a magazine or a video game and distribute it as bits over the network to billions. At least in theory. Brilliant Digital is marketing a developers' tool kit that makes it relatively simple to cobble together your own interactive cartoons. "You don't need any programming experience," insists Cheri Grand, a company spokeswoman. "I could create a Heather Locklear character, animate her and do whatever I want with her." Traditional Hollywood studios, she notes, have lots of overhead and immense production costs. "Not us. Everything is done inside the computer." *Deus ex machina*. Amen.

For people who have one, the computer has already shown itself to be the great equalizer, the final flattener, making all of us the creator and the created. With every advance in technology, art and entertainment—its cuter, more popular sister—change in radical, unpredictable ways. And at each turn they become more democratic, more accessible. The printing press starts with Bibles and ends up with pulp fiction. Radio popularizes rock 'n' roll. TV spawns the sitcom. Now consider the possibilities that will open up as the computer meets the Net—not the network of today, with piddly, slow connections that are mainly good for relaying e-mail. But the Net of a hundred years from now, when media can move at the speed of light.

In the next century anyone will be able to create a movie, music, literature, a magazine or a video game and distribute it as bits over the network to billions.

Perhaps all the newfound interactivity will work on our brains in more salutary ways. This is your brain on TV. And this is your brain on "Very Distributed Storytelling," as one futuristic project is called at M.I.T.'s Media Lab. Any questions?

Plenty. Lots of people like just watching. The road to interactive entertainment has been rockier than a walk in a quarry, and with good reason. Who wants to cook when you can eat at a four-star restaurant? Entertainment should be...entertaining! Not work. And who wants to wade through all the awful stuff that's certain to crowd out the brilliance? Attempts at forging serious art from random accessibility have been interesting in an experimental way. But not accessible in a random kind of way.

Entertainment should be . . . entertaining! Not work.

"There is no popular need right now for multimedia. That's obvious," sighs Michael Joyce, the father of hypertext fiction—nonlinear storytelling in which plot lines unfold in different ways upon subsequent readings. Joyce, an associate professor of English at Vassar College, wrote the "classic" hypertext novel, *afternoon, a story.* The piece is told one screenful of text at a time; by clicking on adjectives and verbs, readers veer off in far-flung narrative directions. While this may sound like the same experience as following hypertext links around the World Wide Web, *afternoon* was written in 1987 and distributed on floppy disks—well before the Web opened its portals.

Curiously, rather than being a boon to the nascent hypertext-fiction movement, the Web is seen as a spoiler: "The regrettable rump faction says we lost the hypertext movement when the Web came along," says Joyce. "No one knows yet how to make this a popular medium." Why? "The Web is all edges and without much depth, and for a writer that is trouble," he says.

But Joyce, who nevertheless created his own Web-based novel, *Twelve Blue,* is not discouraged. He believes the forking paths of computer narrative will help some artist somewhere create a new medium that is truer to life than anything that's come before: "People have a complex sense of their own lives, which isn't often accounted for in popular art—they're capable of very complex relationships. New media have to be faulted—ironically!—for the failure to express that complexity."

Joyce believes, though, that the artistic failures that litter the cybserscape are good, a hopeful sign. Art, after all, is not produced easily or without struggle, even in the digital age. "We're very close to some shared moment, a transformative medium," he insists. In other words, something big is happening. We'll know it when we see it.

Pundit Forecasts Portable, Praying PCs in *The Age of Spiritual Machines*[5]

Let's start with a quick quiz: When is your mother's birthday? How about Thomas Jefferson's? When was Mickey Mouse born? When was the right triangle born?

If you can't answer the first question right away, you know the answer will come to you. If you can't answer the second, you realize it immediately, and you know where to find the response. Because Mickey was created, not born, you know that it's impossible to answer the third question. And you know that the last question makes no sense, because birth and triangles are unrelated.

Notice that you were able to respond to each sentence immediately upon reading it, which says a lot about the difference between human and digital intelligence. You answered more quickly than even the fastest computer. You immediately understood my seemingly simple questions, which presuppose a good deal of common sense and information. You did so without parsing the sentences, sorting through lists of facts, or evaluating alternative responses. In other words, you acted like a person, not a machine.

Keep my little quiz in mind if you're reading the latest book by prolific inventor Ray Kurzweil, *The Age of Spiritual Machines*, published in January (Viking Press, $25.95). It goes far beyond the old and traditional notion that computers will one day outthink man. In the 21st century, Kurzweil writes, there won't be a clear difference between human beings and robots. Within 20 years, virtual sex will provide sensations that are more intense and pleasurable than conventional sex, and digital prostitutes are likely to be legal. Before the year 2100, machines will pray and worship. Brain scanners routinely will download our histories and personalities into robots. We will become software, and life expectancy will no longer be a viable term in relation to intelligent beings.

Such fanciful speculations, while entertaining fiction, shouldn't be taken too seriously. Still, Kurzweil's accomplishments do command attention and respect. For more than a quarter-century, he's been a pioneer on the computer frontiers—in scanner technology, optical-character and speech-recognition systems, speech synthesis, and digital music synthesis. He holds an MIT degree and several honor-

In the 21st century, Kurzweil writes, there won't be a clear difference between human beings and robots.

ary doctorates. A previous work, *The Age of Intelligent Machines*, was named the outstanding computer science book for 1990 by the Association of American Publishers. And he has founded and sold several successful companies, one while still an undergraduate.

In addition, some of his predictions from a decade ago seem prescient today. He was correct, for example, about the timing of commercially useful speech recognition, and off by only a year in predicting when a computer would defeat the human champion at chess. Despite his fantasies of a post-biological era a century from now, Kurzweil's new book may actually be useful as a forecast of computer industry advances in the next ten years. Let me cite a few examples.

Despite his fantasies of a post-biological era a century from now, Kurzweil's new book may actually be useful as a forecast of computer industry advances in the next ten years.

- Most computers will be portable, not desk-bound, hidden in our cellular phones, credit cards, watches, and even our clothing.
- PCs won't have moving parts. No hard drives. No keyboards.
- Instead of typing, most people will talk to their computers.
- In place of PCs in our dens and bedrooms, we'll rely on household servers that will feed digital information to a network of audio and video systems and to booklike displays around the home.
- Vast amounts of information will be wirelessly accessible all the time.
- Music, software, and books will be distributed wirelessly, never assuming a physical form.
- Books, magazines, and newspapers will be read on displays that have the resolution, contrast, and viewing angle of paper.
- Many business transactions will take place between a human and what the author calls a "virtual personality."

The key here is not the direction but the time frame. Kurzweil expects all this within a decade. He may be right.

However, I question his vision and assumptions as he looks further out. As we approach the new millennium and digital technology assumes a more significant economic and social role, it's important to recognize why we haven't built machines that outsmart us, and why trying is a waste of time and resources. Computers prevail at chess, guide missiles more accurately, and provide better stock-trading advice. It will become increasingly appropriate and economical for digital intelligence to assist humans in carefully defined areas like these that don't require general knowledge or the ability to comprehend language.

But the reason computers don't yet have the intelligence of a child isn't that our electronic circuits aren't fast enough. Thought is more than the manipulation of symbols. Contrary to what Kurzweil envisions, the state of every atom inside a living skull will never be determined and programmed into a computer. But if this were possible, the effort would reveal no more of that brain's thoughts than a circuit diagram of a radio reveals about the music playing on it. The real reason we can't yet turn a machine into a mind: We don't know how. We never will.

The Future of Intimacy: A Search for Soul in the New Machines[6]

What will happen to people's personal lives—their intimate, daily relationships—as we pass into the new era of the 21st century? Mark Kingwell, author of Dreams of Millennium *and* Better Living: In Pursuit of Happiness from Plato to Prozac, *brings the future down to a human scale, arguing that the only technological developments that will truly matter are those that will improve our ability to connect with our fellow human beings:*

There is a quality of early morning light in Vancouver that you don't find in the rest of the country, a Turneresque wash of greys and blues that suffuses English Bay in romantic obscurity and makes the nearby Coastal Range look like a pod of humpback whales moving out to sea with infinitesimal slowness. It feels like the birthplace of the world—except for the foreground: blocks of half-completed buildings, piles of concrete rubble and the lurking silhouettes of high-load cranes. The joggers and Rollerbladers, inevitable and ubiquitous even at 6 a.m., pick their way nimbly through all this ambiguous evidence of Pacific Rim optimism. If there has been a downturn in the local economy—20,000 jobs lost in January alone, an 11-per-cent decline in house prices, a 40-per-cent drop in volume—you wouldn't know it from the building sites or the packed restaurant patios. Vancouver really is the every-city of *The X-Files*, a generic urban location of hustle and intrigue, and it seems to represent the future—a future confident, multiracial, physically fit, comfortable with technology and happily, even ecstatically, capitalistic.

Is it also a likely future? The economic doomsayers would have us believe that all the pan-Asian and Pacific revivalism is just empty currency-driven puffery. And perhaps they are right: there is quite enough evidence to suggest that the reality of globalization is not the liberalizing dream of modern economics, but instead a nightmare of emergent class conflict, tribal hatred and technological imperialism.

Neal Stephenson's 1992 novel *Snow Crash*, a cult phenomenon of cyberpunk action and inventively dystopian speculation, fills in the details of this not-so-rosy picture. The book, set in a near-future California of gated communities (or "Burbclaves"), private freeways and quasi-governmental companies known as "franchulates," has become an underground best-seller, one of those defining documents of the culture that never quite show up on the radar screens of network television or mainstream newspapers. The central action concerns the efforts of L. Bob Rife, a global media magnate, to resurrect an ancient religion—also an ancient computer virus—to reprogram the brains of the world's population. His point of entry is The Raft, a floating country of refugees, displaced persons and pirates, which is moving towards the vulnerable west coast of North America, whose distracted, drug-addled, materialistic and self-interested inhabitants are powerless to resist. The U.S. federal government has been reduced to Fedland, a bureaucratic non-entity, with a glad-handing president who can't get anyone to take him seriously.

It might seem capricious to consider a science-fiction novel significant in shaping the future, but as the American philosopher Richard Rorty noted recently in his careful assessment of *Snow Crash*, visions of the future can have an unusually powerful bearing on the present. Rorty chided the "pessimism" of Stephenson's vision, and lamented its tendency to induce a sense of impotence. How we imagine the future dictates, in larger part than we know, the kind of future we will actually create.

Any simple dichotomy of optimism and pessimism is too crude to capture the nuances of the issue, however. Advocates would have us believe that the question of life a hundred years hence is one either of utopia or dystopia, wondrous emancipation or dark enslavement—a form of bipolar thinking that is particularly prevalent at cultural-limit times like the much-discussed, entirely arbitrary and yet immensely compelling millennium. Both options sport hidden dangers.

The trouble with utopian visions is that they hide the realities of the messy transition—think of the blithe elimination of poverty and hunger in the *Star Trek* series. They can also become a platform for intolerant, occasionally violent social change: witness the dominant political movements of our bloody century. Not least, utopias run the risk of making any actual, step-wise reform look paltry, and therefore somehow contemptible. It is in this sense that, as the saying goes, the perfect is the enemy of the good.

Similarly, dystopian visions are often an invitation to gloomy inaction, rather than a needed wake-up call. They stunt feelings of hope that might translate into political action. They feed on our fears and anxieties, working them up into fully formed bad dreams of a dark future. They make us feel powerless or overwhelmed: instead of acting, we quiver in a depressed stasis.

There is good evidence that such cultural pessimism has been widespread throughout history, but there is also something that must be acknowledged as unique to our times. In his book *Amusing Ourselves to Death*, the media critic Neil

Postman discusses what he calls the problem of "the information-action ratio"—the structure of human responsiveness that determines how much, and what sort, of information is usefully assimilable. Our current mass-information media offers virtually limitless information. This triggers a kind of overpowering ennui which steals upon us when we think of how many impossible demands there are for action.

It is essential that we bring all issues tangled in the ball of thread we call the future—technology, globalization, environmental changes—down to a level where we can think about them productively.

Consider a small example. Anyone who knows me personally is aware that my favorite techno-toy is a cordless headset phone. This little machine has changed my life more than almost any other piece of technology, in large part because it facilitates the interplay of work and leisure. Using the headset, I can glimpse a future in which we all achieve, on demand, what computer programmers like to call seamless ubiquity: the ability to access a communications or computation system from any point. I am now able to carry on phone conversations not only from every corner of my apartment, but can do so with my hands free. I can talk to a friend while signing for a parcel delivery, or do a radio interview while chopping vegetables.

Sometimes, in moments of self-indulgent adolescent vanity, I even imagine I look pretty cool with the headset on. This is surely part of its appeal, at least for men of my generation, raised as we were on Gerry Anderson's Supermarionettes, Captain Scarlet and the Thunderbirds, and with more recent echoes in John Cusack's well-equipped professional killer in *Grosse Point Blank*—not to mention Pierce Brosnan as James Bond, or Madonna and Bobby Brown on stage during a concert tour. Of course, it's entirely possible that I just look geeky, not so much savvy gadget king as stock-control boy at The Gap.

Most of us, in thoughtful moments, realize that technology is entirely devoid of interest unless it makes some aspect of daily life easier or more interesting—or if it, in rare cases, increases the degree of justice in our world.

The headset is only a minor piece of technology, but it hints at the real issues in thinking about the future. We have spent a lot of time lately either decrying or celebrating technology, with the hype-masters of *Wired* magazine squaring off against various neo-Luddites and advocates of media fasting. But most of us, in thoughtful moments, realize that technology is entirely devoid of interest unless it makes some aspect of daily life easier or more interesting—or if it, in rare cases, increases the degree of justice in our world.

The base-level facts of existence—that we must rise and face each day, and that at some point this circadian cycle will cease for each one of us—will not be altered by the passage of a century. Whatever changes, these will remain the same. And they cast any technological, economic and social changes in their only worthwhile light. What happens to the people around the globe, what happens in their daily lives of seeking security, love and happiness, as we pass into the new era of the 21st century?

What particularly fascinates me in this attempt to bring the future down to a human scale is the concept of intimacy, the phenomenon of closeness, one person to another. How is it that we are able to form and maintain relationships, to carry on conversations that build up a web of interpersonal connections so vast and complicated they can only be captured by the nearly banal phrase "human civilization"?

This daily miracle, which we rarely pause to acknowledge, let alone celebrate, is the key to thinking about imaginable future. It is unlikely that the next hundred years will change one of the key features of human life: namely that consciousness is irreducibly inward, forcing us to find our connections to others by outward means. Intimacy will continue to play its joyful, vexing, complex role in our lives, and the subtle dialectic of private and public will continue to dominate our institutions, occupations, entertainments and, most of all, our sense of ourselves.

Our machines will always change, often in ways that technological cheerleaders will choose to call progress, but beneath the faster and better wiring, our longing for connection will remain the same.

I have been away from home a lot lately, travelling from city to city across this country and south of the border. On a recent Sunday, I had breakfast with my wife in Boston, lunch with a friend in Toronto, and dinner with a colleague in Ottawa. I started writing this essay in Montreal, worked on it in Vancouver, Edmonton and Calgary, fiddled with the first few paragraphs in Winnipeg, fleshed out some other parts in upstate New York, and then finished it in Toronto. Covering all those miles, trundling in and out of departure lounges and putting in hours in rental cars gives you an appreciation for the vastness and variety of Canada: the way provincial politics dominates Edmonton in a way it doesn't in Winnipeg; the way Vancouver has, like Paris, apparently cornered the regional market on beautiful people; the way the smog and the driving habits get worse every year in Toronto.

This kind of travel also forces an awareness of technology's gifts. Many of us now board transcontinental planes with all the excitement of commuters entering a subway car, and I boot up my laptop absentmindedly in a hotel restaurant, the way I might open a door. These are the small miracles of modern life, incredible privileges, ones within the grasp of less than a fifth of the planet's inhabitants. And there are many more on the way, things that will alter the details of daily life in ways we can hardly guess at.

What matters to me, or anyone else, in all this? That I could have dinner with my parents and brothers in Vancouver last month, the first time in four years that we had all been together, with my mother passing around old snapshots

Intimacy will continue to play its joyful, vexing, complex role in our lives, and the subtle dialectic of private and public will continue to dominate our institutions, occupations, entertainments and, most of all, our sense of ourselves.

of her and my father when they were first together—wonderful black and white portraits, my father with his lanky good looks and Harry Connick haircut, my mother sprightly at 19, the sweet little messages she wrote to him on the back of each photo. That I can check my e-mail in Calgary and read a welcome message from a friend in England, saying that he has a new son. That I can, finally, come home again and find the restful, familiar comfort of my little apartment, the reassuring and human routine of doing the laundry, watering the plants, shopping for food, and cooking a meal for myself.

We all realize that as humans we find much of our deepest happiness in intimacy, in the sharing of ourselves with each other. This communion is the texture of life, the cross-hatching beneath our fingers as we run them over the passage of time. There is a mystery here, a deeply human thing that must be acknowledged before we can move on into the future, a future that is coming whether we like it or not. The critic Walter Benjamin once said that we don't move into the future facing forward so much as we back into it, gazing out over the past. It might be even more accurate to say that we back into it, gazing fixedly down at our feet.

The critic Walter Benjamin once said that we don't move into the future facing forward so much as we back into it, gazing out over the past. It might be even more accurate to say that we back into it, gazing fixedly down at our feet.

The word intimate contains an illuminating contradiction that is worth dwelling on before we take our next backward steps. As an adjective, "intimate" means personal: the intimate details of your life that only you can know. It comes from the Latin word *intimus*, which means "inmost." In this sense, "intimate" captures the strange opacity of individual consciousness, that irreducible first-personal character of identity, that is, at some level, impenetrable by anyone outside.

To be intimate in this sense is to be inward. But the adjective is also used, more commonly, to describe the act of sharing that inwardness with another: an intimate conversation, an intimate friendship. This hints at the ambiguity in the word, and the concept.

Considered as a verb now, "intimate" also means to declare, to communicate, to set out a message. In English we change the pronunciation to distinguish the two uses of the word, and the verb form derives more proximately from the Latin verb *intimare*, meaning to announce. But the deep connection is clear: to intimate is to share a message, though not always an inward one; to be intimate is to be inward, though not always in a way that can be shared.

This play of closeness and distance, of inside and outside, is at the centre of human life. Trapped, of necessity, inside our own minds, we try, with the crude but wonderful tools of language and touch and expression, to bridge the unbridgeable gap between one person and another. We intimate things and hope, thereby, to become intimate: to join our private lives together in the public space that lies between us, where meaning resides. It doesn't always work: our words are misconstrued, our intentions twisted, our messages changed in the telling like the comical distortions of the telephone game. But we go on trying because otherwise we are nothing, our stories fall untold and therefore, somehow, unlived.

We also hear intimations from elsewhere. Intimations of immortality, as Wordsworth said, where life and experience hint at the transcendent possibilities buried in our limited selves: the way we can go beyond ourselves, can feel a sense of purpose or belonging that is not illusory because we sense our connection to a scheme of things. We may also hear intimations of mortality, those whispers of the shade that throw life suddenly into high relief and, if we are listening closely enough, may clarify the possibilities of happiness in this life.

Finding our way into the future is not a matter of deciding which big picture is most likely. It is not, perhaps, a matter of big pictures at all. Like Socrates' basic question—"What is the life worth living?"—the question of the future is one that must start with a thousand smaller ones. What are you going to do today? Tomorrow? Next month? The future is constructed of the infinite number of present moments passing through our hands. With each one we have an opportunity to make our inwardness responsive to the needs of others.

We need ideals to guide us in that responsiveness: justice, primarily, and the respect for other entities on which it is ultimately based. Indeed, we can no longer restrict our pursuit of these connections to other members of our race, our nationality, even our species. Nor can we allow the triumph of private life and private goods that has been wrought in these past three centuries of modernity to atrophy the public life and public good that alone makes a society, or a civilization, worth while.

We therefore have to countenance the possibility that some of the private luxuries we have enjoyed—ones which are too rapacious of resources, too disproportionate in their distribution—will no longer be tolerable as time goes on. Our intimate lives may change in ways we do not always like because we can no longer ignore the voices in our ears—and in our hearts—that intimate we must share even more.

The problem is that if we let the question spin off into trying to imagine the future as such, the result can only be an overwhelming set of demands that will, paradoxically, have the effect of deadening our responsiveness. People defect from responsibility then, hiding in gated communities and surrounding their property with private police forces. Taxpayers begin to see themselves more as clients than as citizens, able to take their purchasing power for social services elsewhere than to inefficient or redistributive governments.

That revolt is rooted in anxiety, in perceived external threats to our security and comfort. We all feel that anxiety now and then, and because it comes from within, it may

Finding our way into the future is not a matter of deciding which big picture is most likely. . . . The question of the future is one that must start with a thousand smaller ones. What are you going to do today?

even seem perfectly justifiable. After all, it is a dangerous world. However, no retreat into isolation will protect our intimate connections if we lack a common destiny to support them and give them purpose. The challenge is to get on with the hard business of making the world a slightly better place, one step at a time, ignoring the increasingly strident prophets of both boom and doom. The truth about the future is, as always, both less spectacular and more demanding—like everyday life itself.

Bibliography with Abstracts and Reviews

For further study, the reader may consult the resources listed below. Abstracts and reviews are from *Book Review Digest*, copyright The H. W. Wilson Company. All rights reserved. *Book Review Digest* is available by subscription from the publisher in both print and electronic formats.

Berry, Adrian. **The Next 500 Years: Life in the Coming Millennium.** W. F. Freeman, 1996.

Abstract:

The author forecasts "life in the third millennium. He sees machines reproducing human personalities and human intelligence. Berry also envisions harvesting the sea to herd and breed whales; privatizing space travel; [and] mining the solar system. . . . He predicts ethics-centered religion, draconian punishments for crime, the replacement of words with icons, and an upsurge of space landscape artists."— *Booklist*

Reviews:

1. Berry's expertise is based in science and played out journalistically as science correspondent of the UK's *Daily Telegraph.* One can see that an appreciation for the history of science informs his mindset early in the book, but loosely conceived conjecture takes over as the underlying concept of his closing chapter, in which he postulates that lifespans will increase, space colonization will disperse future communities such that politics will become increasingly insignificant, and religion will be based on ethics rather than faith. Although marginally interesting, most futurists will find the book devoid of any new ideas.—M. Evans, *Choice* (Nov. 1996)

2. Berry has collected comprehensive and convincing evidence to back his fascinating ideas and arguments. And the book is meticulously referenced and indexed.—Justin Mullins, *New Scientist* (Dec. 11, 1995)

3. [This is a] thought-provoking, well researched book. . . . Who cannot welcome a world where people live to 140, politics are passe, and Shakespeare (as performed by holograms) is as popular as ever?—Patricia Hassler, *Booklist* (Mar. 15, 1996)

Canto, Christophe, and Faliu, Odile. **The History of the Future: Images of the 21st Century.** Flammarion, 1993.

Celente, Gerald. **Trends 2000: How to Prepare for and Profit from the Changes of the 21st Century.** Warner Books, 1997.

Abstract

The author aims to predict trends that will occur in the twenty-first century. "Though he emphasizes economic and technological trends, he also identifies 'trendposts' in the areas of politics, health, the environment, and culture."
—*Booklist*

Reviews:

1. The book is written in a crisp nontechnical style and should appeal to a wide spectrum of readers.—W. C. Struning, *Choice* (June 1997)

2. [Celente] presents a solid, substantive analysis of major national and international forces that will help readers make profitable business, career, or personal decisions for the future. The founder of Trends Research Institute (TRI), he focuses here on the interconnectedness of these trends rather than specialized expert predictions. Celente uses a curious past-perfect tense, writing as if it were January 1, 2000, describing events that 'have happened,' a style that may confuse some readers. Just a few of the cited 'trendposts' include the perfection of the video phone, longevity centers, a stronger emphasis on weight control, clean water and food, life-extension services, microfarms, and more home businesses. There are more trends cited here than in the more faddish *The Popcorn Report* (1992), but both are useful, popular, futurist additions for informed lay readers and academic and larger public libraries.—Dale F. Farris, *Library Journal* (Jan. 1997)

Clarke, Arthur C. **Arthur C. Clarke's July 20, 2019: Life in the 21st Century.** Macmillan, 1986.

Clinton, Bill**. Between Hope and History: Meeting America's Challenges for the 21st Century**. Times Bks., 1996.

Abstract:

"This book continues the conversation I have had with the American people about our destiny as a nation, our duty to prepare for the new century, and our need for a shared vision of twenty-first century America that will enable us to grasp the extraordinary opportunities of this age of possibility. . . . In the three main sections of this book—Opportunity, Responsibility, and Community—I explore the most important challenges we face today, the progress we have made in the last four years and what still must be done, and what responsibilities individuals and families, businesses and labor, community leaders and government have as we move toward the next century." (Preface).

Reviews:

1. [This book] tries to weave all the disparate, often incremental accomplishments of the past four years into a grander vision. At its heart is the great straddle that Mr. Clinton has attempted since his days with the Democratic Leadership Council: one foot in liberalism, one in conservatism, an insistence that there is, in fact, a third way between the two. . . . Sometimes his argument that he has found it is less than compelling; even he acknowledges . . . that the welfare legislation he recently signed is 'far from perfect.' The reader also gets hungry for more reflection on what this conservative moment in political time means for a man like Mr. Clinton, who clearly had aspirations earlier in his Administration for a Government that does more. It is a little sad to see health care reform dealt with in a scant four pages. But this is, first and foremost, a political document for a President seeking a second term. For a better sense of the frustrations of the 'third way' for this child of the 1960's, we may have to wait for the memoirs.—Robin Toner, *New York Times Book Review* (Sept. 22, 1996)

2. This work is better than the usual puffery written to produce votes through a rosy assessment of one's performance. Certainly, the president can be questioned

about a number of his assertions. Have more and better jobs been created? Are there more police officers on patrol? Will the new welfare reform bill succeed without day-care and jobs provisions? However, he clearly articulates his agenda in a style reminiscent of his best speeches. Clinton's plans for environmental protection, deficit reduction, expanded educational and training opportunities, public/ private partnerships, and peace and security are worthy of bipartisan support. . . . Recommended for public libraries. Purchase as demand warrants.—Karl Helicher, *Library Journal* (Oct. 15, 1996)

Dimde, Manfred. **Nostradamus: Predictions for the 21st Century.** Sterling Pub., 1998.

Dunn-Mascetti, Manuela. **Nostradamus: Prophecies for Women.** Simon & Schuster, 1995.

Erdoes, Richard. **A.D. 1000: Living on the Brink of Apocalypse.** Harper and Row, 1988.

Freed, Josh, and Mosher, Terry, eds. **2000 Reasons to Hate the Millennium: A 21st Century Survival Guide.** Simon & Schuster, 1999.

Friedman, George, and Friedman, Meredith. **The Future of War: Power, Technology, and American World Dominance in the 21st Century.** Crown, 1997.

Abstract:

"The authors argue that [the] Age of Ballistics is ending and we are entering a fundamentally new period, the Age of Precision-Guided Munitions (PGMs), the so-called smart weapons that will antiquate the traditional way of making war. . . . The authors [aim to] show how the innovations in weapons technology will affect America's defense strategies on land and sea, in the air and in space, reshaping our military forces, while confronting us with new strategic challenges as America enters the next century." (Publisher's note.)

Reviews:

1. The book is, as the Friedmans admit, 'not really about war today.' . . . It offers some decent analysis of the evolution of battleships, carriers, tanks, and aircraft, but it comes nowhere near matching the astonishing vision of the late Marshal Nikolai Ogarkov, former Chief of the Soviet General Staff. In fact, their work doesn't even cite him or some other key foreign strategists who have written at length about this subject. Perhaps the Friedmans should rerun their model. An optional purchase.—John J. Yurechko, *Library Journal* (Dec. 1996)

2. For those whose libraries can't possibly subscribe to the numerous specialty periodicals covering military technology, the Friedmans corral the openly available information concerning the ongoing revolution in precision weaponry. . . . Their thesis implies a fundamental reorientation of weaponry development toward hypersonic, intercontinental munitions. Bureaucratically, the thesis would compel the U.S. Navy to wean itself from aircraft carriers in favor of controlling the seas from space. For interested civilians, a provocative glimpse into the issues roiling America's military professionals.—Gilbert Taylor, *Booklist* (Oct. 15, 1996)

Gould, Stephen Jay. **Questioning the Millennium: A Rationalist's Guide to a Precisely Arbitrary Countdown.** Harmony Books, 1997.

Abstract:

In three essays entitled 'What?,' 'When?,' and 'Why?,' Gould . . . analyzes why humans are . . . fascinated by the year 2000."—*Library Journal*

Reviews:

1. Gould in conclusion says that he has 'always and dearly loved calendrical questions because they display all our foibles in revealing miniature'—our foible, that is, of looking to nature for anthropocentric order and, not finding it there, seeking to impose it. Gould's ability to empathize with failed science, to retrace its awkward but earnest steps, is perhaps his outstanding quality as an essayist.—John Updike, *New Yorker* (Oct. 20-27, 1997)

2. It is no great revelation that millennial passions are fueled in part by apocalyptic yearnings as well as by an innate human compulsion to measure and organize time, but, as always, Gould puts his own clever spin on these observations. Hardcore fans may be disappointed, for this book contains more religion and numerology than science. Any book by Gould will generate demand, but while this one is witty and entertaining, it is not especially illuminating. An optional purchase.—Gregg Sapp, *Library Journal* (Aug. 1997)

3. Gould poses three questions about the millennium in this delicious science-historical jeu d'esprit: What does millennium mean? When does a millennium arrive? Why are we interested in it and other divisions of time? . . . There is an emotional rabbit punch at the very end of the book--but don't let that warning scare you away from what may be the most enjoyable millennium book of the second millennium.—Ray Olson, *Booklist* (July 1997)

Halberstam, David. **The Next Century.** William Morrow and Company, 1991.

Abstract:

The author discusses what he sees as "America's declining world position and how its economic dominance has been eroded by more industrious and dynamic rivals."—*Library Journal*

Review:

[The author] weaves memories, ideas and insights from his life's work into a concise warning about the bad habits we have introduced into American life, and he offers fresh hope for our ability to overcome them. Mr. Halberstam's is not the only book published recently to scour the past for hints about the future, but it is the shortest and the best. . . . Mr. Halberstam's is one of the few books to recognize that the challenge facing the United States is not finding a scapegoat for our economic blunders but making the most of our physical and mental capabilities, improving our productivity in an open, democratic structure. He pinpoints our failures in education, sees we are practicing 'the politics of anxiety and uncertainty rather than the politics of confidence' and urges us to judge ourselves by our own norms of what 'a harmonious and decent society' should be.—Bill Bradley, *New York Times Book Review* (Feb. 17, 1991)

Hammond, Allen L. **Which World? Scenarios for the 21st Century.** Island Press, 1998.

Abstract:

Looking toward the 21st century, Hammond "presents an array of global and regional scenarios with . . . different outcomes. In 'Fortress World,' civil order collapses as capitalism brings increased income disparity and planet-threatening levels of pollution. In 'Market World,' capitalism is the hero, spawning innovation and progress. Still, there are pockets of poverty and environmental decay. In the 'Transformed World' scenario, pollution taxes, philanthropy, and the Internet . . . bring about an era of good feeling where pollution and child abuse are in decline and spiritualism and technology advance."—*Choice*

Reviews:

1. Hammond shows his capacity to highlight clearly options for long-term sustainability to a broad audience. His assessment and summary of 1990's research data is well organized and should be studied by anyone with serious concerns about the future.—Jack DeForest, *Science Books and Films* (Nov. 1998)

2. Hammond (director, Strategic Analysis, World Resources Inst.) bases the title of this work on the results of the 2050 Project, a joint research program of the Brookings Institution, the World Resources Institute, and the Sante Fe Institute. Given the fairly liberal bent of these organizations, it is not surprising that the most enlightened and socially productive path centers around the 'Transformed World' scenario, which requires some enlightened social engineering, significant environmental payoffs, and enlightened self-interest among international market forces. The other two scenarios are 'Market World' and 'Fortress World.' Market World pictures a number of positive social and economic indicators but also significant degradation of environmental quality. . . . Fascinating and thought-provoking, this is an excellent choice for all academic and larger public libraries.—Stephen W. Green, *Library Journal* (Aug. 1998)

3. Looking toward the 21st century, Hammond "presents an array of global and regional scenarios with . . . different outcomes. In 'Fortress World,' civil order collapses as capitalism brings increased income disparity and planet-threatening levels of pollution. In 'Market World,' capitalism is the hero, spawning innovation and progress. Still, there are pockets of poverty and environmental decay. In the 'Transformed World' scenario, pollution taxes, philanthropy, and the Internet . . . bring about an era of good feeling where pollution and child abuse are in decline and spiritualism and technology advance."—E. Kacapyr, *Choice* (Dec. 1998)

Hewitt, V. J., and Lorie, Peter. **Nostradamus: The End of the Millennium: Prophecies 1992-2001.** Simon & Schuster, 1991.

Judy, Richard W., and D'Amico, Carol. **Workforce 2020: Work and Workers in the 21st Century.** Hudson Inst., 1997.

Kaku, Michio. **Visions: How Science Will Revolutionize the 21st Century.** Anchor Books, 1997.

Abstract:

The author provides a number of "forecasts about the shape of human life in the 21st century and [beyond]."—*New York Times Book Review*

Kaplan, Robert D. **The Ends of the Earth: A Journey at the Dawn of the 21st Century.** Random House, 1996.

Abstract:

Kaplan's book takes the form of a travelogue, beginning with his tour of West Africa, and continuing . . . [through] countries in the Near East and Central, South, and Southeast Asia.—*New Yorker*

Reviews:

1. Kaplan, author of Balkan Ghosts and a contributing editor to *Atlantic Monthly*, provoked extensive debate when he initially set out the theme of this book in an article in that magazine. . . . Kaplan argues that patterns of traditional ethnic conflict will influence much of non-Western international affairs in the 21st century. Like any travel journalist, Kaplan spoke to many people to contribute to his impressions, but one senses that he rarely got below the surface to discover the strength and resiliency of the cultures he encountered. The narrative is fascinating; the conclusions merely impressionistic. Of interest to larger public libraries.— Bill Rau, *Library Journal* (Jan. 1996)

2. As a piece of travel literature alone, *The Ends of the Earth* succeeds in providing a tangible sense of the sweaty, smelly reality of many exotic points on the map, with glimpses of their cruelty but also, occasionally, of beauty and human kindness. As a piece of analysis, it is deeply thought-provoking.—Francis Fukuyama, *Commentary* (Apr. 1996)

3. [The author] admits to being 'addicted to political analysis.' It comes as no surprise, then, to find an account of his travels throughout Africa and Asia to be no mere travelogue, but rather a stimulating journey distinguished by detailed observations of economic and social conditions he encountered. Often, Kaplan's timely viewpoint may be all too bleak. . . . Still, the dense yet fluid reportage shows Kaplan to be an objective seeker of truth. His keen observations are shocking at times, but they sound an alarm difficult to ignore.—Alice Joyce, *Booklist* (Mar. 1, 1996)

4. In the final pages, Kaplan abandons the possibility of a "general solution" to the "complexity and apparent hopelessness'"he has described. . . . The white man's burden still rests heavily on him as, near the end of his journey, he gazes at the strange beings who inhabit Cambodia—"those buttery, cocoa-brown faces . . . bearing an archetypal forest-spirit quality, enhanced by eyes of such smiling brightness that each face was like a charity poster.'" Kaplan assures his American readers that such suffering faces "are closer than we think." But Kaplan has done everything in his power to render them completely alien, and his chief complaint about the troubled world is "We are not in control."—Philip Gourevitch, *New Yorker* (Apr. 8, 1996)

Kennedy, Teresa. **Welcome to the End of the World: Prophecy, Rage, and the New Age.** M. Evans and Co., 1997.

Khalilzad, Zalmay M., and Lesser, Ian O., eds. **Sources of Conflict in the 21st Century: Regional Futures and U.S. Strategy.** Rand, 1998.

Abstract:

In "Overview of the Future Security Environment," contributors advance nine propositions about the evolving world order and the role of the US in that order, and they develop three alternative scenarios of future worlds. The regional surveys . . . [concern] Asia, the Greater Middle East, and Europe and the former Soviet Union.—*Choice*

Reviews:

1. It is one of the puzzles of the time. The range of security threats facing the established industrial democracies seems to be changing with bewildering and often alarming speed. But the debate about how to head off these challenges is mostly stale, bureaucratic and confined, not least by impenetrable jargon, to an introverted elite. Anyone who doubts the first proposition and was therefore preparing to lie back and enjoy a world where history has almost ended should study the list of 'wild cards' drawn up by the Rand Corporation, the Pentagon's favourite think-tank, in a study for the United States Air Force on possible future sources of conflict—*Economist* (July 11, 1998)

2. A product of the Rand Corporation's long-running Project Air Force, this useful book is aimed primarily at defense planners, whose task, it is argued, has become more difficult since the Cold War's end. . . . Asia-Pacific is thought to be 'poised to become the new strategic center of gravity in international politics.' Trends, 'drivers of change,' and possible conflicts in the Northeast Asian, Southeast Asian, and South Asian 'security complexes' are highlighted. Similar serviceable surveys of the Greater Middle East and Greater Europe follow. What it all means for the US Air Force is the subject of a concluding chapter. For faculty, advanced undergraduates and graduate students, and researchers and practitioners.—A. L. Ross, *Choice* (Oct. 1998)

Kolodny, Annette. **Failing the Future: A Dean Looks at Higher Education in the Twenty-first Century.** Duke Univ. Press, 1998.

Abstract:

This book "deals with the future of higher education. . . . [Kolodny examines] the threat posed by increased enrollments and the costs associated with the maintenance of facilities even as funding from both federal and state sources dwindles. She . . . [discusses] the politics involved in tenure, debating its pros and cons, and outlines the special problems women face in the world of academe. . . . Kolodny also addresses the issues of family-friendly practices, such as offering onsite child care, and cognitive as well as cultural diversity, as they relate to higher education."—*Library Journal*

Reviews:

1. Kolodny uses her personal and professional experiences to identify structural changes necessary if higher education is to respond successfully to demographic trends that are altering the publics that universities will serve in the 21st century. .

. . Recommended for all levels.—J. F. Biter, *Choice* (Sept. 1998)

2. This is a book of great good will and impeccable good intentions. Drawing on her five years as a self-described 'change agent' as the dean of humanities at [the University of] Arizona, Kolodny makes a persuasive case for the reworking of higher education in anticipation of a new century. She is clear and effective when describing problems. . . . Strikingly original on some topics, Kolodny's critical analysis also has moments of lethargy. . . . Incomplete explorations and unresolved issues cluster around Kolodny's chapter on kindergarten through 12th-grade education.— Patricia Nelson Limerick, *New York Times Book Review* (Apr. 26, 1998)

3. Will the future find college classes 'taught' by computer programs and video tapes, what Kolodny . . . terms 'the professor in a can'? This is just one scenario presented in her work. . . . Kolodny recognizes that quality education must be offered at all levels, beginning with grade school, or else all levels of education suffer. Her insights will appeal primarily to those in the academic field, but they may find an audience in larger public libraries as well.—Terry A. Christner, *Library Journal* (Mar. 15 1998)

Koppeschaar, Carl. **Moon Handbook: A 21st Century Travel Guide**. Moon Publs., 1995.

Abstract:

Combining established scientific facts with his own speculations, Koppeschaar discusses the moon as a possible tourist destination in the 21st century.

Review:

If you are one of those people who gaze at the moon at night, fascinated by its glow, its shadows and by all of the folklore that surrounds it, you'll probably enjoy this account of Carl Koppeschaar's fanciful trip in the year 2020. From his position in the next century, Koppeschaar looks back on reports of a comet hitting the moon in the 12th century, NASA littering the moon with space technology in the 20th century and folklore about the moon's effect on everything from menstrual cycles to rainfall on earth. Following a dissertation on moon geography and climate, he slips into a soaring flight of whimsy as he outlines travel tips for visits to the moon. Moonsuits, of course, are mandatory. And don't worry about the news, the Lunarian Tribune and the Mont-Blanc Herald Gazette are published locally while major newspapers from Earth are beamed up daily by satellite!—Peter Lord, *Small Press* (July/Aug. 1996)

Kurian, George Thomas, and Molitar, Graham T. T., eds. *Encyclopedia of the Future.* Macmillan, 1996.

Abstract:

Contributors to this volume of 450 articles write "about the future of such matters as agricultural technology, cities, family planning, museums, pharmaceuticals, railways, sexual harassment, voting, and the women's movement. In addition to social phenomena, public policy issues, and individual countries, the encyclopedia covers topics [such as] . . . Buddhism, minerals, and . . . death and taxes. It also includes articles on noted futurologists (e.g., Buckminster Fuller, Herman Kahn, Nostradamus) and on methods used to forecast the future. . . . Every article concludes with a bibliography. . . . Appendixes list the most influential futurologists, the most influential books about the future, and a [chronology].”—*Booklist*

Review:

The editors have assembled an impressive group of contributors, including John Naisbitt (Global Paradox), William F. Buckley, Jr. (Conservatism, Political), Joseph A. Califano (Health Care Costs), F. Wilfrid Lancaster (Libraries: Electronic Formats), and Ben Bova (Space Flight). Approaches vary. Some authors couch their sketches of the future in if-then qualifiers; others confidently lay out statements about what the future will be like. . . . However, since most cited items deal with the present, they offer readers leads on sources that provide context for the topics but that will be of less help in judging the probable validity of an article's conclusions. . . . Accuracy is a bedrock criterion for judging reference books. However, in the case of this one-of-a-kind encyclopedia, readers will be able to judge better its accuracy as time passes. . . . It will stimulate thinking and provide a useful starting point for anyone contemplating the future of any of the topics it engages.—*Booklist* (June 1-15, 1996)

Kurzweil, Ray. **The Age of Spiritual Machines: When Computers Exceed Human Intelligence.** Viking Penguin, 1999.

Abstract:

Moore's Law on Integrated Circuits was first formulated by Gordon Moore, the former head of Intel, in the mid-Sixties. . . . The basic idea is that better chip technology will produce an exponential increase in computer power. Every two years you get twice as much computer power and capacity for the same amount of money. . . . [Kurzweil's] new book is an extended reflection on the implications of Moore's Law, and is a continuation of a line of argument begun in his earlier book, The Age of Intelligent Machines [1990]. He begins by [attempting to] place the evolution of computer technology within the context of evolution in general, and he [seeks to] place that within the history of the universe, . . . beginning at the Big Bang and going to 2099. . . . [Kurzweil concludes that] we will soon have computers that vastly exceed us in intelligence.—*New York Review of Books*

Reviews:

1. Kurzweil does more than simply prognosticate about the future--he provides a blueprint for the next stage of human evolution, in which we will begin to develop computers more intelligent than ourselves. . . . This superb work is a thoughtful melding of technology, philosophy, ethics, and humanism.—Joe J. Accardi, *Library Journal* (Dec. 1998)

2. In another age Kurzweil would be an sf fantasist, but the underlying facts of the computer revolution's next stages compel readers to take him seriously. Kurzweil is articulate and sardonic, which makes his work highly readable, if no less uncomfortable concerning the ethics and fate of human identity—Gilbert Taylor, *Booklist* (Dec. 1, 1998)

3. [This book] provides a vivid window on the state of the art in artificial intelligence research, and offers provocative speculations on where we might be heading as the information age advances. . . . [It] is more detailed, thoughtful, clearly explained and attractively written than *Robot*, by Hans Moravec, and *When Things*

Start to Think, by Neil Gershenfeld—though all three are creditable efforts at popularization. Since the books cover much of the same ground, with some difference of emphasis, Kurzweil's gives you the most bits for your buck. . . . If our three authors are wobbly on the philosophy of mind and artificial intelligence, they are strong on computer technology itself; and here is where their books are particularly interesting.—Colin McGinn, *New York Times Book Review* (Jan. 3, 1999)

4. In Kurzweil's vision, there is no conflict between human beings and machines, because we will all soon . . . become machines. . . . There will not be any difference between us and robots. . . . This is seriously intended. Kurzweil does not think he is writing a work of science fiction. . . . He is making serious claims that he thinks are based on solid scientific results. He is himself a distinguished computer scientist and inventor and so can speak with some authority. . . . I believe that Kurzweil's book exhibits a series of conceptual confusions, . . . common to the prevailing culture of information technology. . . . For the sake of argument, I am just going to assume that everything Kurzweil says about the increase in computational power is true. . . . My point is that to the issues that really concern us about human consciousness and cognition, these successes are irrelevant. . . . When it comes to understanding consciousness, ours is not the age of spiritual machines. It is more like the age of neurobiological infancy.—John R. Searle, *New York Review of Books* (Apr. 8, 1999)

Lanza, Robert Paul. **One World: The Health and Survival of the Human Species in the 21st Century.** Health Press, 1996.

Abstract:

Lanza has compiled a book of . . . essays by 40 contributors from 16 countries. . . . Lanza expresses concern that preoccupation with technological developments may cause people to lose sight of the basic needs of humanity. . . . Francisco Ayala and Audrey Chapman, AAAS officers, speak of 'The Way Forward: Health and Human Rights.' Hiroshi Nakajima, director-general of the World Health Organization, discusses 'Charting the Future: Health Goals for the Next Century.' . . . [Another] view is offered by Dr. Christiaan Barnard in 'Medicine Negated.' . . . Other articles discuss technological and scientific developments such as advances in genetics and reproductive medicine, vaccines, climate, and AIDS. The last section provides statements from the ministries of 8 nations.—*Science Books and Films*

Reviews:

1. The contributors are scientists, educators, statesmen, and experts. The ethical dimension is a recurrent theme, with stress on social justice, human rights, the quality of life, and the security and sustainability of the planet. . . . This book is highly recommended as a stimulating volume of great breadth and many perspectives.—Elizabeth Price, *Science Books and Films* (May 1996)

2. Medical researcher Lanza has brought together an impressive diversity of contributors to make the point that health and medicine are necessarily central to any realistic conception of international stability. The world population continues to increase, and poverty and politics continue to influence patterns of disease. . . . Jimmy Carter, Robert Gallo, Jonas Salk, Linus Pauling, Christiaan Barnard, Carl Sagan, and the heads of international agencies and medical ministries in leading countries come together with dozens of others in the 39 essays ranging over political, biochemical, medical, and humanistic aspects of our global medical challenges. . . . This volume makes an important contribution by raising awareness of

the absolutely central role of disease as a global factor affecting prospects for peace and war. It should be read by a wide audience. General undergraduate through faculty.—J. Maienschein, *Choice* (July/Aug. 1996)

Linden, Eugene. **The Future in Plain Sight: Nine Clues to the Coming Instability.** Simon & Schuster, 1998.

Lorie, Peter, and Murray-Clark, Sidd. **History of the Future: A Chronology.** Doubleday, 1989.

Macrae, Norman. **The 2025 Report: A Concise History of the Future, 1975-2025.** Macmillan, 1985.

Abstract:

An editor of the *Economist*, a computer expert, and a scientist look back from the year 2025 and explain how the world became reasonably safe, sane, and equitable for the first time. The process had to begin with cooperation between the USSR and the United States, then universal use of TCs ("free-as-air telecommunicating computer terminals"), which had become the key to a series of subsequent developments: rational economic policies implemented by a new Centrobank; highly decentralized and customized entrepreneurship; individualized educational and human services; narrow-casting in place of broadcasting; and . . . the disappearance of big government and welfare states.—*Science Books and Films*

Reviews:

1. More optimistic and less authoritarian than Butler's Erewhon and Bellamy's Looking Backward [BRD 1968], this book provides many thought-provoking insights about the possible effects of the information and biological revolutions currently under way.—Alan Rabinowitz, *Science Books and Films* (Nov./Dec. 1985)

2. A spate of recent futurist books predict a conservative happyland. The 2025 Report is a libertarian vision. . . . [Macrae's] forecast has technical merit but appears politically implausible. Yet 2025, with its interspersed biographies of individual success stories, is well written, sharply executed, and rather intriguing.—Clifton E. Wilson, *Library Journal* (Mar. 15, 1985)

3. Unfortunately, while wit and sophistication are present in full measure, absent is the discipline enforced by the need to react to actual events in the real world. Macrae's altogether optimistic 'history' is thus likely to leave even the most hopeful reader skeptical. . . . In a classic article written in the late 1970's, Norman Macrae himself compellingly showed the foolishness of relying on computer models to forecast economic behavior in the real world. . . . How he came to write this book, then, must remain a mystery.—Jeffrey Marsh, *Commentary* (Sept. 1985)

Markley, Oliver W., and McCuan, Walter R., eds. **21st Century Earth: Opposing Viewpoints**. Greenhaven Press, 1996.

Abstract:

This book focuses on "futuristic issues. Five major topics are considered: demographic trends, impact of new technologies, global ecology, international relations, and 'wild card' items that include effects of human longevity and the realms of robots and aliens. Thirty-two opposing viewpoints, originally published between 1990 and 1995 [are presented]."—*Booklist*

Reviews:

1. Each section contains a brief periodical bibliography, and the editors attempt to focus the debates with a general introduction, an introduction to each article, a brief bibliography of books, and a selected list of future-oriented organizations. Inevitably, contributions vary in quality despite the editors' evident efforts to be scrupulously fair in the selection of viewpoints. Given the necessarily circum-scribed space available (each article consumes no more than eight pages), most authors attempt to crowd in more argument than their cited research supports, leading in some cases to polemic rather than rational analysis. Nonetheless, any-one with any point of view regarding the 21st century will find ideological support somewhere in these pages. As with many such volumes, it will be interesting to see which views have held up best by, say, 2050!—J. R. McDonald, *Choice* (May 1996)

2. Will the earth be overpopulated in coming decades? . . . Is global warming less disastrous than we usually suppose? This Opposing Viewpoints title tackles these and many other futuristic issues. . . . For its depth of coverage and provocative points, the Opposing Viewpoints series is hard to beat. As is customary, a short preface and a few guiding questions introduce each pair of viewpoints and help readers focus on main points. Students researching topics for speeches, science, social studies, and persuasive essay assignments on futuristic topics will find the readings and their supplemental bibliographies invaluable. Teachers will find much useful material for supplementary class readings as well.—Anne O'Malley, *Booklist* (Apr. 1 1996)

Mazarr, Michael J., ed. **Nuclear Weapons in a Transformed World: The Chal-lenge of Virtual Nuclear Arsenals**. St. Martin's Press, 1997.

Abstract:

This book proposes to shunt nuclear weapons to 'marginal relations' by replacing operational weapons systems with virtual (i.e., disassembled) nuclear arsenals (VNAs). It embraces Jonathan Schell's proposal to disarm except for disassembled nuclear weapons that would take 5-7 weeks to reassemble.—*Choice*

Review:

This is an ambitious and imaginative look at one of the most urgent and yet com-plicated issues today--the future of nuclear weapons and their role in international politics of the 21st century. Mazarr, editor of the *Washington Quarterly* and direc-tor of the New Millennium Project at the Center for Strategic and International Studies, has assembled a group of scholars and other policy experts to ponder the future role of nuclear weapons. Notwithstanding their diverse backgrounds, the contributors address how nuclear weapons can be rendered less effective as a politico-military tool by placing them in 'virtual' condition. . . . The positions of the current nuclear powers as well as the emerging ones are analyzed in detail. Recommended for academic libraries and those interested in the future of arms control and nuclear weapons—Nader Entessar, *Library Journal* (Feb. 1, 1998)

McCorduck, Pamela, ed. **The Futures of Women: Scenarios for the 21st Century.**

Perseus, 1996.

McRae, Hamish. **The World in 2020: Power, Culture, and Prosperity.** Harvard Business School Press, 1995.

Abstract:

The author presents his predictions for the year 2020. "As well as charting the rise and fall of nations, McRae examines the structural changes within and beyond them—changes in demography, the environment, economics, government and technology."—*New Scientist*

Reviews:

1. Hamish McRae, economist and associate editor of the *Independent*, is a talented and powerful painter of scenarios. . . . McRae sets technology's role in shaping the future firmly in its economic and social context. His book should be required reading for everyone involved in Britain's Technology Foresight Programme. . . . One of the few weaknesses in the book is its superficial treatment of medicine and bio-technology. . . . One of the most thought-provoking subthemes of the book is the dwindling power of governments, as international markets and private agents become stronger. . . . In businesses, in governments, and even in private life, a coherent view of the future makes for better decisions today. McRae's view is not the only possible outcome for 2020, but it is a plausible and challenging one.—Ian Harvey, *New Scientist* (Oct. 15, 1994)

2. [This book] lacks an outrageously optimistic (or pessimistic) thesis around which to twist its evidence. Its analysis is grounded in penetrating reflections on the present. It looks forward one generation, rather than farther ahead to an entirely unknowable future. It is thoughtful, sensible and extremely well written. . . . In what [Mr. McRae] says about the next 25 years of material progress in today's rich countries, however, [he] is probably not quite cheerful enough. This is partly because he is rather too gloomy about how well the West is doing at the moment. . . . As the American economy becomes less a maker of goods and more a supplier of services (which are harder to count than cars or washing machines), figures for output and productivity understate the truth by an ever wider margin. The failure of the personal computer to make any visible impression on the productivity statistics tells you not that computers do not matter but that the statistics are wrong.— *Economist* (June 18, 1994)

3. [McRae] offers no bold, futuristic scenarios but instead extrapolates from current demographic and economic trends to paint a picture of what the world will be like for its next generation. McRae argues that it is in a nation's own economic interest to pursue a course of 'good behavior,' and he suggests that the world will be better off economically and see more political stability 25 years from now. He virtually ignores Latin America and Africa, acknowledging their social and political importance but claiming they will continue to be insignificant economic producers. Given this major limitation and the emphasis on the knowable rather than the unpredictable, McRae, nonetheless, provides a sensible, readable look at the near future.—David Rouse, *Booklist* (Mar. 1, 1995)

O'Neill, Gerard K. **2081: A Hopeful View of the Human Future.** Simon & Schuster, 1981.

Postrel, Virginia. **The Future and Its Enemies: The Growing Conflict Over Creativity, Enterprise, and Progress**. The Free Press, 1998.

Abstract:

This is a "work of political and cultural commentary. . . . In recent years, according to Postrel, the line separating liberals and conservatives has been blurred. . . . The issues and controversies of our day have sparked . . . new alliances that defy the familiar divide between Left and Right. . . . The source of this shift, Postrel argues, is a deepening conflict in American society between two basics outlooks on the future. Arrayed on one side are . . . those who fear and resist change, seeking 'stability and control' in a 'regulated, engineered world.' These 'stasists,' as she calls them, run the political gamut from Right to Left. . . . [On the other side are 'dynamists' who, according to Postrel], celebrate the future in all its promise and uncertainty. . . . Believers in the possibility of progress, [dynamists] are devoted to learning and experimentation, free markets and technological innovation."—*Commentary*

Reviews:

1. Postrel wants us to replace 'left' and 'right' political categories with 'stasists' and 'dynamists.' Who are they, you ask? Stasists include radical environmentalists, Pat Buchanan, supporters of big government programs, and technophobes. Postrel also calls them reactionaries. Dynamists are learners, experimenters, risk-takers, entrepreneurs, and subscribers, perhaps, to her libertarian magazine Reason. So this is her dynamist manifesto, support for whose ideological precepts is offered in dozens of critical examples of our government at work. . . . An off-beat treatise for serious politicos.—Gilbert Taylor, *Booklist* (Nov. 1, 1998)

2. [This is] a lively, engaging, and thought-provoking book. [Postrel] is surely correct that temperamental factors such as the fear of change transcend the political categories of left and right. She is also correct to note that we seem to be going through something of an intellectual revolution; . . . scholars and theorists are voguishly emphasizing unplanned dynamic change. Still, translating all this ferment into an appealing political outlook is no easy task. Postrel fails at it. For there is no compelling evidence that the way systems evolve in nature or in technology holds any lessons at all for understanding how societies grow or people develop.—Alan Wolfe, *New Republic* (June 7, 1999)

3. What is one to say of this sweeping analysis and the agenda that goes with it? First and most obviously, there is the problem of labeling. It is not just that Postrel's clumsy coinages are unlikely to find their way onto the Sunday political talk shows. More fundamentally, her division of the political world into stasists and dynamists is misleading, even—one suspects—intentionally diversionary. [This book] seems like nothing so much as an attempt to repackage libertarianism, giving it the appealing name of 'dynamism' while throwing together into one 'stasist' camp those who happen to oppose it in some way, however different their grounds for doing so. This may explain why Postrel's taxonomy is so unhelpful once one looks beyond the handful of highly contested issues, like immigration and free trade, on which some elements of the Left and Right have indeed come together in recent years against mainstream 'dynamist' opinion.—Daniel Casse, *Commentary* (Apr. 1999)

Renner, Michael. **Fighting for Survival: Environmental Decline, Social Conflict, and the New Age of Insecurity.** Norton, 1996.

Abstract:

Renner argues that the focus of post-Cold War national security be shifted from military concerns to the global social, economic, and environmental pressures threatening peace today. After analyzing the recent transformation of national security, Renner uses global examples to illustrate the sources of conflict that have replaced political ideologies: the degradation of lands, forests, and marine ecosystems, plus ozone depletion and climate change. He posits that the social, economic, and political repercussions of these environmental changes—poverty, population growth, and refugees—lead to conflicts that transcend national boundaries. Then Renner offers his vision of security in the 21st century.—*Choice*

Reviews:

1. For a green-minded author, it is tempting to blame all wars and violence on some sort of environmental problem. Mr. Renner, however, is careful not to underplay the other causes of conflict. . . . Only when it comes to his prescriptions for a new worldwide security policy, does Mr. Renner lose touch with the real world. He suggests that governments should make big cuts in their spending on arms in order to increase their spending on environmental measures. He also wants much more debt relief for poor countries. Neither of these recommendations, however worthy, is likely to be implemented by today's political leaders.—*Economist* (Feb. 15, 1997)

2. Clearly organized, the book is written for everyone. Extensive endnotes. Adequate subject/author index.—S. Cable, *Choice* (Mar. 1997)

Reston, James, Jr. **The Last Apocalypse: Europe at the Year 1000 A.D.** Doubleday, 1998.

Abstract:

This is an account of European history in the years surrounding the first millennium. Reston argues that the year 999 A.D. "marked a turning point in Europe's 40-year battle against three . . . invasions: by the Viking fleets from the north, the Moors in Spain and the Magyar horsemen of Hungary. Christianity finally succeeded in driving paganism from the continent."—*New York Times Book Review*

Revews:

1. Reston, the author of ten previous books, including Galileo: A Life, reveals how medieval kingdoms overcame foreign military forces and established Christianity as the dominant sociopolitical force in Europe. . . . Reston brings to life some of the major personalities of the era (e.g., Gerbert of Aurillac, a 'kingmaker' and Pope Sylvester II) in his often wry account of the turning of the military tide. The book bears comparison to Norman F. Cantor's The Civilization of the Middle Ages (1993), and the author's scholarship and writing style make this work suitable for both public and academic libraries.—Norman Malwitz, *Library Journal* (Mar. 15, 1998)

2. Reston is a wonderful storyteller, and here he has an epic tale to tell. . . . As the year A.D. 1000 approaches, Christianity is conquering the pagan world, though not always by the most religious of means. . . . Reston jumps into this sweeping saga and discovers more thrilling action, more heroes and villains than could be found in an Old English epic. . . . Reston's seemingly encyclopedic knowledge of the tenth century, combined with his disarming interpretations of the period's events, makes for fascinating reading. His intermittent reflections on what the turn of the millennium meant to Europeans gives the book an additional level of interest. Fans of Barbara Tuchman's *A Distant Mirror* (1978) are the logical audience for this one.—Ilene Cooper, *Booklist* (Jan. 1-15, 1998)

Rostow, W. W. **The Great Population Spike and After: Reflections on the 21st Century.** Oxford University Press, 1998.

Abstract:

As the author "sees it, the decline in population growth in the industrialized world below 'replacement levels' will fall to a zero level circa 2100, with the exception of southern Africa, and will have a major impact on employment, social services for a decelerating population, diminished work forces, and other population-related investments."—*Library Journal*

Reviews:

1. Rostow (emeritus, Univ. of Texas at Austin) [is a] former consultant to the Eisenhower, Kennedy, and Johnson administrations. . . . His projections present significant challenges for developing countries, as well as those entering what he terms the fourth industrial age. . . . This is a critical, thought-provoking work dealing with highly technical, macroanalysis of international demographics and economics and is recommended for major academic libraries supporting graduate curricula in these areas.—Dale F. Farris, *Library Journal* (May 1, 1998)

2. Rostow, always rather deterministic about demographics and technology, sees the coming end of 200 years with a rate of population growth above zero as defining the twenty-first century's challenges. He projects supply-side strains and rising food prices early in the century, urging that we need to respond to these problems with 'more rational water policies,' research on nonpolluting energy sources and genetic engineering-based improvements in grain production, and workforce expansion.—Mary Carroll, *Booklist* (June 1-15, 1998)

Skinner, Stephen, and King, Francis X. **Nostradamus: Prophecies of the World's Greatest Seer: Prophecies Fulfilled and Predictions for the Millennium and Beyond.** St. Martin's Press, 1994.

Solso, Robert L. **Mind and Brain Sciences in the 21st Century**. MIT Press, 1997.

Abstract:

Sixteen "workers in scientific psychology and cognitive neuroscience have contributed speculative chapters about their expectations for the near future. . . . Authors include Hilgard, Baars, Sagan, Thompson, Tulving, Smith, Posner, Gevins, Pribram, Gazzaniga, Roediger, Snodgrass, Kagan, Sperling, Miller, Eysenck, and editor Solso."—*Choice*

Reviews:

1. [This is] a series of essays differing wildly in style and approach. Some of [Solso's] more senior authors, like the veteran Ernest Hilgard, . . . probably feel themselves towards the end of their scientific careers and so take the opportunity to review their own achievements in an appropriately kindly light. Of the others, some take their task seriously, some send it up, some attempt fiction. Yet others (notably Carl Sagan and his co-author Ann Druyan) unabashedly recycle earlier articles. . . . The best approach comes from Endell Tulving, to my mind the deepest thinker among cognitive psychologists, who elegantly parodies a great deal of the vacuous guff which neuroscientists, artificial intelligencers and even physicists straying too far from their own terrain have been writing about consciousness this past decade.—Steven Rose, *Times Literary Supplement* (Mar. 13, 1998)

2. Comprising 16 essays by noted psychologists and brain scientists whose profound thinking is matched by their lucid prose, this volume brings the serious amateur as well as the professional a real appreciation of the state of the field and its future. Solso (psychology, Univ. of Nevada) sets an exemplary standard in editing the papers, all of which are readable and stimulating, and he provides a summary chapter at the end that some readers may find helpful as a beginning. Prediction is hazardous, but the writers—many of the most important names in the field—take risks prudently and with good humor. . . . The practical impact of the work comes through, especially in 'The Memory Trainers' by Gay Snodgrass, . . . who pursues the idea that we can determine whether and when we will lose essential brain functions as we age. Other topics are less sensational but equally important. . . . Essential for most libraries.—E. James Lieberman, *Library Journal* (Aug. 1997)

3. The writing and editing are excellent. . . . A competent index and half-page biographies of the writers are included. One weakness: there is little reference to the background knowledge from which these projections and speculations were made. That would be impossible in a single volume, but it still leaves this book appropriate only for those with a current understanding of either of these disciplines.—R. A. Drake, *Choice* (Mar. 1998)

Stableford, Brian M. **The Third Millennium: A History of the World, AD 2000-3000.** Sidgwick & Jackson, 1985.

Stearns, Peter N. **Millennium III, Century XXI: A Retrospective on the Future.** Westview Press, 1996.

The Top 100 : The Fastest Growing Careers for the 21st Century. J. G. Ferguson, 1998.

Abstract:

"This guide profiles 100 careers that are projected by the U.S. Department of Labor and a variety of other sources as the fastest growing careers for the next decade. . . . Among the careers covered are accountants and auditors, biologists, computer programmers, food service workers, hotel and motel managers, nurses, physical therapists, secretaries, teachers, and Web masters. . . . [Entries include] sections on definition, nature of the work, educational and/or training requirements, opportunities for experience and exploration, methods of entering the career, advancement, employment outlook, earnings, conditions of work, and sources of additional information (containing names, addresses, phone numbers, and in some cases Web or e-mail addresses for relevant associations, unions, and government agencies)."—*Booklist*

Review:

The index identifies more than 600 occupations referred to in the text. Of the 100 careers profiled, 29 percent require at least a bachelor's degree, and 8 percent require at least a master's degree. . . . A helpful feature is that all career subspecialties mentioned in the text are italicized. Entries are drawn from the same publisher's *Encyclopedia of Careers and Vocational Guidance* (10th ed., 1998) and follow the same format. . . . Although everything here (and more) can be found in Encyclopedia of Careers and Vocational Guidance, it is convenient to have so much information about the most promising careers available in a low-cost large-format paperback edition. Recommended for secondary schools, colleges, and guidance and counseling offices.—*Booklist* (Jan. 1-15, 1998)

Turner, Frederick. **Tempest, Flute, and Oz: Essays on the Future.** Persea Books, 1991.

Tyl, Noel. **Predictions for a New Millennium**. Llewellyn Pubs., 1996.

Vanderpool, Harold Y., ed. **The Ethics of Research Involving Human Subjects: Facing the 21st Century.** University Pub. Group, 1996.

Abstract:

This book provides historical, current, and future perspectives on . . . [the issue of using human subjects for research]. . . . It is divided into four parts with a 'road map' essay providing an overarching perspective and context for the chapters in each section.—*Choice*

Reviews:

1. [This] collection of essays . . . is serious and scholarly, and has a comprehensive bibliography, a boon to anyone writing about the problem. . . . The book is divided into four sections, to each of which Vanderpool contributes an introduction. The various authors do not all agree with each other, and it is sometimes difficult to keep one's head among conflicting recommendations and differing priorities. Understandably, the issue of informed consent is a constant theme, as it is in all the declarations and guide-lines that have ever been published. But the difficulty of determining what is to count as informed consent, and what to do about those who are, for one reason or another, deemed incapable of consent, is not resolved, nor can it be, in general terms. . . . Vanderpool's book is to be read now by anyone interested in medical research, and kept on the shelf for future reference.—Mary Warnock, *Times Literary Supplement* (Mar. 14, 1997)

2. Many of the contributed essays are structured in a debate-like format around points of controversy. Each of the contributing authors is a noted expert in their own right and, as a whole, bring a valuable diversity and perspective to this very complex field of thought. Useful notes and appendixes. A well organized, user friendly, comprehensive, and excellent resource on research ethics.—R. L. Jones, *Choice* (Dec. 1996)

Weatherford, J. McIver. **The History of Money: From Sandstone to Cyberspace.** Crown, 1997.

Abstract:

The author discusses the meaning and use of money through history. "Money, according to Weatherford, has experienced three revolutions: the first, with the invention of metallic coins (gold, silver) 3000 years ago; the second, the development of paper money (now the most prevalent form of money) in Renaissance Italy; and today, on the cusp of the 21st century, the rise of electronic money (the all-purpose electronic cash card), which, he believes, will radically change the international economy. . . . Weatherford traces the rise of banking systems and other financial institutions and [seeks to show] . . . how national governments are playing a dominant role in managing the money supply."—*Library Journal*

Reviews:

1. Anthropologist Weatherford (*Savages and Civilization*) has written an interesting and informative book about money, a subject often treated in a dry-as-dust technical manner. . . . There is much peripheral but fascinating material in this anecdotal account. Well recommended for all readers.—Harry Frumerman, *Library Journal* (Jan. 1997)

2. Existing only by government fiat or popular consensus, money has been changed into many forms over thousands of years. Yet it has always had what Weatherford calls a 'cultural configuration,' meaning money exerts a social force beyond its abstract value. . . . Weatherford, building his reputation for skilled storytelling, which extends back to such popular books as *Indian Givers* (1988), surveys offbeat tales of money's impact in such disparate episodes in economic history as hyperinflation in Weimar Germany, the etymology of the word dollar, and the dominance and demise of the gold standard. Weatherford concludes his history of Mammon on an interesting note: cash will increasingly be used by the poor for daily transactions while wealthier classes will rely on electronic forms of money, such as 'smart' cards and Internet exchanges. Could garner wide interest.—Gilbert Taylor, *Booklist* (Jan. 1-15, 1997)

Weber, Eugen. **Apocalypses: Prophecies, Cults, and Millennial Beliefs through the Ages.** Harvard University Press, 1999.

Wyke, Alexandra. **21st Century Miracle Medicine: RoboSurgery, Wonder Cures, and the Quest for Immortality.** Plenum Press, 1997.

Abstract:

Part of the book is "devoted to chronicling current and anticipated scientific discoveries and describing the technological marvels they portend. These include drug delivery systems customized to the genetic code of particular patients (and/or their specific disease-causing microorganisms), ubiquitous access to computerized medical records, online consultants providing remote-controlled medical and surgical interventions, and tiny monitoring devices that can diagnose illness or injury and communicate with appropriate health professionals. Concluding chapters predict the future of medicine as a social institution and describe the role of medicine in the mid-21st century."—*Choice*

Reviews:

1. As Wyke tells us, the research for her book involved numerous interviews conducted with the executives of major medical corporations. . . . It is their language and messages that are being relayed, and their version of the future which is being publicised. As a result, the account Wyke offers of medicine fifty years hence is partial and partisan. Many of her predictions are surely sound: there is little doubt that genetic therapies will increase, and robots will become as normal in the operating theatre as they are in car-assembly plants. But *21st Century Miracle Medicine* fails to analyse the wider implications of these developments. . . . There is something appealing about Wyke's technological optimism. But when she writes that 'tomorrow's healthcare setting will see the quality of medical services shift into the position of becoming a supreme requirement for the accolade of good doctoring', the impenetrability of the prose is symptomatic of the woolliness of the thinking.— Roy Porter, *New Scientist* (May 31, 1997)

2. [This is an] entertaining book. . . . The view here is unabashedly technologically utopian; indeed, the book's final sentence states, 'Technology will literally transform medicine, dismissing all possible doubt that we can look forward to a universally hale and hearty future.' One wonders how the author can acknowledge, but so easily dismiss, the ethical issues and technical glitches inherent in complex technologies, problems of equity of access to these marvels, and biological harms that may be caused by the technologies themselves. General readers.—L. A. Crandall, *Choice* (Dec. 1997)

Index